THE
BOOK OF LUKE

the Smart Guide to the Bible™ series

Joyce L. Gibson
Larry Richards, General Editor

THOMAS NELSON
Since 1798

NASHVILLE   DALLAS   MEXICO CITY   RIO DE JANEIRO   BEIJING

The Book of Luke
The Smart Guide to the Bible™ series
Copyright © 2007 by GRQ, Inc.

Published in Nashville, TN by Thomas Nelson. Thomas Nelson is a trademark of Thomas Nelson, Inc.

Thomas Nelson, Inc. titles may be purchased in bulk for educational, business, fundraising, or sales promotional use. For information, please email SpecialMarkets@ThomasNelson.com.

Originally published by Starburst Publishers under the title *Luke: God's Word for the Biblically-Inept*. Now revised and updated.

Scripture quotations are taken from The New King James Version® (NKJV), copyright © 1979, 1980, 1982, 1992, Thomas Nelson, Inc., Publishers.

General Editor: Larry Richards
Managing Editor: Lila Empson
Associate Editor: W. Mark Whitlock
Scripture Editor: Deborah Wiseman
Assistant Editor: Amy Clark
Design: Diane Whisner

ISBN-13: 978-1-4185-0996-5

Printed in the United States of America
09 9 8 7 6 5 4 3 2

Introduction

Welcome to *The Book of Luke—The Smart Guide to the Bible*™, another in a series that makes the Bible easy to understand. This is not a traditional Bible study! It's a new commentary designed to uncomplicate the Bible and change your outlook on this book forever so that you will turn to it often for enjoyment and instruction.

To Gain Your Confidence

The Book of Luke—The Smart Guide to the Bible™ is for you if you want an easy walk-through of the book Luke wrote to introduce people to Jesus Christ. In writing about Luke's account I have tried to fill you in on historically correct background information, but mostly I have kept the focus on Jesus Christ, as Luke did. The Bible was written for you, so you'll want to read Luke's words, which we have included throughout this book.

What Is the Bible?

When you hold a Bible in your hand you see one book. But it's really a collection of sixty-six books written by a number of authors over a long period of time. You'll find a list of those books in the front of the Bible. You'll also notice that the books are listed under two headings: Old Testament (thirty-nine books) and New Testament (twenty-seven books).

Many years after the Bible was written, scholars took the books and divided them into chapters and verses. Today when you see a reference, such as Luke 19:10, you can find it quite easily by locating first the book, then the chapter, and then the verse.

The Bible was written by ordinary people, but the Bible is not an ordinary book. God himself was the source of their writing. These ordinary people wrote what God inspired them to write. God gave them the wisdom and insight to write what he wanted. That's why we call the Bible the Word of God.

Why Study the Bible?

One good reason to study the Bible is that it is the only book that has God's message for us. As you turn the pages of your Bible, you'll see again and again—more than 2,600 times—that the writers claimed that they were recording what God said. In other words, these writers put down what God told them to say.

Another reason to read the Bible is that it tells you the truth—about God, about the world we live in, about you, and about how much God loves you and wants you to know him. And the truth in your Bible has power to change your life—far more than you may think—because the living God speaks to you through its pages. You can get to know God as a real, living Person when you believe what you read and do what he says.

Why Study the Life of Jesus Christ?

Actually, Luke is one of four Bible books that give us the life of Christ. Those books are Matthew, Mark, Luke, and John. You may wonder why the first four books of the New Testament are devoted to the life of one person. When Jesus came to earth, he came as the focal point of all history!

All the years from Creation to the end of the Old Testament were years of preparation for Jesus's coming. God was at work in the nation of Israel to prepare them for the arrival of his Son to be the Savior of all people. The first four books of the New Testament tell about Jesus's

- birth,
- three years of ministry,
- death on the cross,
- resurrection from the tomb, and
- return to his Father in heaven.

The rest of the New Testament tells how Jesus changed the world by taking his followers and forming the church. He gave the apostles power to lead many others to have faith in him. Today the church is still growing all around the world.

Who Wrote the Four Gospels?

God chose three Jewish men and one Greek to write about the life of Jesus. These men were convinced without even the slightest doubt that Jesus is the Son of God, the Messiah-King promised by Old Testament prophets, the Savior of the world who will come again as King.

Let's look briefly at the men who wrote three of the books: Matthew, Mark, and John. That will help us see how Luke's Gospel account is unique. Matthew was a tax collector before he met Jesus. Matthew directed his Gospel to the Jewish people. He quoted Old Testament Scriptures to prove that Jesus was the Messiah they were looking for.

John Mark (also called John or Mark) traveled with Peter, one of Jesus's disciples. In his Gospel, Mark recorded what he learned from Peter's close association with Jesus. He wrote for the Romans.

John was a fisherman who arranged his Gospel thematically and included lengthy conversations in which Jesus revealed his true nature. John wrote for everyone and showed Jesus as the divine Son of God.

Why Study Luke's Gospel?

Luke was Greek and was a doctor. He must have loved to write too. When we count the actual number of verses, he wrote more of the New Testament (in Luke and Acts) than any other writer. Though Luke never met Jesus in person, he did thorough research and must have conducted in-depth interviews, because through his Gospel he clearly reveals Jesus's great heart of compassion, and he includes parts of Jesus's life and teaching that are not in the other Gospels.

Luke addressed his book (as well as the book of Acts) to an individual—Theophilus, thought to be a Gentile official of some kind who believed in Jesus. Luke wanted him to have an "orderly account" of Jesus's life, which would give him confidence that he had heard the truth about Jesus (Luke 1:3–4 NKJV).

Though Luke never mentions himself in his Gospel, he leaves the distinct impression that he loved Jesus as the Son of Man—completely human as well as completely divine. He understood that Jesus came as a servant "to seek and to save that which was lost" (Luke 19:10 NKJV). In his Gospel account he shows how Jesus went out of his way to reach out to ordinary people, especially to those who were ignored or despised by the religious leadership of his day.

what others say

Larry Sibley

Luke's Gospel has several main themes. Christ is presented as the Savior of the world; the friend who stands with the poor and powerless, the sick and the brokenhearted. Luke emphasizes the urban setting of Jesus' life and work. Women play a prominent role in this gospel. The Holy Spirit is given an important place. Most important of all is Jesus' purpose to give his life in Jerusalem for the sinners he called to repentance.[1]

Luke must have shared some of Jesus's deep understanding of people's heartaches because he shows amazing insight as he notes again and again how Jesus related to people, especially those who had needs: women, children, the sick and disabled, the poor, and the oppressed. Luke also makes special mention that in addition to the twelve disciples who traveled with Jesus, there were other followers, including women, who used their personal funds to pay the bills as they moved from place to place. Luke's care in telling about specific individuals not mentioned in the other Gospels—widows, children, and babies—points to him as a heart specialist, a doctor of the soul.

Feelings Flow

Luke wasn't a stuffy academic-type doctor. He wasn't afraid of emotions. God's love for all people—not only the Jews—flows through the pages, both in Jesus's actions and in the stories he told. Because of that love, the spirit of joy brightens Luke's book. In one form or another, the word *joy* appears more than twenty times. Praise to God pervades Luke's accounts of the birth of John the Baptist and Jesus. He includes four songs in his first two chapters:

- The Magnificat (Luke 1:46–55)
- The Benedictus (1:68–79)
- The Nunc Dimittis (2:29–32)
- The Gloria (2:14)

The Language of the Gospels

The Jews in Jesus's day were trilingual! That's what archaeologists and Bible students tell us.

Aramaic was used in everyday conversation.

Hebrew was used in the synagogues and the Temple, but was also spoken in everyday conversation.

Greek, however, was the universal language. Most Jews spoke it fluently. They used it for communication with Roman authorities and foreign traders. Jews in Israel used spoken and written Greek.

The writers of the New Testament used common Greek so that their books could be read by people all over the Roman Empire.

A Word About Words

There are several interchangeable terms: *Scripture, Scriptures, Holy Scriptures, the Word, Word of God, God's Word, Gospel.* All these mean the same thing and come under the broad heading called the Bible. I may use each of these terms at various times.

The word *Gospel* may refer to one of the four books written about the life of Jesus, of which the Gospel of Luke is one. Or *gospel* may refer to the good news about Jesus.

One Final Word

As you read Luke, you'll see God's love for the Jews and how that love extends to the rest of us. You'll see Jesus's wisdom and compassion for all. You'll see how Jesus willingly gave his life for us. God promises that when we acknowledge our guilt and trust Jesus as

Savior, God will forgive our sins and make us his own children. When you open your heart to God and ask him to speak to you, he will. Ask God to speak to you as you read Luke, and you'll be amazed how wonderfully the Bible will enrich your life!

> **what others say**
>
> **Ken Gire**
>
> The words He speaks are words of life. That is why we must reach for them, receive them, and respond to them. Whatever they may say, however they may sound, whatever implications they may have for our lives, the words that proceed from his mouth offer life to our world.
>
> Those words are how our relationship with God grows. Living reflectively is how we receive them.[2]

About the Author

Joyce L. Gibson, who was born in Toronto, Ontario, spent her first four years in Nigeria with her missionary parents. When the family returned to Canada, where she grew up, she knew she wanted to write and to teach the Bible. This became her passion. After attending Prairie Bible College and Wheaton College, she became a Bible curriculum editor, writing and developing curriculum, at Scripture Press Publications in Wheaton, Illinois, a position she held for thirty-seven years. During that time she taught children in Sunday school, children's church, vacation Bible school, and club programs. She has edited *Anchor*, Haven Ministries' monthly devotional, for thirty years. Her great love for storytelling and teacher training has taken her across the U.S. and Canada to Jamaica and Egypt.

For relaxation, Joyce enjoys cooking and is ever ready to try a new recipe and invite friends over for a meal. Her two nieces and their young families keep her occupied. Currently she is dividing her time between Wheaton and Oostburg, Wisconsin.

About the General Editor

Dr. Larry Richards is a native of Michigan who now lives in Raleigh, North Carolina. He was converted while in the Navy in the 1950s. Larry has taught and written Sunday school curriculum for every age group, from nursery through adult. He has published more than two hundred books, and his books have been translated into some twenty-six languages. His wife, Sue, is also an author. They both enjoy teaching Bible studies as well as fishing and playing golf.

Understanding the Bible Is Easy with These Tools

To understand God's Word you need easy-to-use study tools right where you need them—at your fingertips. The Smart Guide to the Bible™ series puts valuable resources adjacent to the text to save you both time and effort.

Every page features handy sidebars filled with icons and helpful information: cross references for additional insights, definitions of key words and concepts, brief commentaries from experts on the topic, points to ponder, evidence of God at work, the big picture of how passages fit into the context of the entire Bible, practical tips for applying biblical truths to every area of your life, and plenty of maps, charts, and illustrations. A wrap-up of each passage, combined with study questions, concludes each chapter.

These helpful tools show you what to watch for. Look them over to become familiar with them, and then turn to Chapter 1 with complete confidence: You are about to increase your knowledge of God's Word!

Study Helps

The thought-bubble icon alerts you to commentary you might find particularly thought-provoking, challenging, or encouraging. You'll want to take a moment to reflect on it and consider the implications for your life.

Don't miss this point! The exclamation-point icon draws your attention to a key point in the text and emphasizes important biblical truths and facts.

death on the cross
Colossians 1:21–22

Many see Boaz as a type of Jesus Christ. To win back what we human beings lost through sin and spiritual death, Jesus had to become human (i.e., he had to become a true kinsman), and he had to be willing to pay the penalty for our sins. With his <u>death on the cross</u>, Jesus paid the penalty and won freedom and eternal life for us.

The additional Bible verses add scriptural support for the passage you just read and help you better understand the <u>underlined text</u>. (Think of it as an instant reference resource!)

How does what you just read apply to your life? The heart icon indicates that you're about to find out! These practical tips speak to your mind, heart, body, and soul, and offer clear guidelines for living a righteous and joy-filled life, establishing priorities, maintaining healthy relationships, persevering through challenges, and more.

This icon reveals how God is truly all-knowing and all-powerful. The hourglass icon points to a specific example of the prediction of an event or the fulfillment of a prediction. See how some of what God has said would come to pass already has!

What are some of the great things God has done? The traffic-sign icon shows you how God has used miracles, special acts, promises, and covenants throughout history to draw people to him.

Does the story or event you just read about appear elsewhere in the Gospels? The cross icon points you to those instances where the same story appears in other Gospel locations—further proof of the accuracy and truth of Jesus' life, death, and resurrection.

Since God created marriage, there's no better person to turn to for advice. The double-ring icon points out biblical insights and tips for strengthening your marriage.

The Bible is filled with wisdom about raising a godly family and enjoying your spiritual family in Christ. The family icon gives you ideas for building up your home and helping your family grow close and strong.

Isle of Patmos
a small island in the
Mediterranean Sea

something significant had occurred, he wrote down the substance of what he saw. This is the practice John followed when he recorded Revelation on the **Isle of Patmos.**

What does that word really mean, especially as it relates to this passage? Important, misunderstood, or infrequently used words are set in **bold type** in your text so you can immediately glance at the margin for definitions. This valuable feature lets you better understand the meaning of the entire passage without having to stop to check other references.

the big picture

Joshua
Led by Joshua, the Israelites crossed the Jordan River and invaded Canaan (see Illustration #8). In a series of military campaigns the Israelites defeated several coalition armies raised by the inhabitants of Canaan. With organized resistance put down, Joshua divided the land among the twelve Israelite

How does what you read fit in with the greater biblical story? The highlighted big picture summarizes the passage under discussion.

what others say

David Breese
Nothing is clearer in the Word of God than the fact that God wants us to understand himself and his working in the lives of men.[5]

It can be helpful to know what others say on the topic, and the highlighted quotation introduces another voice in the discussion. This resource enables you to read other opinions and perspectives.

Maps, charts, and illustrations pictorially represent ancient artifacts and show where and how stories and events took place. They enable you to better understand important empires, learn your way around villages and temples, see where major battles occurred, and follow the journeys of God's people. You'll find these graphics let you do more than study God's Word—they let you *experience* it.

Chapters at a Glance

Part Two: Miracles, Teachings, and Actions

Part Three: Betrayal, Death, and Resurrection

Part One
Babyhood, Boyhood, and Manhood

Luke 1 Visitors from Heaven

Chapter Highlights:
• **An Angel Visits the Temple**
• **Mary's Song**
• **Birth of a Messenger**
• **A Father's Song**

Let's Get Started

Welcome to a true story about encounters with a heavenly being! But this heavenly being didn't come without prior notice. For years **prophets** told people about God's promise to send a **Messiah**, a king from heaven, and everybody had high hopes for him. They hoped he would rescue them from the domination of foreign powers. They hoped he would establish a kingdom of justice and prosperity. How they yearned for this promise to be fulfilled in their lifetime! But God had been silent for four hundred years. Was he still coming? Had God forgotten his promise? Some of his people, the Jews, had become weary and indifferent to the promise. But in the hearts of the faithful, anticipation lived on.

At the beginning of the first century an incredible series of events began to unfold, and the Messiah—Jesus Christ—was sent to earth. Jesus bewildered the religious authorities because many of the prophecies that foretold his coming and purpose were not fulfilled as they had expected. Nevertheless, Jesus changed the course of history, and even today our lives are touched by his thirty-three-year visit to our planet.

prophets
people who declare a message on behalf of God

Messiah
"anointed one" whom God would send; the Christ

A Reliable Account

LUKE 1:1–4 *Inasmuch as many have taken in hand to set in order a narrative of those things which have been fulfilled among us, just as those who from the beginning were eyewitnesses and ministers of the word delivered them to us, it seemed good to me also, having had perfect understanding of all things from the very first, to write to you an orderly account, most excellent Theophilus, that you may know the certainty of those things in which you were instructed. (NKJV)*

go to

Felix
Acts 24:3

Festus
Acts 26:25

tax collector
Matthew 9:9–13

apostle
Christ's ambassador
sent out; Jesus's
twelve disciples,
Paul, and other
New Testament
missionaries

disciples
learners, students

the Twelve
original group of
disciples who trav-
eled with Jesus and
were taught by him

This One's for Theo

Read a book's dedication or the personal comments in the preface and you'll discover at least some of the author's motivation for writing. Most authors have a purpose that fuels them throughout the often tough and painful process of writing. Luke is no exception. The birth of Jesus Christ and his life on earth caused such a stir that many of Luke's contemporaries wrote accounts of Jesus's life to get the truth out. We have four of these in the Bible—the Gospels—written by Matthew, Mark, Luke, and John, each having a distinct emphasis.

Luke made it his responsibility to investigate all aspects of Jesus's life. Though Luke was not an eyewitness to Jesus's life and teachings, he did thorough research. Some think he interviewed Mary (the mother of Jesus) and others who knew Jesus personally. He organized the material chronologically and highlighted particular themes, keeping in mind the needs and interests of his main recipient, Theophilus, and other Gentiles.

To this day Theophilus is somewhat of a mystery man. His name, which means "lover of God" or "dear to God," was common. He seems to have been a Christian Gentile, recognized as an official of some kind. Luke addresses him as "most excellent," a title he quoted the **apostle** Paul as using in reference to <u>Felix</u> and <u>Festus</u>.

what others say

Paul N. Benware

In the introduction to his gospel, Luke explained his purpose for writing. He wrote to present a historically accurate and chronologically correct account of the life and ministry of Jesus Christ. He wanted his readers to be well grounded in their faith.[1]

The Gospels were written by two of Jesus's twelve **disciples** and by two who were not:

Matthew does not identify himself, but tradition holds the book was written by the <u>tax collector</u> whom Jesus called to be one of **the Twelve**.

Mark was written by John Mark, who was not one of the twelve disciples. He was, however, a close associate of <u>Peter</u>, who was an original disciple. John Mark also traveled with Barnabas and Paul on their first <u>missionary journey</u>.

Luke was written by a Greek physician who worked closely with <u>Paul</u>. He was not one of the twelve disciples. Luke also wrote the book of <u>Acts</u>. Luke wrote from the perspective of a physician. Throughout his books of Luke and Acts you'll find medical references that are not included in the other Gospel accounts. He gives insight into his own heart when he writes about Jesus's compassion for those who were sick or in special need.

John was written by one of Jesus's inner circle of disciples and was recognized as the disciple "whom Jesus loved" (John 13:23 NKJV).

Peter
1 Peter 5:13

missionary journey
Acts 13:1–5

Paul
Colossians 4:14;
Philemon 24;
2 Timothy 4:11

Acts
Acts 1:1–2

An Angel Visits the Temple

LUKE 1:5–10 *There was in the days of Herod, the king of Judea, a certain priest named Zacharias, of the division of Abijah. His wife was of the daughters of Aaron, and her name was Elizabeth. And they were both righteous before God, walking in all the commandments and ordinances of the Lord blameless. But they had no child, because Elizabeth was barren, and they were both well advanced in years. So it was, that while he was serving as priest before God in the order of his division, according to the custom of the priesthood, his lot fell to burn incense when he went into the temple of the Lord. And the whole multitude of the people was praying outside at the hour of incense. (NKJV)*

Meet Zacharias, a model citizen and devout follower of the Lord. Both he and his wife, Elizabeth, were serious about obeying all God's laws. They were faithful in this practice, even though God had withheld the gift that their hearts ached to receive. They were childless! Their voices must have choked when they sang the old Hebrew song, "Children are a heritage from the LORD, the fruit of the womb is a reward" (Psalm 127:3 NKJV). Still they remained faithful, even though old age had crept up and all hope of having a child had long since faded.

divisions of priests
1 Chronicles
24:7–18

custom
1 Chronicles 24:5

Zacharias was also faithful in his professional life as a priest, honored to perform duties at the Temple in Jerusalem. Many years before, King David had set up twenty-four groups of priests from the sons of Aaron. These <u>divisions of priests</u> were assigned duties for one week twice a year. Zacharias was born into the division of Abijah, the eighth division, and as part of a long line of priests he followed the job descriptions set up by David hundreds of years before. According to <u>custom</u> the priests drew **lots** to determine who would have the once-in-a-lifetime honor of entering the Holy Place, an inner room of the Temple (see illustration below), to offer prayers for the nation and to offer **incense** at the **altar**.

Illustration #1
Temple Diagram—
This diagram shows
the Temple as it
appeared in Jesus's
day.

lots
devices used to
determine God's
will, much like
drawing straws

incense
resin that emits a
fragrant aroma when
burned

altar
a stone or metal
construction used
for offering sacrifice

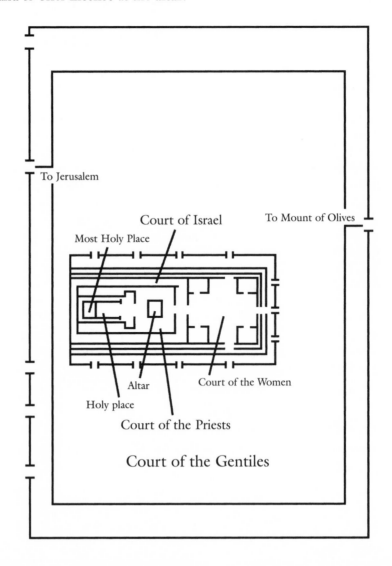

Zacharias and Elizabeth lived with embarrassment and humiliation. In Bible times children were viewed as evidence of God's blessing on the parents. Many people probably assumed their barrenness was the result of some hidden sin. Zacharias and Elizabeth also lived with anxiety. Children and grandchildren were expected to provide for the elderly in their declining years. Who would care for Zacharias and Elizabeth when they were no longer able to care for themselves?

Isaac
Genesis 21:1–7

Samson
Judges 13:1–5, 24

Samuel
1 Samuel 1:1–20

what others say

The Bible Knowledge Commentary

[Zacharias and Elizabeth] were both well along in years and thus had no prospect of children. This fact was a constant embarrassment to Elizabeth as is evident from her statement later on (verse 25). God's allowing a barren woman to have children occurred several times in the Old Testament (e.g., the mothers of Isaac, Samson, and Samuel).[2]

Zack Is Taken Aback

LUKE 1:11–17 *Then an angel of the Lord appeared to him, standing on the right side of the altar of incense. And when Zacharias saw him, he was troubled, and fear fell upon him. But the angel said to him, "Do not be afraid, Zacharias, for your prayer is heard; and your wife Elizabeth will bear you a son, and you shall call his name John. And you will have joy and gladness, and many will rejoice at his birth. For he will be great in the sight of the Lord, and shall drink neither wine nor strong drink. He will also be filled with the Holy Spirit, even from his mother's womb. And he will turn many of the children of Israel to the Lord their God. He will also go before Him in the spirit and power of Elijah, 'to turn the hearts of the fathers to the children,' and the disobedient to the wisdom of the just, to make ready a people prepared for the Lord." (NKJV)*

Zacharias was performing his priestly duty when suddenly an angel appeared at the right side of the altar when he was offering incense (see Illustration #2). He was more than surprised—he was gripped with terror. Ironic, isn't it? Zacharias had given his life to serving God and speaking for God, but when God actually appeared to him in the person of an angel, godly Zacharias responded with absolute terror!

Elijah
Old Testament
prophet whose mes-
sages and prayers
were accompanied
by miracles

The angel quickly assured him that he had come with good news. God had heard his priestly prayer for the nation and was about to answer it in an amazing way. God had also heard Zacharias's and Elizabeth's prayers for a child. He was about to bestow on them the gift they had so earnestly desired. Elizabeth—even in her old age— would bear a son, and his name would be John.

This child would delight his parents' hearts. He would also be infused with the spirit and power of **Elijah** to fulfill a God-given mission of leading many of his people back to the Lord. He would have the special role of preparing the people for an awesome event that God would orchestrate.

what others say

J. C. Ryle

Prayers are not necessarily rejected because the answer is long delayed. Zechariah, no doubt, had often prayed for the blessing of children, and to all appearances he had prayed in vain. At his advanced age he had probably stopped mentioning the subject before God long ago and had given up all hope of being a father. Yet the very first words of the angel show clearly that Zechariah's prayers of long ago had not been forgotten: "Your prayer has been heard" (verse 13).[3]

Illustration #2
Altar of Incense—
Pictured is an altar
like the one that
Zacharias may have
used in Luke 1.

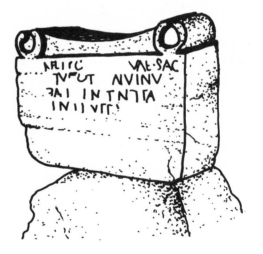

Gabe Sets Him Straight

*Luke 1:18–20 And Zacharias said to the angel, "How shall I know this? For I am an old man, and my wife is well advanced in years." And the angel answered and said to him, "I am **Gabriel**, who stands in the presence of God, and was sent to speak to you and bring you these glad tidings. But behold, you will be mute and not able to speak until the day these things take place, because you did not believe my words which will be fulfilled in their own time." (NKJV)*

last promise
Malachi 4:5–6

Gabriel
high-ranking angel who appears in both the Old and New Testaments

Zacharias was stunned, but not speechless. Filled with doubt, he asked how this incredible miracle could be accomplished. After all, it was humanly impossible for Elizabeth to bear a child. Zacharias recognized that his visitor was a heavenly being, but when the messenger spoke, his response was based on earthly information. His questioning heart left no room for faith.

The angel responded with authority. He gave Zacharias:

- HIS NAME: Gabriel

- HIS CREDENTIALS: Gabriel stood in the presence of the living God and was sent with a specific message from God.

- PROOF OF HIS MESSAGE'S AUTHENTICITY: Zacharias would be unable to speak until the birth of the promised son.

what others say

R. C. Sproul

Zechariah would not have missed the fact that the angel was quoting from the book of Malachi. . . . The angel's announcement links the last promise of the Old Testament with the first promise of the New. Zechariah was given the message that he and his wife would be parents of the prophet who would announce the Messiah![4]

God decided when it was time to send the Messiah. Perhaps we can get a better understanding of God's timing by looking at first-century society. Rome provided roads that enabled relatively easy travel. Greece provided a language that was widely understood, and the faithful Jews were looking for the Messiah to be sent. The time was ripe to launch the Messiah's mission!

miracle
an occurrence that
cannot be explained
apart from the
power of God

A Long Silence

LUKE 1:21–25 *And the people waited for Zacharias, and marveled that he lingered so long in the temple. But when he came out, he could not speak to them; and they perceived that he had seen a vision in the temple, for he beckoned to them and remained speechless. So it was, as soon as the days of his service were completed, that he departed to his own house. Now after those days his wife Elizabeth conceived; and she hid herself five months, saying, "Thus the Lord has dealt with me, in the days when He looked on me, to take away my reproach among people." (NKJV)*

It's hard to imagine the scene outside the Temple as the people waited for Zacharias to appear. What was going on in there? What was taking Zacharias so long? And when he emerged from the Holy Place, they probably looked at each other in bewilderment. Why couldn't he speak to them? Why didn't Zacharias offer the usual benediction that followed the burning of incense?

It's even harder to imagine the scenes in Zacharias's home when he returned unable to speak of his awesome encounter with Gabriel and Elizabeth discovered she had become pregnant. Elizabeth must have poured out her joyous thoughts to Zacharias, but all he could do was gesture and write notes. This **miracle** was not random good luck in a game of chance—it was God invading Zacharias and Elizabeth's life with loving-kindness. Though Zacharias could not articulate the thoughts and feelings that welled up, they must have drawn closer to each other as they opened their hearts more and more to the Lord.

Zacharias doubted God's promise to give him the child of his hopes and dreams. Abraham, Isaac, Moses, and many other Bible heroes also doubted God's promises. Unbelief began in the Garden of Eden when Eve questioned God's word.

Let's avoid looking down on these individuals, as if we're superior. Like them, we doubt God's promises sometimes. The old washing machine gives up and the car breaks down—again. We complain, "Why me?" instead of trusting God to supply our needs. Rumors fly around that the company is going to downsize. We panic instead of believing that God is in control. A family member hurts us deeply. We write "hopeless" over the situation rather than trusting God to change hearts on both sides of the relationship. God still speaks today. Are we listening? Do we believe and act on what he tells us? It is not wrong to ask God questions, but it is wrong to doubt his ability to keep his Word.

Meanwhile, in an Obscure Village . . .

LUKE 1:26–33 *Now in the sixth month the angel Gabriel was sent by God to a city of Galilee named Nazareth, to a virgin betrothed to a man whose name was Joseph, of the house of David. The virgin's name was Mary. And having come in, the angel said to her, "Rejoice, highly favored one, the Lord is with you; blessed are you among women!" But when she saw him, she was troubled at his saying, and considered what manner of greeting this was. Then the angel said to her, "Do not be afraid, Mary, for you have found favor with God. And behold, you will conceive in your womb and bring forth a Son, and shall call His name JESUS. He will be great, and will be called the Son of the Highest; and the Lord God will give Him the throne of His father David. And He will reign over the house of Jacob forever, and of His kingdom there will be no end." (NKJV)*

An Astounding Encounter

In the village of Nazareth, within a small region in northern Israel called Galilee, a young woman, actually a teenager, was engaged to be married. Mary's engagement had not been heralded in the social observations of the more elite Judea to the south. For her, village life was simple and predictable. Her daily tasks involved cooking, cleaning, visiting the village well, and preparing for marriage to Joseph.

Suddenly, like a bolt of lightning, the angel Gabriel appeared, piercing and forever shattering the tranquility of Mary's life. When Gabriel greeted her, he told her she was highly favored by God, who was actually right there with her, knowing her every thought and motive!

Naturally Mary was astounded. Immediately, the angel assured her that she did not need to be afraid. God favored her so much he chose her to give birth to a child who would be unique in every way.

- The child would be called the Son of the Highest—equal with Jehovah, whom Mary worshiped. This would be **blasphemy** if Mary had thought of this without the angel's prompting. How could her son be equal with God?

Immanuel
name meaning
"God with us"

- God would give him the throne of his ancestor King David. A throne? What poor village girl would ever have aspired to such a privilege for her son?

- He would rule over the house of Jacob forever—as king of the nation Israel. How could this be when the Jews were then being ruled by the hated Romans?

- His kingdom would never end. What mystery was this? A mother has dreams for her child's well-being for a lifetime—but forever?

The angel was saying that Mary had been chosen to give birth to the Messiah, the one who had been promised throughout ages past. Could it be true? For her?

This was no time for theological debate. Hundreds of years before, the prophet Isaiah had written, "Therefore the Lord Himself will give you a sign: Behold, the virgin shall conceive and bear a Son, and shall call His name **Immanuel**" (Isaiah 7:14 NKJV). Whether Mary knew this or not, the fact was there: God had chosen her, a virgin, to bear a son who would be both God and man.

Angelic Explanation

LUKE 1:34–38 *Then Mary said to the angel, "How can this be, since I do not know a man?" And the angel answered and said to her, "The Holy Spirit will come upon you, and the power of the Highest will overshadow you; therefore, also, that Holy One who is to be born will be called the Son of God. Now indeed, Elizabeth your relative has also conceived a son in her old age; and this is now the sixth month for her who was called barren. For with God nothing will be impossible." Then Mary said, "Behold the maidservant of the Lord! Let it be to me according to your word." And the angel departed from her. (NKJV)*

Mary could have raised a number of panicky questions. "What will Joseph do to me?" "How will my parents handle the disgrace that I will bring on them?" "What will the village leaders say?" Instead, Mary asked a perfectly logical question as she prepared her heart to cooperate with God's plan for her: "How can this be?" No matter how honored she was to be the mother of the long-promised Messiah, no matter how convincingly the angel Gabriel had spoken, the practical question arose: How could a virgin possibly give birth to a son? Further, how could a human give birth to a child whose father was God?

Gabriel was not caught off guard. The answer was ready. The conception of Jesus would be an act of God. The Holy Spirit would come upon Mary and his presence would perform a unique miracle—once and only once in the history of humankind—so that she would give birth to a "holy" child, the only child ever born without sin of any kind. To bolster her trust in God's ability to do the impossible, Gabriel informed Mary that her elderly relative Elizabeth was already in her sixth month of pregnancy—another miracle of God.

Mary's response to God's plan for her has remained one of the most beautiful statements ever expressed: "Behold the maidservant of the Lord! Let it be to me according to your word" (Luke 1:38 NKJV). She did not argue or question. She submitted to the will of God for her and for the son she would bear.

A Study in Contrasts

Both Zacharias and Mary were visited by the angel Gabriel, who delivered God's promise of a child (Luke 1:19, 26). Note the contrasts in the following chart.

Two Angelic Visits, Two Birth Announcements

Zacharias	Mary
A man "well advanced in years" (1:7 NKJV)	A teenager engaged to be married (1:27)
A priest with temple duties (1:8–10)	A peasant girl who lived in the small village of Nazareth (1:26)
Response to angel: "troubled, and fear fell upon him" (1:12 NKJV)	Response to angel: filled with wonder at the meaning of his greeting (1:29)
Doubted: How can I be sure? My wife and I are old (1:18)	Asked: "How can this be, since I do not know a man?" (1:34 NKJV)
Because of his unbelief, made unable to speak until birth of son—proof that God had given the promise (1:20)	Believed the message and submitted to God's will (1:38); was articulate, filled with praise to God (1:46–55)

A virgin gave birth to Jesus Christ. Is this fact or fiction? Students of the Bible have long wrestled with this question while skeptics have laughed it off as utter fiction. However, it is a question on which hinges everything else the New Testament tells us about Jesus. If his virgin birth is fiction, then how much else in the New Testament is fiction?

If we believe Gabriel's statement that "with God nothing will be impossible" (Luke 1:37 NKJV), then we can accept as fact that Jesus was born of a virgin and that he was actually God in human form. Much as Mary had to have faith to believe that she, a virgin, would conceive a son, so we must have faith that the conception actually occurred as stated in the Bible. Will we respond to God's Word as Mary did—with reverence and acceptance—or as Zacharias did—with doubt and disbelief?

Mary's submission to God's will was not something she piously expressed, hoping to impress the messenger from heaven. She spoke spontaneously from her heart, revealing an attitude that was there even before the angel appeared. We should respond to God's Word with simple faith and a readiness to do whatever he says.

what others say

Gilbert Bilezikian

The significance of the virgin birth (or, more accurately, the virginal conception) of Christ is twofold. It demonstrates Christ's complete identification with the human race and his uniqueness as the Son of God.[5]

Charles C. Ryrie

The virgin birth was the means of the Incarnation. The **Incarnation**, once accomplished, is a lasting state for our Lord. It began at his birth and continues (albeit in a resurrection body now) forever. The virgin birth was an event that lasted only a matter of hours.[6]

Kindred Hearts

LUKE 1:39–45 *Now Mary arose in those days and went into the hill country with haste, to a city of Judah, and entered the house of Zacharias and greeted Elizabeth. And it happened, when Elizabeth heard the greeting of Mary, that the babe leaped in her womb; and Elizabeth was filled with the Holy Spirit. Then she spoke out with a loud voice and said, "Blessed are you among women, and blessed is the fruit of your womb! But why is this granted to me, that the mother of my Lord should come to me? For indeed, as soon as the voice of your greeting sounded in my ears, the babe leaped in my womb for joy. Blessed is she who believed, for there will be a fulfillment of those things which were told her from the Lord." (NKJV)*

Of all the people Mary knew, one would understand her experience better than any other. Elizabeth, her elderly relative (possibly her cousin), was also to be the mother of a miracle child. She was already in her sixth month of pregnancy.

Mary hurried to the town where Elizabeth and Zacharias lived, assured of a welcome. She could hardly have anticipated, however, the joyful, Spirit-guided reception Elizabeth gave her. As soon as Mary greeted her, Elizabeth felt her baby leap within her. Instantly Elizabeth sensed that her unborn child recognized that Mary was the mother of the yet-to-be-born Messiah, and she herself acknowledged that she was favored to be visited by Mary, whom she referred to as "the mother of my Lord" (Luke 1:43 NKJV). Mary's heart must have welled up with thankfulness for the confirmation that she was indeed blessed by God and that he would reward her obedience.

Mary's Song

LUKE 1:46–56 *And Mary said:*
"My soul magnifies the Lord,
And my spirit has rejoiced in God my Savior.
For He has regarded the lowly state of His maidservant;
For behold, henceforth all generations will call me blessed.
For He who is mighty has done great things for me,
And holy is His name.
And His mercy is on those who fear Him
From generation to generation.
He has shown strength with His arm;
He has scattered the proud in the imagination of their hearts.
He has put down the mighty from their thrones,
And exalted the lowly.
He has filled the hungry with good things,
And the rich He has sent away empty.

go to

Hannah's song
1 Samuel 2:1–10

The Magnificat
the liturgical name
given to Mary's song
of praise

glorify
to praise God for
who he is and to
submit to him in
worship and
obedience

He has helped His servant Israel,
In remembrance of His mercy,
As He spoke to our fathers,
To Abraham and to his seed forever."
And Mary remained with her about three months, and
returned to her house. (NKJV)

Mary was so eager to express her praise to God that she burst into song! Her song is so remarkable that it is still celebrated as **"The Magnificat."** Her words are amazing when we remember that she was a young teenager living in a quiet village that had no resources for enrichment in the fine arts. Her song is somewhat like <u>Hannah's song</u>, in which Hannah praised God for giving her the son for whom she had prayed.

Mary begins by expressing her desire to **glorify** the Lord and rejoice in him as her Savior. She praises him for his favor on her, such favor that future generations would call her blessed. She then turns her focus on God. Her lyrics are lavish with references to the Old Testament as she praises him for his mercy, mighty deeds, power, loving-kindness to the humble, his faithfulness in keeping his promises to Abraham and his descendants.

Mary's song has 133 words, as translated in the New King James Version of the Bible. The opening 49 words relate to her personal wonder and joy in the amazing blessing the Lord had given her, and the remaining 84 words express praise to God for who he is.

> ### what others say
>
> #### Larry Sibley
>
> Mary's words are called "The Magnificat" from the first word in the Latin translation. Her praise was couched in phrases drawn from the Old Testament. . . . Her mind was saturated with Old Testament language. When she spoke her praise, it was largely with words that were already part of the Bible.
>
> When one realizes that Mary had no personal copy of the Old Testament it is clear that she must have listened very carefully to synagogue readings.[8]

Luke records that Mary stayed with Elizabeth for about three months, probably returning to Nazareth just before Elizabeth gave birth to her son.

Matthew, who records these events from a different angle in Matthew 1:18–25, gives us some interesting information. Soon after Mary returned to Nazareth, she must have told Joseph the news. Understandably he was distraught. His engagement to Mary was legally binding, yet it would appear that she had been unfaithful. To avoid seeing her publicly disgraced, he decided to seek a quiet divorce from her. But God sent an angel, perhaps Gabriel, to assure him of the truth of Mary's message. Joseph's heart was opened to God. He accepted the news and immediately took Mary to be his wife.

At that time in that culture, a betrothal was regarded as binding as a marriage. The main difference was the man and the woman simply didn't live together yet.

Birth of a Messenger

LUKE 1:57–66 *Now Elizabeth's full time came for her to be delivered, and she brought forth a son. When her neighbors and relatives heard how the Lord had shown great mercy to her, they rejoiced with her. So it was, on the eighth day, that they came to circumcise the child; and they would have called him by the name of his father, Zacharias. His mother answered and said, "No; he shall be called John." But they said to her, "There is no one among your relatives who is called by this name." So they made signs to his father—what he would have him called. And he asked for a writing tablet, and wrote, saying, "His name is John." So they all marveled. Immediately his mouth was opened and his tongue loosed, and he spoke, praising God. Then fear came on all who dwelt around them; and all these sayings were discussed throughout all the hill country of Judea. And all those who heard them kept them in their hearts, saying, "What kind of child will this be?" And the hand of the Lord was with him.* (NKJV)

Excitement surged through a little town in the hilly area near Jerusalem. Word spread quickly that Elizabeth had just given birth to a son, and just as quickly people praised God for his great mercy in giving Zacharias and Elizabeth a child in their old age.

A celebration was held on the eighth day. Obeying God's law, they performed the rite of circumcision, which set the baby boy apart as a Jew. Then came the naming of the child. Friends and relatives assumed that custom would be followed and the child would be named Zacharias after his father Zacharias, whose name meant "Yahweh remembers." But Elizabeth spoke up, correcting them. The child would be called John!

Surely Elizabeth had made a mistake! No relative had that name. So they turned to Zacharias. To everyone's amazement he wrote, "His name is John" (Luke 1:63 NKJV).

What was the significance of giving the baby the name of John, meaning "Yahweh is gracious"? When Zacharias agreed with Elizabeth, he was obeying what the angel had directed, "You shall call his name John" (Luke 1:13 NKJV), and demonstrated his faith in God. Immediately his ability to speak was restored, and understandably his first words were praises to God.

Everyone in that town and in the surrounding area could not stop talking about what was happening. Surely John was a child to be watched as he grew up, for it was evident that God's special blessing was on him.

what others say

The Bible Knowledge Commentary

Word then spread through the whole hill country (in the Jerusalem area) that this was an unusual child. The people continued to note that the Lord's hand was with him. Years later, when John began his preaching ministry, many went out from this district who no doubt remembered the amazing events surrounding his birth (Matthew 3:5).[9]

A Father's Song

LUKE 1:67–75 *Now his father Zacharias was filled with the Holy Spirit, and prophesied, saying:*
"Blessed is the Lord God of Israel,
For He has visited and redeemed His people,
And has raised up a horn of salvation for us
In the house of His servant David,
As He spoke by the mouth of His holy prophets,
Who have been since the world began,
That we should be saved from our enemies
And from the hand of all who hate us,
To perform the mercy promised to our fathers
And to remember His holy covenant,
The oath which He swore to our father Abraham:

To grant us that we,
Being delivered from the hand of our enemies,
Might serve Him without fear,
In holiness and righteousness before Him all the days of
*   our life. (NKJV)*

horns
Deuteronomy 33:17

anoint
1 Samuel 16:1, 13

salvation
Psalm 18:2

enemies
Psalm 132:17–18;
Jeremiah 30:8–9

Star
Numbers 24:17

Sun of Righteousness
Malachi 4:2

Zacharias's joy could not be repressed. During his months of silence he had opportunity to reflect on both Gabriel's words to him and on the Old Testament Scriptures he had loved for so long. Now he was filled with the Holy Spirit and burst out in a song that was full of praise to God for his faithfulness in keeping his promises to Israel. His hymn focused not on his newborn son, but on the one John would be introducing to the world, the Messiah.

Balaam
a practitioner of
the occult through
whom God gave
a prophecy

Zacharias's reference to Israel's "horn of salvation" (verse 69) was significant. The <u>horns</u> of an animal, such as an ox, were symbolic of his strength. A horn was filled with oil, which was used to <u>anoint</u> kings. Zacharias was picturing the power of the Messiah, the horn of salvation, who was coming to bring <u>salvation</u> and to fulfill God's promise that the Messiah would save them from their <u>enemies</u>.

Praise for a Precious Child

Luke 1:76–80
And you, child, will be called the prophet of the Highest;
For you will go before the face of the Lord to prepare His ways,
To give knowledge of salvation to His people
By the remission of their sins,
Through the tender mercy of our God,
With which the Dayspring from on high has visited us;
To give light to those who sit in darkness and the shadow
*   of death,*
To guide our feet into the way of peace."
So the child grew and became strong in spirit, and was in the
deserts till the day of his manifestation to Israel.

Zacharias also sang of the mission his son would fulfill. John would become a prophet of God to prepare the way for the Messiah. Through his preaching many people would turn to God for forgiveness and thus would be prepared to welcome the Messiah, who would come as the "Dayspring from on high." Centuries before, **Balaam** had prophesied of the Messiah, saying a <u>Star</u> would come. Malachi, in the last Old Testament book, prophesied that the Messiah would come as the <u>Sun of Righteousness</u>. Those living in the darkness of sin and death would welcome John's message that the Messiah was coming to bring light and life.

Under the watchful eyes of his parents, John grew both physically and spiritually. Gabriel had announced that John would work "in the spirit and power of Elijah" (Luke 1:17 NKJV). It was fitting that when John grew up and was preparing himself for his work, he lived briefly in the wilderness, as Elijah had done so long before. In the silence of those lonely surroundings, John discovered the message he was to bring—a message Israel had not heard for many generations.

what others say

Stephen Fortosis

We worship the same God Zechariah and Elizabeth worshiped. Yet sometimes we actually imply to God, either directly or indirectly, that we don't believe he can act in supernatural ways. We should never underestimate God's ability to do anything he wills. His grace and power have no limits.[10]

Chapter Wrap-Up

- Luke wrote his Gospel to give Theophilus and others a carefully researched and organized account of Jesus's life on earth (Luke 1:1–4).

- Though Zacharias and his wife, Elizabeth, grieved because they were still childless in their old age, they followed God's laws and lived without blame before God. Zacharias faithfully performed his duties as a priest (Luke 1:5–10).

- An angel told Zacharias that Elizabeth would bear a son whose name would be John and whose mission would be to prepare people for the arrival of the Messiah. Zacharias questioned this possibility, and God took away Zacharias's ability to speak until John was born. God kept his promise: Elizabeth became pregnant; Zacharias became dumb (Luke 1:11–25).

- Gabriel was sent by God to announce to Mary that she had been chosen to be the mother of the Messiah. Though Mary was a virgin, the conception would take place through the Holy Spirit overshadowing her. She would give birth to Jesus, the God-man. Gabriel assured Mary that "with God nothing will be impossible" (Luke 1:26–38).

- When Mary visited Elizabeth, the Holy Spirit gave Elizabeth insight to see that Mary would be the mother of God. Mary burst into a song of praise that exalted God, first for his favor on her, and then for his favor on all her people in showing mercy, mighty deeds, power, loving-kindness, and faithfulness in keeping his promises (Luke 1:39–56).

- When John was born, people rejoiced, acknowledging that God had given Zacharias and Elizabeth a son in their old age. The people were in awe in the way both Elizabeth and Zacharias confirmed that their child would be named John, and Zacharias's speech returned immediately afterward (Luke 1:57–66).

- After nine months of silence, Zacharias expressed praise to God in a song. He praised God for his faithfulness in keeping his promise to Israel. He also acknowledged that John would grow up to be God's prophet who would prepare people to receive the Messiah (Luke 1:67–80).

Study Questions

1. After four hundred years of silence, how did God set in motion his timetable for sending the promised Messiah?

2. God sent Gabriel to give announcements to Zacharias and Mary. In what ways were Zechariah and Mary alike in their responses? How were they different?

3. What did God say would be John's unique mission?

4. What purpose was served by Zacharias's inability to speak throughout Elizabeth's pregnancy?

5. Why is it important for you to accept and believe in the virgin birth of Jesus Christ?

6. What events led the people to see that "the hand of the Lord" was with John?

Luke 2 Birth and Boyhood

Let's Get Started

One birth is celebrated today with far more joy and pageantry than could have been imagined when the actual birth occurred two thousand years ago. There's a great contrast between the humble arrival of the Son of God and the lavish displays of Christmas decorations that compete for our attention and entice us to spend money on merchandise that is not remotely related to the one whose birth we celebrate.

Micah
Micah 5:2

Luke, ever a realist, did not garnish his account of Jesus's arrival with tinsel and glittering lights. Instead, he causes a hush to come over our hearts as he takes us into what really happened that holy night when God came in the person of his Son to live among us.

The Birth of Jesus

> **LUKE 2:1–5** *And it came to pass in those days that a decree went out from Caesar Augustus that all the world should be registered. This census first took place while Quirinius was governing Syria. So all went to be registered, everyone to his own city. Joseph also went up from Galilee, out of the city of Nazareth, into Judea, to the city of David, which is called Bethlehem, because he was of the house and lineage of David, to be registered with Mary, his betrothed wife, who was with child.* (NKJV)

Through his prophet <u>Micah</u>, God had announced that Bethlehem would be the birthplace of the coming Messiah. (The word *Messiah* comes from the Hebrew word for "anointed one." The word for *anointed* in Greek is *christos*, from which we get the title "Christ.")

Mary, however, lived in the Galilean town of Nazareth—a village ninety miles north of Bethlehem (see appendix A). So, how did God relocate Mary in time for Jesus's birth? He used the Roman emperor's census. The custom was for people to register for the census at their hometown, and Joseph's hometown was Bethlehem.

Why did Caesar Augustus take a census? He needed money for the imperial treasury. The best way for the emperor to get money was to increase taxes. The best way to increase taxes was to take a census.

Artists show Mary riding on a donkey to Bethlehem. Fact or fiction? Luke makes no mention of a donkey, so we shouldn't claim this as fact. Mary was pregnant, however, and we know from other Scriptures that Joseph did his best to look after her. So it's certainly possible Joseph provided his pregnant fiancée with a donkey or some other means of transportation less toilsome than walking.

Birth in Bethlehem

LUKE 2:6–7 *So it was, that while they were there, the days were completed for her to be delivered. And she brought forth her firstborn Son, and wrapped Him in swaddling cloths, and laid Him in a manger, because there was no room for them in the inn. (NKJV)*

Because of the influx of census registrants, there was no room for Mary and Joseph in the inn. The Son of God was born in unsanitary surroundings with only Mary and Joseph and a few animals to hear his first cry.

Was Jesus born in the muck and grime of an animal stable? Though this isn't explicit in Scripture, most Bible students conclude such, because Mary laid him in a **manger**. Was the newborn baby surrounded by soft lights, sweet-smelling hay, the rhythmic munching of cattle, and the soft cooing of doves? Probably not. Typically a first-century "inn" was a series of stalls where guests built fires and cooked the food they had brought with them. They could look out toward a cave or common area where animals were tethered. If this was the case in Bethlehem, Mary and Joseph could not find an open stall, so Mary gave birth in less-than-pleasant surroundings among animals.

what others say

R. Kent Hughes

If we imagine that Jesus was born in a freshly swept, county fair stable, we miss the whole point. It was wretched—scandalous! There was sweat and pain and blood and cries as

> Mary reached up to the heavens for help. The earth was cold and hard. The smell of birth mixed with the stench of manure and acrid straw made a contemptible bouquet. Trembling carpenter's hands, clumsy with fear, grasped God's Son slippery with blood—the baby's limbs waving helplessly as if falling through space—his face grimacing as he gasped in the cold and his cry pierced the night.[1]

Luke gives particular emphasis to the birth of Jesus, providing details that may have come from personal interviews with Mary herself. As he notes the place where Mary gave birth to her son, we can almost sense his sympathy for the shattering disappointment Mary and Joseph must have felt when there was no room for them in the inn.

As Mary placed her newborn son in the manger, Luke notes that she followed the common practice of their day, called "swaddling." She wrapped his whole body in long strips of cloth, as the medical profession recommended. People of that day thought the snug wrapping helped ensure straight limbs and prevented broken bones.

Angel Announcement

LUKE 2:8–14 *Now there were in the same country shepherds living out in the fields, keeping watch over their flock by night. And behold, an angel of the Lord stood before them, and the glory of the Lord shone around them, and they were greatly afraid. Then the angel said to them, "Do not be afraid, for behold, I bring you good tidings of great joy which will be to all people. For there is born to you this day in the city of David a Savior, who is Christ the Lord. And this will be the sign to you: You will find a Babe wrapped in swaddling cloths, lying in a manger." And suddenly there was with the angel a multitude of the heavenly host praising God and saying:*
"Glory to God in the highest,
And on earth peace, goodwill toward men!" (NKJV)

Just like always, shepherds were out in the fields near Bethlehem. Just like always, they were keeping track of the sheep that huddled around them in the darkness.

Suddenly the silence was shattered and the darkness was pierced by an unearthly light. An angel appeared to them and the heaven's

Mary
Luke 1:46–55

Zacharias
Luke 1:67–79

Lamb of God
John 1:29

glory shone around the trembling shepherds. They were terrified, but the heavenly messenger assured them they had no need to fear. The angel came with good news for them and for all people. A Savior had been born in Bethlehem. They would find the newborn "wrapped in swaddling cloths, lying in a manger" (Luke 2:12 NKJV).

The startled shepherds listened breathlessly as the angel was joined by a huge choir of angels that filled the sky, praising God in heaven and blessing people on earth.

Who Is This Newborn?

The angel spoke of the newborn as Savior, Christ, and the Lord, names that spoke volumes:

- *Savior:* the one who would deliver his people. Though the shepherds would not have known it, the name confirmed what both <u>Mary</u> and <u>Zacharias</u> had acknowledged in their songs.
- *Christ:* the Anointed One of God, the promised Messiah, for whom faithful Jews had waited for many generations.
- *The Lord:* God, who became one of us in a human body.

The shepherds were humble men not highly thought of by the law-keeping religious leaders of their day. Their outdoor duties of caring for sheep prohibited them from observing rigid ceremonial rules demanded by the orthodox Jews. Still, they probably were sincere in their faith in God. Some scholars of this period believe shepherds tended sheep that would be offered in temple sacrifices. Perhaps, uneducated as they were, they understood the significance of their roles as shepherds of such sheep. Perhaps when they heard the angel's message, they gained insight into the true identity of the newborn child—the Savior who would give his life as the <u>Lamb of God</u> and would forever remove the need for sacrificing sheep, for he would take away the sins of the world.

Shepherds Are Not Sheepish

LUKE 2:15–20 *So it was, when the angels had gone away from them into heaven, that the shepherds said to one another, "Let us now go to Bethlehem and see this thing that has come to pass, which the Lord has made known to us." And they came with haste and found Mary and Joseph, and the Babe lying in a manger. Now when they had seen Him, they made widely known the saying which was told them concerning this Child. And all those who heard it marveled at those things which were told them by the shepherds. But Mary kept all these things and pondered them in her heart. Then the shepherds returned, glorifying and praising God for all the things that they had heard and seen, as it was told them. (NKJV)*

The shepherds made a quick decision to investigate what they had heard. There was no question in their minds that the God of Israel had given them the announcement. They hurried off to Bethlehem and found the baby with Mary and Joseph, exactly as the angel had said.

Immediately they spread the word, sharing with everyone who would listen what the angel had said. Townspeople were amazed at the news. But Mary was more than amazed. She "kept all these things" that had happened and "pondered them" deeply "in her heart" (Luke 2:19 NKJV). She kept as a precious jewel the confirmation of what the angel Gabriel had told her: she was the mother of the Savior of the world. The shepherds were filled with joy as they returned to their sheep. Their hearts overflowed and their voices proclaimed their praises to God.

As God revealed his plan for saving the world, the reaction was consistent. People responded with praise. Take Zacharias in the Temple. First, he was fearful and full of doubt. But when John was born, he expressed wholehearted praise. Elizabeth received Mary with joyful praise to God. When Mary learned God was keeping his promise to send the Savior, she responded with a song of praise. After the birth of Jesus, the shepherds were unrestrained in their praise to God for all they had seen and heard.

What is your PQ (praise quotient) as you consider the birth of Jesus? Every reason we have for rejoicing is linked to God's love for us and for his unfathomable mercy in sending his Son to be our Savior.

apply it

go to

circumcision
Genesis 17:9–14

naming
1 Samuel 1:20

Gabriel
Matthew 1:21;
Luke 1:31

purification
Leviticus 12:1–4,
22–24

what others say

William Barclay

In Palestine the birth of a boy was an occasion of great joy. When the time of the birth was near at hand, friends and local musicians gathered near the house. When the birth was announced and it was a boy, the musicians broke into music and song, and there was universal congratulation and rejoicing. If it was a girl the musicians went silently and regretfully away! There was a saying, "The birth of a male child causes universal joy, but the birth of a female child causes universal sorrow."[2]

By the Book

LUKE 2:21–24 *And when eight days were completed for the circumcision of the Child, His name was called JESUS, the name given by the angel before He was conceived in the womb.*

Now when the days of her purification according to the law of Moses were completed, they brought Him to Jerusalem to present Him to the Lord (as it is written in the law of the Lord, "Every male who opens the womb shall be called holy to the LORD"), and to offer a sacrifice according to what is said in the law of the Lord, "A pair of turtledoves or two young pigeons." (NKJV)

Mary and Joseph were careful to obey the laws that God had given and to follow the customs of Jews who were new parents. This involved three ceremonies.

First, on the eighth day of their baby's life, Mary and Joseph observed the ceremony of <u>circumcision</u> and <u>naming</u> the child.

Naming a new child seems to have been the responsibility of the mother usually, but the responsibility could be assumed by the father. In this case Mary and Joseph named their baby Jesus, as <u>Gabriel</u> had directed.

Second, forty days after the birth of Jesus, Mary and Joseph took him from Bethlehem to the Temple in Jerusalem for the ceremony of <u>purification</u>. Women who gave birth were unclean, according to the law, until they participated in this ceremony. The mother was to make two offerings—a lamb and a dove. However, the law allowed those who could not afford a lamb to offer two doves or two young pigeons. Mary chose the alternate offering—a public indication that she could not afford a lamb.

The third ceremony was for the redemption of the firstborn son. The law said that every <u>firstborn son</u> should be "presented to God" or dedicated for service to him. Then the son would be **redeemed** for the "redemption price" of five shekels.

go to

firstborn son
Numbers 18:15–16

Simeon's Dreams Come True

redeemed
to "buy back"

what others say

J. C. Ryle

The word *Jesus* means simply "Savior" . . . a name which speaks of mercy, grace, help, and deliverance for a lost world. It is as a deliverer and redeemer that he desires principally to be known.[3]

LUKE 2:25–35 *And behold, there was a man in Jerusalem whose name was Simeon, and this man was just and devout, waiting for the Consolation of Israel, and the Holy Spirit was upon him. And it had been revealed to him by the Holy Spirit that he would not see death before he had seen the Lord's Christ. So he came by the Spirit into the temple. And when the parents brought in the Child Jesus, to do for Him according to the custom of the law, he took Him up in his arms and blessed God and said:*

"Lord, now You are letting Your servant depart in peace,
According to Your word;
For my eyes have seen Your salvation
Which You have prepared before the face of all peoples,
A light to bring revelation to the Gentiles,
And the glory of Your people Israel."

And Joseph and His mother marveled at those things which were spoken of Him. Then Simeon blessed them, and said to Mary His mother, "Behold, this Child is destined for the fall and rising of many in Israel, and for a sign which will be spoken against (yes, a sword will pierce through your own soul also), that the thoughts of many hearts may be revealed." (NKJV)

Simeon was old and ready to die—but not yet! He had been waiting for God to send the Messiah, and lived in such a close relationship with God that he knew from the Holy Spirit that he would not die before seeing that Promised One.

go to

sword
Luke 2:35

Gentiles
non-Jews

rejection
refusal to accept

crucifixion
form of capital punishment whereby the victim was tied or nailed to a cross

On the day Mary and Joseph brought Jesus to the Temple, Simeon was gently nudged by the Spirit to meet them there. Taking the baby in his arms, he praised God for sending the one who would be the light of the world—not only to the Jews for whom he was promised, but also to the **Gentiles** who needed a Savior just as badly.

Turning to the astonished parents, Simeon made predictions that were fulfilled both within their lifetimes and afterward. Mary's child would have a pivotal effect on people. Those who refused him would fall, while those who received him would rise and be blessed. Her son would also be "a sign which will be spoken against" (Luke 2:34 NKJV), meaning his sinless life and his open relationship with God his Father would provoke hatred in the hearts of the unbelieving. Simeon concluded his speech with a special word for Mary. The privilege of being the mother of Jesus came with a cost. Her soul would be pierced when she witnessed the **rejection** of her son and his eventual **crucifixion** as a common criminal.

what others say

Frederick Buechner

What [Simeon] saw in [Mary's] face was a long way off, but it was there so plainly he couldn't pretend. "A <u>sword</u> will pierce through your soul," he said.

He would rather have bitten off his tongue than said it, but in that holy place he felt he had no choice. Then he handed her back the baby and departed in something less than the perfect peace he'd dreamed of all the long years of his waiting.[4]

Luke includes words from Simeon's song that articulate a perspective on death that believers may enjoy. For Simeon, the pleasures of earthly life had lost their appeal and the fear of the grave had lost its terror. As a physician who had doubtless observed the agonizing passing of his patients, Luke must have marveled at the testimony of this righteous man who had complete confidence that he was in God's hands. He had a secure future beyond physical death and was ready to go whenever God called him.

Not Your Average Little Old Lady

LUKE 2:36–38 *Now there was one, Anna, a prophetess, the daughter of Phanuel, of the tribe of Asher. She was of a great*

age, and had lived with a husband seven years from her virgin-
ity; and this woman was a widow of about eighty-four years, who
did not depart from the temple, but served God with fastings
and prayers night and day. And coming in that instant she
gave thanks to the Lord, and spoke of Him to all those who looked
for redemption in Jerusalem. (NKJV)

Having been married for seven years and widowed for eighty-four,
Anna must have been more than a hundred years old. She may have
been frail, but her spirit was lively. Anna's devout heart kept her
always at the Temple, worshiping, fasting, praying, seeking. A
prophetess, Anna lived so close to God that he gave her revelations
to share with others. We can easily imagine a youthful curiosity
drawing Anna to the temple doors whenever they opened. On the
day Mary and Joseph presented Jesus at the Temple, she sensed
instantly the longed-for Messiah! She lifted her heart in praise to
God and spoke to all the faithful that God had kept his promise. The
Savior had come.

Medical professionals see them every day—the elderly and frail,
the very old whose minds and bodies are wasting away. They often
hole themselves up in their homes or apartments and rarely go out.
Surely Luke had seen his fair share of such people. Their needs were
great and their caregivers could do little to bring comfort or relief,
for old age cannot be reversed. Some elderly people are exceptional,
however. Though bodies age and frailty creeps in, the inner spirit
does not have to harden or become brittle with disillusionment or
disappointment. Even in their advanced years, Simeon's and Anna's
hopes were vibrant; their spirits sang with youthful praise to God.
They did not consider cocooning an option. They were out and
about. They were actively engaged in public worship and daily contact with people of faith. Just to hear about the radiance that shone
through the eyes of aged Simeon and Anna must have brightened
Luke's heart so much that he included their visits in his Gospel.

what others say

John Piper

I think Luke tells us about Simeon and Anna to illustrate the
way holy and devout people feel about the promise of Christ's
coming, and how God responds to their longings. They see
more than others see. They may not understand fully all the

details about how the Messiah is coming—Simeon and Anna surely didn't—but God mercifully gives them, before they die, a glimpse of what they so passionately wanted to see.[5]

Boyhood Briefly

LUKE 2:39–40 *So when they had performed all things according to the law of the Lord, they returned to Galilee, to their own city, Nazareth. And the Child grew and became strong in spirit, filled with wisdom; and the grace of God was upon Him.* (NKJV)

In one sentence Luke summarizes the next few years of Jesus's life. The child Jesus grew normally, becoming strong in body and spirit and filled with unusual wisdom. Clearly, God's grace was on this very special boy.

gospel harmony

For more of the story we must turn to Matthew's account of Jesus's early years in Matthew 2. After Mary and Joseph presented Jesus at the Temple, Matthew says the young family returned to Bethlehem. After living there approximately two years, their circumstances suddenly changed.

Wise men, the Magi from the East, arrived unannounced in Jerusalem and inquired about a new "king of the Jews." Their query upset King Herod—an evil ruler who was paranoid of losing his position and brutally killed anyone he wished. God guided the wise men by a star to the house where they found Jesus. After they bowed down and worshiped him, they presented him with gifts of gold, incense, and myrrh. They returned to their country without reporting back to King Herod, disobeying his orders. Furious, Herod ordered his troops to go to Bethlehem and kill every male child two years old and younger.

But Jesus was not there. An angel had warned Joseph, urging him to take Mary and the young child to Egypt. They were to stay there until the threat had passed.

Contrary to popular thinking, we don't know for a fact that there were three wise men. Plus, we do know for a fact that these wise men did *not* worship the infant Jesus at the manger in Bethlehem. Nowhere does the Bible record how many wise men arrived. The idea that there were three wise men arose from the number of gifts the wise men presented. Furthermore, by the time the wise men arrived, Joseph had moved his family from the stable to a house. King Herod found it necessary to kill all boys two years old and younger, which means Herod knew it was possible Jesus was no longer a newborn. The wise men required months to travel from Babylon to Jerusalem, so it's likely Jesus was between six months and two years old when the wise men arrived to worship him.

A Missing Messiah

LUKE 2:41–50 *His parents went to Jerusalem every year at the Feast of the Passover. And when He was twelve years old, they went up to Jerusalem according to the custom of the feast. When they had finished the days, as they returned, the Boy Jesus lingered behind in Jerusalem. And Joseph and His mother did not know it; but supposing Him to have been in the company, they went a day's journey, and sought Him among their relatives and acquaintances. So when they did not find Him, they returned to Jerusalem, seeking Him. Now so it was that after three days they found Him in the temple, sitting in the midst of the teachers, both listening to them and asking them questions. And all who heard Him were astonished at His understanding and answers. So when they saw Him, they were amazed; and His mother said to Him, "Son, why have You done this to us? Look, Your father and I have sought You anxiously." And He said to them, "Why did you seek Me? Did you not know that I must be about My Father's business?" But they did not understand the statement which He spoke to them. (NKJV)*

When Jesus reached age twelve, he became a **"son of the commandment."** He was a member of the synagogue and was accountable for obeying the law of Moses. He was also allowed to accompany Mary and Joseph on their annual trip to Jerusalem where they celebrated the **Feast of Passover**. When it was time to return to Nazareth, the celebrants left in groups. Mary enjoyed the companionship of other women, while Joseph traveled with men. Both assumed Jesus was with the other group. When evening came and it was time to set up camp for the night, they discovered Jesus was missing.

Mary and Joseph set off for Jerusalem, anxiously looking for their son. On the third day they found him in the Temple. He was perfectly comfortable, seated with members of the Jewish **Sanhedrin**, listening and contributing to their theological discussions and raising such perceptive questions that the religious elders were amazed

son of the commandment
English for *bar mitzvah*

Feast of Passover
celebration of Israel's freedom from Egyptian slavery

Sanhedrin
seventy leaders who served as the high council and supreme court in Hebrew law

please him
John 5:30

at his understanding and insights. What happened in the Temple revealed how Jewish leaders trained young rabbis. Students not only listened to their teachers, but they also were encouraged to raise questions.

Mary's frustration erupted as she announced to Jesus that she and Joseph had been frantically searching for him for three days. Jesus was surprised. He thought it was obvious that if he wasn't with Mary and Joseph, they would know he was about his "Father's business" (Luke 2:49 NKJV). Jesus already knew his father was God, not Joseph.

> ### what others say
>
> ### R. C. Sproul
>
> How significant that the first recorded words of Jesus are ones that go to the heart of his own destiny, to his vocation and calling as the Messiah. Here Jesus is consciously identifying himself as the Son of God, because it was his Father's house.[6]
>
> ### Leon Morris
>
> Jesus had a relationship to God shared by no other. Joseph and Mary did not understand this. They learned what Jesus' Messiahship meant bit by bit.[7]

Home Sweet Home

> LUKE 2:51–52 *Then He went down with them and came to Nazareth, and was subject to them, but His mother kept all these things in her heart. And Jesus increased in wisdom and stature, and in favor with God and men.* (NKJV)

We may wonder what the threesome talked about as they made the trip from Jerusalem back to Nazareth. Jesus quickly shifted gears from his intellectual discussions in the Temple to the more simple interests of his parents. Mary must have looked at Jesus with wonder, tucking away in her memory the insights she had gathered about her unusual son. She treasured these as evidence that Jesus was indeed who the angel had promised he would be. For the next eighteen years, Jesus fit into the everyday life of Nazareth and was obedient to his parents in all ways. But he never forgot even for a moment who his real Father was, and he lived to please him in every way.

Luke made a special comment on Jesus's total fitness. As an adolescent growing into manhood, Jesus was perfectly balanced. He grew "in wisdom"—intellectually. He grew "in stature"—physically. He grew "in favor with God"—spiritually. And he grew in favor with the people of Nazareth—socially.

Jesus did not overemphasize any aspect of growth. While our culture may favor one aspect of healthy growth over another, we need to remember that what was important to the perfect Son of God should also be important to us: to strive for healthy growth intellectually, physically, spiritually, and socially.

Chapter Wrap-Up

- Caesar Augustus ordered a census that required Joseph to go to Bethlehem to register. While there, Mary gave birth to Jesus. Angels announced the birth of Jesus the Savior to shepherds who were watching their sheep in the fields near Bethlehem. After the shepherds went to see the baby lying in the manger, they rejoiced and spread the happy news of the Savior's birth. (Luke 2:1–20)

- Mary and Joseph fulfilled the requirements of the law at the Temple and presented the sacrifice allowed for the poor. (Luke 2:21–24)

- Simeon, a devout man in Jerusalem, was eagerly looking for the coming of the promised Messiah. The Holy Spirit alerted him to go to the temple court, where he met the baby Jesus. Simeon, recognizing that he was the Messiah, gave glory to God. Anna, an elderly woman who worshiped frequently at the Temple, also recognized who Jesus was and shared the good news with others who were looking for God's promised Messiah. (Luke 2:25–38)

- Mary and Joseph took Jesus to live in Nazareth, where Jesus grew as a normal, healthy boy. (Luke 2:39–40).

- When Jesus was twelve years old, Mary and Joseph took him to Jerusalem for the Feast of Passover. As they returned, they discovered Jesus was missing. Hurrying back, they found Jesus in the Temple discussing important theological issues. He was surprised that they did not understand where he would be—in his Father's house. Jesus went back to Nazareth, where he lived in obedience to them and matured into perfect manhood. (Luke 2:41–52)

Study Questions

1. What event led Jesus to be born in Bethlehem, as foretold in Micah?

2. In Bethlehem, where was Jesus born? Why was he born in such inhospitable surroundings?

3. What was the significance of the angel announcing to shepherds the birth of the Savior?

4. What did Simeon and Anna say and do that showed they recognized the true identity of the baby Mary and Joseph presented at the Temple?

5. What did Jesus reveal about himself when he was twelve years old and visited Jerusalem for the Feast of the Passover?

Let's Get Started

In the last chapter we found out about the amazing events that surrounded the birth of two babies, John and Jesus. Both births were miracles—John's because Zacharias and Elizabeth were too old to have children and Jesus's because Mary was a virgin.

John grew up and chose a rugged life in the desert. Luke accounts for Jesus's life up to when Jesus astonished teachers and religious leaders in the Temple at age twelve. Then Luke leaves Jesus in Joseph's carpenter shop in Nazareth where Jesus grew from boyhood to manhood. These have been called the "hidden years" of Jesus. Luke's third chapter turns to the public ministry of John.

go to

orderly account
Luke 1:3

John's Message

LUKE 3:1–6 *Now in the fifteenth year of the reign of Tiberius Caesar, Pontius Pilate being governor of Judea, Herod being tetrarch of Galilee, his brother Philip tetrarch of Iturea and the region of Trachonitis, and Lysanias tetrarch of Abilene, while Annas and Caiaphas were high priests, the word of God came to John the son of Zacharias in the wilderness. And he went into all the region around the Jordan, preaching a baptism of repentance for the remission of sins, as it is written in the book of the words of Isaiah the prophet, saying:*

"The voice of one crying in the wilderness:
'Prepare the way of the LORD;
Make His paths straight.
Every valley shall be filled
And every mountain and hill brought low;
The crooked places shall be made straight
And the rough ways smooth;
And all flesh shall see the salvation of God.'" (NKJV)

In keeping with his promise to deliver an <u>orderly account</u>, Luke placed events in their historical context by telling the reader who was ruling and who the high priests were. Back then people didn't assign

go to

prepare
Malachi 3:1

announce
Malachi 4:5–6

Elijah
2 Kings 1:8

purification
Exodus 30:17–21

baptism
a sacred rite involving water, symbolizing purification from sin

repentance
turning to God and changing one's way of living

numbers to years the same way we do today, so people didn't go around saying so-and-so happened in 2002. Instead they referred to who was in power, as Luke did above, to let people know when in history an event occurred.

Years before, God told his people that he would send a special messenger to <u>prepare</u> the way for and <u>announce</u> the coming of the Messiah. He told them to look for Elijah, so it was not by chance that John bore a striking resemblance to <u>Elijah</u>.

John dressed like Elijah, went to the desert where Elijah had lived, and preached a message every bit as fiery as Elijah's had been. Like Elijah, John hated being politically correct. He did not preach in the courts of the Temple in Jerusalem, inviting the religious leaders to share the platform with him. He stayed in the desolate wilderness with the windswept rocks providing the backdrop for his stern words. He had no public relations staff to enhance his image, no promotional agents to whip up interest in his campaign. Still, people flocked to him, their attention riveted on his message. They were overcome with an awareness of how far they were from God.

As people confessed their sins, John baptized them in the Jordan River. This **baptism** was a public statement of their sincere repentance. Up to this point the Jews had followed the Old Testament directions for personal <u>purification</u>, but John used baptism as an outward sign of inward spiritual cleansing. John was doing something new.

An Unlikely Public Speaker

> LUKE 3:7–9 *Then he said to the multitudes that came out to be baptized by him, "Brood of vipers! Who warned you to flee from the wrath to come? Therefore bear fruits worthy of **repentance**, and do not begin to say to yourselves, 'We have Abraham as our father.' For I say to you that God is able to raise up children to Abraham from these stones. And even now the ax is laid to the root of the trees. Therefore every tree which does not bear good fruit is cut down and thrown into the fire." (NKJV)*

key point

John broke every rule in the book for effective public speaking. He didn't start with a good joke. He made no promises to win votes. On the contrary, his razor-sharp words cut deep into the hearts of his listeners. As descendants of Abraham, the Jews who listened to

John considered themselves so favored by God they would not face God's judgment, which was certain to come to other nations. They believed their status of being favored by God was guaranteed. John destroyed the foundation on which all their beliefs were built. He called for a complete change of heart! God looks at one's heart attitude, not national heritage.

what others say

R. Kent Hughes

In characterizing his hearers as "vipers," he was saying they were like snakes fleeing a brush fire, trying to escape but having no intention of allowing their evil natures to be changed. John's language was also meant to convey the repulsive nature of their hypocritical smugness.[1]

Gilbert Bilezikian

If sin is telling God to move over because we're taking over, repentance is falling on our knees so he can take over.[2]

Something for Everyone!

LUKE 3:10–14 *So the people asked him, saying, "What shall we do then?" He answered and said to them, "He who has two tunics, let him give to him who has none; and he who has food, let him do likewise." Then tax collectors also came to be baptized, and said to him, "Teacher, what shall we do?" And he said to them, "Collect no more than what is appointed for you." Likewise the soldiers asked him, saying, "And what shall we do?" So he said to them, "Do not intimidate anyone or accuse falsely, and be content with your wages." (NKJV)*

John's fiery warnings got through to the people. Terror gripped their hearts. Knowing they needed to do something to avoid God's wrath, they asked what they should do. True repentance is a heart attitude, but it shows itself in one's behavior.

Tax collectors and soldiers were in positions of authority in the first-century world. Tax collectors routinely asked for more money than the law required because they were allowed to keep any extra money for themselves. The Roman government knew this happened and didn't do anything to stop it. Soldiers had the influence of military force. Today in the United States if police get carried away with their authority and unduly beat people up, often they are taken to court for excessive use of force. They can lose their jobs and get thrown into jail. The Roman "police" didn't worry about getting punished for excessive force. In fact, we can tell from what John said that at least some soldiers made a practice of taking people's money by force and falsely accusing people for their own selfish ends.

People from the crowd, tax collectors, and soldiers asked John what they should do. In each case John's response had to do with either their possessions or their money. John knew that the way people handled their material goods and wealth reflected the condition of their hearts.

John was saying clearly that for everyone true inner repentance will be revealed in outer actions. We demonstrate our change of heart in the way we treat other people even if we live in a society filled with injustice and suffering. We are to hold our possessions in open hands and show compassion by making available what we have to those who have less. We should demonstrate our righteous attitudes in the workaday world. This involves being fair, even when being so is not required of us.

Contrary to the standards of today's society, true success is not measured by how much we get but by how much we give. When the desire of our hearts is to follow God, we will give evidence of this desire in the way we treat people around us.

Stop Thinking What You're Thinking

LUKE 3:15–18 *Now as the people were in expectation, and all reasoned in their hearts about John, whether he was the Christ or not, John answered, saying to all, "I indeed baptize you with water; but One mightier than I is coming, whose sandal strap I am not worthy to loose. He will baptize you with the Holy Spirit and fire. His winnowing fan is in His hand, and He will thoroughly clean out His threshing floor, and gather the wheat into His barn; but the chaff He will burn with unquenchable fire." And with many other exhortations he preached to the people. (NKJV)*

The crowds came for Elijah, but they could see plainly John wasn't Elijah. Still, they could not account for the power of his words and the grip he had on their hearts. As they came to be baptized by him in the Jordan River, they began to wonder if he was more than a prophet. Could he possibly be the promised Messiah, the One whose coming they had anticipated for hundreds of years? John addressed the speculation as forthrightly as he had dealt with their sins. John told the people his role was only to prepare the way for the Promised One, and that he was not worthy to untie Jesus's sandals (see Illustration #3), let alone fulfill his mission.

John told people about the differences between the baptism he was offering and the baptism Jesus would offer. Getting baptized by John was to participate in an outward water baptism of repentance. Getting baptized by Jesus was to participate in the inward life-transforming work of the Holy Spirit. Only the Messiah could bring the work of the Spirit. He would baptize with fire. And he would remove the useless chaff from the lives of all who turned to him. Only Christ can transform a person's life from the inside out.

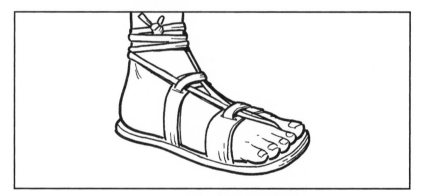

Pharisees
teachers of Jewish law and religious tradition

Sadducees
rich priestly leaders who ran the Temple

Illustration #3
Sandals of Commoners— Common people in first-century Israel wore sandals like the one pictured here. Sandals left people's feet exposed to the sand of the desert, so people often washed their feet or received a foot washing from slaves upon entering a home. Here you can see the "thongs" or straps to which John refers in Luke 3:16.

what others say

Paul N. Benware

John's baptism could not forgive and remove sins, since the Scriptures clearly teach that the removal of sin is based on blood, not water. The removal of sin begins with repentance, and baptism is the outward declaration that the person has a new spiritual identity. John demanded that those who wished to be baptized give some evidence that they had indeed repented of their sins.[3]

Other Gospel writers tell "the rest of the story" of John's dynamic ministry:

• Matthew points out that John's sternest words were directed to many **Pharisees** and **Sadducees**, the religious elite of Jewish society (Matthew 3:1–12).

go to

foretold
Isaiah 40:3

furious
Mark 6:18–25

- Mark includes John's clear statement: "There comes One after me who is mightier than I, whose sandal strap I am not worthy to stoop down and loose" (Mark 1:7 NKJV).

- John, writer of the fourth Gospel, fills in some of the details about priests who were sent from Jerusalem to demand that John identify himself and present his credentials for baptizing people (John 1:15–28). John responded by referring to himself as "the voice of one crying in the wilderness" (John 1:23 NKJV), publicly acknowledging that he was the messenger whose coming was <u>foretold</u> hundreds of years before.

Sin Accumulation

LUKE 3:19–20 *But Herod the tetrarch, being rebuked by him concerning Herodias, his brother Philip's wife, and for all the evils which Herod had done, also added this, above all, that he shut John up in prison. (NKJV)*

John's scathing indictments reached Herod's palace. John rebuked the tyrant for dismissing his wife and replacing her with his sister-in-law, an act forbidden by God. He also addressed his many other evil deeds, spelling out what nobody else would dare to say. Herod was <u>furious</u> to be confronted in this way. He was also fearful that John would incite the masses into a political uprising. Here Luke leaps ahead and records what happened later. Herod added one more transgression to his already large and ever-growing pile of sins when he arrested John and threw him into a dungeon. Later, because Herodias hated John for his stern rebuke, Herod had John beheaded (Luke 9:7–9).

Jesus's Baptism

> LUKE 3:21–22 *When all the people were baptized, it came to pass that Jesus also was baptized; and while He prayed, the heaven was opened. And the Holy Spirit descended in bodily form like a dove upon Him, and a voice came from heaven which said, "You are My beloved Son; in You I am well pleased." (NKJV)*

Promised One
John 15:26

Note Luke's introductory phrase: "When all the people were baptized . . ." Luke seems to be emphasizing how Jesus identified himself with the common people—the sinners. Jesus didn't get a special mountaintop baptism. He was right there with the rest of them, wading into the grime of sin that was being washed down the Jordan with each immersion.

Water and Wellness

Don't be mistaken. We know from elsewhere in Scripture that Jesus was "without sin" (Hebrews 4:15 NKJV), so he was not getting baptized for the same reason everyone else was, namely, to participate in the outward symbol of an inward spiritual cleansing. Jesus did not need a spiritual cleansing.

After Jesus's baptism the Holy Spirit descended upon him, affirming that he was God's Anointed, the Messiah. It was not until after this anointing—his baptism—that Jesus performed miracles.

We turn to other Gospel writers for more details of this incredible scene:

- Matthew records that when Jesus came to be baptized, John tried to deter him. John knew immediately Jesus was no sinner. Jesus should baptize him! Jesus responded that it was right for him to be baptized by John (Matthew 3:13–17).

- Mark makes the point that it was as Jesus was coming up out of the water that the heavens opened and the Spirit came down (Mark 1:9–11).

- From Gospel writer John we learn that at least one of the descending Spirit's purposes was to show John the Baptist who the <u>Promised One</u> was (John 1:29–34). When John the Baptist saw the dove rest on Jesus, he knew this was the Messiah. John recounted what he saw and heard at Jesus's baptism as evidence that Jesus was the Christ.

David
Israel's greatest king

Abraham
father of the Jews

Adam
first man

Robert C. Girard

By presenting himself for baptism, Jesus was not confessing that he was a sinner. He was saying,

"I am with John."

"I'm committed to live a righteous life."

"I want to live under God's reign."

"I'm one of you."[5]

Jesus's Genealogy

LUKE 3:23–38 *Now Jesus Himself began His ministry at about thirty years of age, being (as was supposed) the son of Joseph, the son of Heli, the son of Matthat, the son of Levi, the son of Melchi, the son of Janna, the son of Joseph, the son of Mattathiah, the son of Amos, the son of Nahum, the son of Esli, the son of Naggai, the son of Maath, the son of Mattathiah, the son of Semei, the son of Joseph, the son of Judah, the son of Joannas, the son of Rhesa, the son of Zerubbabel, the son of Shealtiel, the son of Neri, the son of Melchi, the son of Addi, the son of Cosam, the son of Elmodam, the son of Er, the son of Jose, the son of Eliezer, the son of Jorim, the son of Matthat, the son of Levi, the son of Simeon, the son of Judah, the son of Joseph, the son of Jonan, the son of Eliakim, the son of Melea, the son of Menan, the son of Mattathah, the son of Nathan, the son of David, the son of Jesse, the son of Obed, the son of Boaz, the son of Salmon, the son of Nahshon, the son of Amminadab, the son of Ram, the son of Hezron, the son of Perez, the son of Judah, the son of Jacob, the son of Isaac, the son of Abraham, the son of Terah, the son of Nahor, the son of Serug, the son of Reu, the son of Peleg, the son of Eber, the son of Shelah, the son of Cainan, the son of Arphaxad, the son of Shem, the son of Noah, the son of Lamech, the son of Methuselah, the son of Enoch, the son of Jared, the son of Mahalalel, the son of Cainan, the son of Enosh, the son of Seth, the son of Adam, the son of God.* (NKJV)

Luke traces Jesus's family tree from Joseph, the assumed father of Jesus, back to **David**, to **Abraham**, and to **Adam**, who was created by God. In doing so Luke confirms Jesus came from the same roots as Jews and Gentiles alike, the first man, Adam.

Matthew 1:1–17 is another genealogy of Jesus. Matthew's purpose was to establish for his Jewish readers that Jesus fulfilled the ancestral requirements of the Messiah as detailed in the Old Testament. Jesus was born into the lineage of Abraham and King David, both of whom had received prophecies that the Messiah would be one of their descendants (Genesis 12:1–3, 7; 2 Samuel 7:16).

It is obvious even to a casual reader that Luke's genealogy is not identical to Matthew's. From David to Jesus's earthly father, Joseph, the genealogies differ, but there are a number of explanations for this. The most common explanation is that "Luke traces the lineage through Mary, and Matthew through Joseph. Thus Joseph who is Jesus's father ("so it was thought") is the son-in-law of Heli in Luke's genealogy rather than son. The word 'son' may indicate either."[6]

Bob Girard has some additional explanations:

1. "Matthew gives the royal descent of Jesus, establishing his right to David's throne [Romans 1:3]. . . .

2. "The differences may be explained by the fact that many Jewish men were known by more than one name [John 1:42].

3. "The differences may be due to the fact that in Jewish culture it was common practice, when a man died, for his brother to marry the widow and raise children in his own name or in the name of the deceased [Deuteronomy 25:5–10]."[7]

what others say

Matthew Henry

[Luke's] genealogy concludes with this, who was the son of Adam, the son of God. He was both the Son of Adam and the Son of God, that he might be a proper Mediator between God and the sons of Adam, and might bring the sons of Adam to be, through him, the sons of God.[8]

Chapter Wrap-Up

- John suddenly appeared on the scene, coming from the desert rather than the religious elite of Jerusalem. He bore a striking resemblance to the Old Testament prophet Elijah (Luke 3:1–3).

- John's mission was to prepare the hearts of the people to receive the Messiah. People who responded to John's message came to him at the Jordan River to be baptized (Luke 3:4–14).

- For people who wondered if he were the Messiah, John had only one answer. He was not the Messiah, but a voice announcing his coming. John publicly rebuked Herod for his immoral personal life and for his many evil acts (Luke 3:15–20).

- Jesus came to John and requested to be baptized by him. God confirmed the identity of Jesus when the Holy Spirit descended on Jesus in the form of a dove, and a voice spoke from heaven confirming that Jesus was God's Son (Luke 3:21–22).

- Luke's genealogy traces Jesus's lineage to Adam. There are multiple valid explanations for the differences between Matthew's genealogy and Luke's (Luke 3:23–37).

Study Questions

1. What was John's God-given mission?

2. Suppose John were preaching today in our society. To whom, do you think, would he direct his most pointed warnings?

3. What specific "fruit of repentance" do you think John would call for? How can you and your circle of family and friends demonstrate this fruit?

4. According to John, in what ways was he inferior to the Messiah, whose coming he was announcing?

5. How did God confirm Jesus's identity when he was baptized by John?

6. How would you account for the differences between the genealogies given by Matthew and Luke?

Luke 4 Temptation and Triumph

Chapter Highlights:
- **Temptation**
- **Rejection**
- **Power over an Evil Spirit**
- **Compassion for All**

Let's Get Started

The curtains part and the scene is one of desolation. One figure, deep in thought, moves alone among the rocks and sandy soil. There's silence in this windswept desert of temptation. Who is he? What's going on? Draw closer and listen. Luke, our narrator, is about to tell us the story.

mountain
Deuteronomy 9:9

son
Exodus 4:22;
Hosea 11:2

Temptation

> LUKE 4:1–2 *Then Jesus, being filled with the Holy Spirit, returned from the Jordan and was led by the Spirit into the wilderness, being tempted for forty days by the devil. And in those days He ate nothing, and afterward, when they had ended, He was hungry. (NKJV)*

Now that Jesus was "filled with the Holy Spirit," what would the Spirit tell him to do? Conquer some illnesses? Beat up some demons? Calm some storms? That's what we might expect, but instead Jesus had some preparation to do before he could begin his public ministry. And the preparation wasn't going to be easy. The Spirit led Jesus into a desert where he was **tempted** by the **devil** for over a month.

tempted
to be enticed to do wrong

devil
evil being, also known as Satan

Luke's first readers probably would have seen parallels between Jesus and Israel, for just as Jesus was in the desert for forty days, Israel was in the desert for forty years. Also, Moses went without food for forty days when he climbed up the <u>mountain</u> to receive God's law. The parallel becomes even more apparent when one remembers that Israel is considered God's "<u>son</u>" in several Old Testament passages.

Did you catch that it was the Holy Spirit who led Jesus into the desert? In other words, though God did not tempt Jesus, God led Jesus to a place where he would be tempted. If Jesus was tempted, Christians should not be surprised when they are tempted. Temptation is part of life. The question is why? Why does God allow

go to

able to help
Hebrews 2:14–18

Satan to tempt us? A little later we'll get an answer, but for now hang close to Jesus as he walks from temptation to temptation to temptation.

Other Names for Satan

Throughout Scripture Satan is described with various names that give word pictures of his evil character. Here are a few:

- Accuser (Revelation 12:10)
- Adversary the devil (1 Peter 5:8)
- Beelzebub or ruler of demons (Matthew 12:24)
- Evil one (Matthew 6:13)
- God of this age (2 Corinthians 4:4)
- Liar and the father of [lying] (John 8:44)
- Murderer (John 8:44)
- One who deceives the whole world (Revelation 12:9)
- Prince of the power of the air (Ephesians 2:2)
- Ruler of this world (John 12:31)
- Serpent of old (Revelation 12:9)
- Spirit who now works in the sons of disobedience (Ephesians 2:2)
- Tempter (Matthew 4:3)

apply it

We are tempted today, but we do not have to face it alone. Jesus stands with us, assuring us that he endured the same pressures we face. He knows from personal experience the pleasures that are offered, the glittering rewards that dance before our eyes, the subtle pull to step away from what God has for us. He withstood it all and is able to help us through our own temptations. God does not tempt us, but sometimes he leads us into tempting situations.

what others say

William MacDonald

The purpose of the temptation was not to see if He would sin but to prove that He could not sin. Only a holy, sinless Man could be our Redeemer.[1]

Spiritual Stomach

LUKE 4:3–4 *And the devil said to Him, "If You are the Son of God, command this stone to become bread." But Jesus answered him, saying, "It is written, 'Man shall not live by bread alone, but by every word of God.'"* (NKJV)

The last verse of the previous passage sets us up for Satan's first ploy. After forty days of not eating, Jesus was hungry. Now, turning a stone to bread is not by itself a sinful thing to do. Most people know that Jesus had no problem with multiplying bread later in his life. Also, Jesus's need was legitimate. He was hungry. Who wouldn't be? And he had the power to perform the miracle. So what could possibly be wrong with turning this stone into bread?

The answer is in Christ's reply, which is a direct quote from Deuteronomy. Deuteronomy is largely comprised of a series of speeches Moses gave to the Israelites when they were waiting to enter the land God had promised them. Moses reminded Israel of God's faithfulness to them, saying, "[God] humbled you, allowed you to hunger, and fed you with manna which you did not know nor did your fathers know, that He might make you know that man shall not live by bread alone; but man lives by every word that proceeds from the mouth of the LORD" (Deuteronomy 8:3 NKJV). Jesus knew his hunger was from God, and he had faith that God would eventually feed him, just as he fed the Israelites with manna. God the Father may have been teaching Jesus by experience (because experience is the best teacher) that life is about more than physical sustenance; it's about spiritual sustenance as well. In short, it would have been wrong for Jesus to turn the stone into bread because doing so would have required Jesus to reject his dependence on God.

Jesus fasted for forty days. As a physician, Luke would know that after Jesus had gone without food for this long, his body would be depleted and he would be near collapse from exhaustion. Further, throughout this time Jesus had been exposed to the elements and

him only
Deuteronomy 6:13

had been deprived of human companionship. Satan tempted Jesus when he was physically and psychologically weak, but Jesus proved strong enough to resist temptation by relying on God's Word and submitting to his Father.

what others say

John Piper

Fasting is God's testing ground—and healing ground. Will we murmur as the Israelites murmured in the absence of bread? For Jesus the question was: Would he leave the path of sacrificial obedience and turn stones into bread? Or would he "live by every word that proceeds out of the mouth of God"? Fasting is a way of revealing to ourselves and confessing to our God what is in our hearts. Where do we find our deepest satisfaction—in God or in his gifts?[3]

A Prickly Proposition

LUKE 4:5–8 *Then the devil, taking Him up on a high mountain, showed Him all the kingdoms of the world in a moment of time. And the devil said to Him, "All this authority I will give You, and their glory; for this has been delivered to me, and I give it to whomever I wish. Therefore, if You will worship before me, all will be Yours." And Jesus answered and said to him, "Get behind Me, Satan! For it is written, 'You shall worship the LORD your God, and Him only you shall serve.'"* (NKJV)

It is not wrong to have "authority" and "glory," but it is wrong to gain them by allegiance to Satan. Jesus recognized what Satan was offering and rejected it immediately. Again he quoted Old Testament Scripture that we are to worship the Lord our God and serve <u>him only</u>.

As with Jesus's previous quote, Moses gave this instruction to the Israelites as they prepared to enter the land God had promised to give them. For years they had labored as slaves in Egypt. And for forty years they had lived as sojourners in the desert. Suddenly, prosperity lay within their reach, and so did danger. As God made the land fruitful and surrounded the Israelites with comfort, the Israelites ran the risk of forgetting the Lord and giving credit for their good fortune to themselves.

Similarly, Satan was promising good things—authority and

glory—to Jesus, luring him away from worshiping and serving God alone. But Jesus resisted firmly and completely.

Satan as Proctor

rescue
Psalm 91:11–12

Moses said
Deuteronomy 6:16;
Exodus 17:7

throughout Scripture
Deuteronomy 33:8;
Numbers 20:1–13,
24;
Psalm 81:7;
Hebrews 3:7–12

LUKE 4:9–13 *Then he brought Him to Jerusalem, set Him on the pinnacle of the temple, and said to Him, "If You are the Son of God, throw Yourself down from here. For it is written:*
'He shall give His angels charge over you,
To keep you,'
"and,
'In their hands they shall bear you up,
Lest you dash your foot against a stone.'"
And Jesus answered and said to him, "It has been said, 'You shall not tempt the LORD your God.'" Now when the devil had ended every temptation, he departed from Him until an opportune time. (NKJV)

Satan swept Jesus to the highest point of the Temple and dared him to make a spectacular leap over the side to the Kedron Valley some 450 feet below (see the map of Jesus's trial and crucifixion, Appendix B). This time Satan quoted Scripture, assuring Jesus that God would <u>rescue</u> him.

Jesus retorted with yet another quote from Moses, saying we should never put God to the test. When <u>Moses said</u> this, he was referring to a time when the Israelites complained about not having anything to drink. They put God to the test in that they did not believe God would provide for them, or at least they were not content with God's timing, so they whined and blamed Moses for their thirst. Moses cried out to God, saying he didn't know what to do with the people, as they were about to stone him. God heard Moses's cry and gave him instructions to produce water from a stone. Despite God's willingness to bend to the Israelites' complaints, <u>throughout Scripture</u> this interaction between God and his people is cast in a dim light. The Israelites failed to trust God and so put him to the test. What Jesus says to Satan reminds us that we are to live in full dependence on God without trying to manipulate him to prove that he is with us.

Satan quoted Scripture to tempt Jesus, which teaches us that just because someone is quoting the Bible doesn't necessarily mean we should heed their teaching or buy their book or do what they tell us

sign
Mark 8:11;
John 2:18; 6:30

to do. Iain Provan, professor at Regent College in Canada, said in a lecture, "It is just as possible to be biblical and wrong as it is to be biblical and right." Discerning whether someone is using the Bible correctly takes thought, prayer, and often research.

Gospel writers Matthew and Mark give their perspective of Jesus's temptation (Matthew 4:1–11; Mark 1:12–13). In Matthew's account, the second and third temptations are the reverse of Luke's. Some Bible students see this as an indication that Jesus endured these temptations simultaneously. Others point out that Matthew's account is chronological while Luke's is thematic. Both Matthew and Mark add that angels came and ministered to Jesus after Satan left him. Mark includes that wild animals were present in the desert.

what others say

Raymond B. Dillard and Tremper Longman

Jesus' replies to Satan . . . are taken from Moses's speech recorded in Deuteronomy (8:3; 6:13; 6:16), in which he admonishes Israel not to behave as they did in the wilderness. Jesus thus demonstrates to his followers that he is obedient precisely where the Israelites were rebellious.[4]

Derek Prime

The timely encouragement of the angels at the end of Jesus' period of temptation gives a clue to the intensity of the testing through which he passed.

That was not the end of the conflict, for it continued throughout the next three years. Jesus was frequently tempted to shrink from full obedience to His Father's will. The people regularly asked him for a sign as a ground for believing in his identity as the Messiah. As the cross drew nearer, the devil made temptation all the greater. But at the beginning, Jesus showed the way he was determined to go.[5]

Rejection

LUKE 4:14–15 *Then Jesus returned in the power of the Spirit to Galilee, and news of Him went out through all the surrounding region. And He taught in their synagogues, being glorified by all.* (NKJV)

Luke 4:14 begins with gusto. Jesus returns to Galilee "in the power of the Spirit." It sounds like Jesus has been energized by his victory in the desert. And look at the results! The news spread. Everyone praised him. In other words, Jesus was effective in his ministry. This is a clue into why God allows people to be tempted. He does so to prepare his people for work that he wants them to do in the future.

John is the only Gospel writer to record the events that took place in Judea and Jerusalem before Jesus arrived in Galilee (John 1:19–4:45). During this period of time (about one year), Jesus called Andrew, John, Simon Peter, Philip, and Nathanael to be his disciples, turned water into wine at a wedding in Cana, talked with Nicodemus and the woman at the well, and healed a royal official's son.

description
Isaiah 11:1–5

Local Man Becomes Celebrity

LUKE 4:16–19 *So He came to Nazareth, where He had been brought up. And as His custom was, He went into the synagogue on the Sabbath day, and stood up to read. And He was handed the book of the prophet Isaiah. And when He had opened the book, He found the place where it was written:*
    "The Spirit of the LORD is upon Me,
    Because He has anointed Me
    To preach the gospel to the poor;
    He has sent Me to heal the brokenhearted,
    To proclaim liberty to the captives
    And recovery of sight to the blind,
    To set at liberty those who are oppressed;
    To proclaim the acceptable year of the LORD." (NKJV)

Imagine the excitement in Nazareth when one of their own returned as a celebrity. We can be sure his family stood on eager tiptoes to see him, backed by enthusiastic neighbors and friends. On the Sabbath, the townsfolk gathered, and Jesus was given an opportunity to participate in the service. As an act of courtesy, the ruler of the synagogue invited Jesus to read the Scripture (see Illustration #4). When handed the sacred scroll, Jesus unrolled it to the writings of Isaiah and began to read the text he selected, Isaiah 61:1–2 (see Illustration #5). Everyone in the synagogue understood that the words Jesus read were a <u>description</u> of the Messiah, but as he read, did they know the reading referred to Jesus? Did they know Jesus was revealing the desires of his own heart?

Illustration #4
Synagogue Reader—It was common in Jesus's day for synagogue officials to invite qualified visitors to read Scripture and make comments, as this illustration depicts.

go to

confession of faith
Deuteronomy 6:4–9; 11:13–21

A Synagogue Bulletin

Here's what a typical order of service was like back then, repeated in synagogues every Sabbath throughout Israel:

- Invocation
- Recitation of <u>confession of faith</u>
- Prayer
- Readings from the Law and the Prophets
- Brief message or sermon (given by a rabbi or one of the men of the congregation)
- Closing prayer and dismissal

Illustration #5
Scroll—Scrolls were made of leather sheets sewn together or river reeds pressed into papyrus paper as shown here. The Scriptures were carefully copied in columns.

Like My Bio?

LUKE 4:20–22 *Then He closed the book, and gave it back to the attendant and sat down. And the eyes of all who were in the synagogue were fixed on Him. And He began to say to them, "Today this Scripture is fulfilled in your hearing." So all bore witness to Him, and marveled at the gracious words which proceeded out of His mouth. And they said, "Is this not Joseph's son?"* (NKJV)

Having read from the prophet Isaiah, Jesus rolled up the sacred scroll and gave it to an attendant to be returned to its honored place. He then sat down, which was the custom of someone who was about to deliver a sermon. That's why "the eyes of all who were in the synagogue were fixed on Him." Jesus began with a message no one had heard before. He said the reading from Isaiah, which everyone associated with the promised Messiah, was about him. Let's look at the Isaiah passage more closely to determine exactly what Jesus was claiming. Jesus was claiming that God's Spirit was on him, that he had been anointed to bring hope and healing and grace to all, especially to those who needed it most: the poor, the prisoners, the blind, and the oppressed.

And the reaction? At first people were won over by a sense of God's grace. The townspeople nodded at each other. You can almost hear them saying, "That's our boy! Amazing, isn't it?" But they were also skeptical. "Isn't he just Joseph the carpenter's son? Who does he think he is?"

God Likes Gentiles Too

LUKE 4:23–27 *He said to them, "You will surely say this proverb to Me, 'Physician, heal yourself! Whatever we have heard done in Capernaum, do also here in Your country.'" Then He said, "Assuredly, I say to you, no prophet is accepted in his own country. But I tell you truly, many widows were in Israel in the days of Elijah, when the heaven was shut up three years and six months, and there was a great famine throughout all the land; but to none of them was Elijah sent except to Zarephath, in the region of Sidon, to a woman who was a widow. And many lepers were in Israel in the time of Elisha the prophet, and none of them was cleansed except Naaman the Syrian."* (NKJV)

Gentile widow
1 Kings 17:8–16

leper
2 Kings 5:1–15

false prophet
Deuteronomy
13:1–11

grace
favor, generosity,
joy, mercy

Jesus knew their thoughts. He knew they wanted him to do miracles in Nazareth like he had done elsewhere. And he understood the problem. They saw him only as Joseph's carpenter-son. They didn't believe he was who he claimed to be.

Further, Jesus knew they were resolutely opposed to the idea of God showing **grace** to Gentiles. Their hearts turned to stone when Jesus reminded them that because of unbelief in Israel, the prophet Elijah had helped a <u>Gentile widow</u> in Sidon, ignoring widows in Israel. Then Elisha had healed a Gentile <u>leper</u> from Syria.

> **what others say**
>
> **Warren W. Wiersbe**
>
> Our Lord's message of grace was a blow to the proud Jewish exclusivism of the congregation, and they would not repent. (Imagine this hometown boy saying that Jews had to be saved by grace just like the pagan Gentiles!)[6]

From Listening to Lynching

LUKE 4:28–30 *So all those in the synagogue, when they heard these things, were filled with wrath, and rose up and thrust Him out of the city; and they led Him to the brow of the hill on which their city was built, that they might throw Him down over the cliff. Then passing through the midst of them, He went His way. (NKJV)*

The Israelites were outraged. Note how quickly they went from marveling "at the gracious words which proceeded out of His mouth" to being "filled with wrath." They wanted a Messiah who would rid them of Gentile oppression and pour out his mighty anger upon them, and here Jesus was talking about how God showed them grace. Without discussion or a trial they were united in their impulse and determination to kill Jesus as if he were a <u>false prophet</u>! They didn't even wait for the Sabbath service to finish but removed him from the synagogue and marched him out of town to throw him over a cliff. But Jesus walked calmly through the crowd and left town.

go to

the truth
John 1:17

In Nazareth's synagogue Jesus defined his mission, and it was unlike anything people had anticipated of the Messiah. He would confront and heal the heartbreaking problems of the human race:

- Poverty: Jesus would preach the gospel to the poor and give them hope.

- Bondage: Jesus would proclaim liberty to the captives.

- Disabilities: Jesus would give sight to the blind.

- Oppression: Jesus would free those who were oppressed.

In other words, Jesus came to "proclaim the acceptable year of the LORD" (Luke 4:19 NKJV). But as Jesus read from the scroll of Isaiah, he stopped short. He did not include the familiar words that followed in Isaiah 61:2, "and the day of vengeance of our God" (NKJV), which may be why the grace of his words is emphasized in Luke 4:22.

something to ponder

Power over an Evil Spirit

LUKE 4:31–37 *Then He went down to Capernaum, a city of Galilee, and was teaching them on the Sabbaths. And they were astonished at His teaching, for His word was with authority. Now in the synagogue there was a man who had a spirit of an unclean demon. And he cried out with a loud voice, saying, "Let us alone! What have we to do with You, Jesus of Nazareth? Did You come to destroy us? I know who You are—the Holy One of God!" But Jesus rebuked him, saying, "Be quiet, and come out of him!" And when the demon had thrown him in their midst, it came out of him and did not hurt him. Then they were all amazed and spoke among themselves, saying, "What a word this is! For with authority and power He commands the unclean spirits, and they come out." And the report about Him went out into every place in the surrounding region. (NKJV)*

go to

destroy
1 John 3:8

When Jesus left Nazareth, he went to Capernaum, which became his headquarters. There he taught the people with amazing authority. What did he teach? We'll find out a little later, but for now let's look at something he did in the synagogue.

An evil spirit interrupted a Sabbath service by speaking through the voice of a man, calling Jesus "the Holy One of God" (Luke 4:34 NKJV). Jesus rebuked the evil spirit and commanded it to come out of the man.

Imagine the immediate effect this had on the congregation. God had enabled Old Testament prophets to perform miracles, but no one knew anything about demon exorcism. Jesus had come to <u>destroy</u> the devil's work, so Luke appropriately records this account as Jesus's first work of healing.

It is no surprise that Jesus's fame spread throughout the area. Jesus taught with authority and proved that his authority extended over and against demonic forces.

Compassion for All

LUKE **4:38–39** *Now He arose from the synagogue and entered Simon's house. But Simon's wife's mother was sick with a high fever, and they made request of Him concerning her. So He stood over her and rebuked the fever, and it left her. And immediately she arose and served them.* (NKJV)

The text says "they" asked Jesus to help Simon's mother-in-law. This is probably a reference to a group of family members who requested Jesus's presence. They must have heard of Jesus's ability to heal, or perhaps one or more of them were in the synagogue during the exorcism.

Luke the physician records the woman's condition—a high fever—which indicates this probably wasn't a twenty-four-hour bug or a slight case of indigestion. Jesus went to her place, which probably means the poor woman wasn't able to go to him. Back then there was no such thing as antibiotics or vaccinations or even aspirin! People routinely died of such fevers as the one mentioned here. The text gives us no room to think Jesus was a showboat when he healed the woman—a word of rebuke, and the fever was gone. Fast. Quiet. Effective. And note the woman's response. Immediately, she got up and served the people in her home.

See what a difference people can make? The people who asked Jesus to heal Simon's mother-in-law were at least partially responsible for her recovery. If they hadn't asked, who knows if she would have recovered? This should encourage us to pray on the behalf of those who are sick, especially for our relatives and close friends, because it is often by the prayers and requests of people that God dispenses his blessings.

Simon's mother-in-law could have done any number of things upon being healed. She could have run out of the house and shouted to the neighborhood what Jesus had done for her. She could have thanked Jesus and sat around talking about it with her family. She could have taken a nap. What she did instead was serve those around her. She's a good role model. The proper way to show gratitude to God and to people is through service.

ineluctable
inescapable, cannot be evaded

constancy
steadfastness, loyalty

apply it

what others say

John Piper

There is a rebuke from Jesus that cannot be resisted. It carries in it, not just the will to stop a thing, but the force to stop it. A fever is a chemical reaction in the cells of the body, producing excessive heat in response to infection. It has to do with molecules and electrons and the laws of physics and chemistry. In his divinity Jesus designed those laws ages ago (Colossians 1:16), and in his divinity he sustains them so that they work for us daily (Colossians 1:17; Hebrews 1:3). In his humanity he entered into those laws and became subject to them so that he could die by their **ineluctable constancy**. But from inside he revealed that his word is also about these laws of physics and chemistry. He spoke, and the force of his word reversed the fever-flaming effect of infection.[8]

Jesus, M.D.

LUKE 4:40–41 *When the sun was setting, all those who had any that were sick with various diseases brought them to Him; and He laid His hands on every one of them and healed them. And demons also came out of many, crying out and saying, "You are the Christ, the Son of God!" And He, rebuking them, did not allow them to speak, for they knew that He was the Christ. (NKJV)*

lineage
1 Kings 2:1–4

In Luke's Gospel, Jesus's healings began with the expulsion of a demon and continued with the healing of Simon's mother-in-law. In this passage we learn that Jesus healed many more people—people "sick with various diseases."

Jesus continued his demon casting, but here Luke includes a curious detail about Jesus's interaction with the demons. Upon being exorcised, many of the demons shouted that Jesus was the Son of God. Luke goes on to say they knew he was "the Christ." You might expect Jesus to be pleased the demons were telling the truth for once, but instead he slapped some spiritual duct tape over their mouths. He "did not allow them to speak." Why? Answers vary, but one possible reason is that he didn't want to draw too much attention to himself this early in his ministry. If word got to the Roman establishment that this teacher, Jesus, had a bunch of followers and that these followers were calling him Christ or "Messiah," the Romans probably wouldn't have been too happy. But to understand why, you need to understand a little more about the Jewish concept of Messiah.

The Messiah Concept

The Jews believed many different things about the Messiah, but one of the most important things they believed was that he would be an unstoppable political ruler from King David's <u>lineage</u>. The Romans knew this, so whenever they heard there was a "messiah" or "Christ" around, they took it as a direct threat to their own power. In addition to crucifying Jesus, the Romans crucified many supposed "messiahs" before and after Jesus's life.

Where did the Jews get this idea of Messiah? From a combination of Scripture and their own misguided hopes. We learn from passages like Zechariah 9:9 that the Messiah was to be a king, but God's idea of kingship was different from the Jews' idea. The Jews wanted God to raise up a king who would stomp on their enemies. God raised up a King on the wooden beams of a cross—a King who cleansed both Jews and their enemies of sin and now sits on a celestial, eternal throne.

So Long, Farewell, Auf Wiedersehen, Adieu

LUKE 4:42–44 *Now when it was day, He departed and went into a deserted place. And the crowd sought Him and came to Him, and tried to keep Him from leaving them; but He said to them, "I must preach the kingdom of God to the other cities also, because for this purpose I have been sent." And He was preaching in the synagogues of Galilee. (NKJV)*

Luke moves quickly from dusk to dawn. We can't know for sure why Jesus sought out a deserted place, but given all that happened the day before, it seems reasonable to think he had grown weary of the attention he was getting. He may have been pondering whether people were as enamored of God as they were of God's gifts. He may have been praising God for all the healing he had done.

Jesus's response to the people who found him that morning must have saddened, humbled, and perhaps shocked them. Suddenly they realized they were not Jesus's only concern. He felt an urgent need to "preach the kingdom of God to the other cities also" (Luke 4:43 NKJV). In addition to telling us about Jesus's target audience, this brief quote gives us some insight into what Jesus was teaching in 4:31–32. To learn all the details of his teaching, you'll have to wait until chapter 6.

Jesus mentioned that he had been sent, and the question that naturally arises from this statement is, Who sent him? The answer: God himself, the Ruler of the kingdom about which Jesus was to spread the good news.

Chapter Wrap-Up

- Jesus was led by the Holy Spirit into the desert to be tempted by the devil. The three temptations Jesus faced were in the areas of (1) not relying on God's promised provision and care, (2) seeking success apart from God's plan, and (3) testing God. (Luke 4:1–13)

- The people of Nazareth rejected Jesus because they refused to believe he was the promised Messiah unless he performed miracles for them. Also they bitterly resented his point that God's grace extends to Gentiles. (Luke 4:14–30)

- Jesus demonstrated his authority over evil spirits by commanding them to keep silent and by commanding that they leave their victims. (Luke 4:31–37)

- As Jesus's popularity grew, he kept his focus on his mission: to demonstrate his power to heal physical illness and to proclaim the good news of the kingdom of God. (Luke 4:38–44)

Study Questions

1. Why was it necessary for Jesus to be tempted?

2. Jesus's forty days in the desert run parallel to what in the Old Testament?

3. In what general areas was Jesus tempted?

4. Why did the people of Nazareth reject Jesus?

5. How did Jesus prove his authority over evil spirits?

6. How did Jesus show compassion on people with physical needs?

Part Two
Miracles, Teachings, and Actions

Luke 5 Breaking the Rules

Let's Get Started

By this point in Luke's record, Jesus's public ministry was in full swing. In this chapter Jesus goes about building a team of followers—followers who become the first Christian missionaries after Jesus leaves the earth. Jesus breaks away from convention as he does more healing and more teaching. As you read through this chapter, remember that Jesus was the ideal human. From him we can learn what it means to be human.

Lake of Gennesaret
known as Sea of Galilee, Sea of Tiberias, or Sea of Gennesaret

Floatable Pulpit

> LUKE 5:1–3 *So it was, as the multitude pressed about Him to hear the word of God, that He stood by the **Lake of Gennesaret**, and saw two boats standing by the lake; but the fishermen had gone from them and were washing their nets. Then He got into one of the boats, which was Simon's, and asked him to put out a little from the land. And He sat down and taught the multitudes from the boat. (NKJV)*

Why did Jesus choose to teach from a lakeshore? There are at least two possible reasons. One is that the acoustics may have been good there, especially if the ground sloped toward the lake, creating an amphitheater effect. Also, he might have anticipated the people would crowd him—the water made an ideal natural boundary between him and them. Note that Peter was either in or near the boat, so he would have had a front-row seat for the sermon.

Jesus taught the "word of God." This phrase or its cousin "the word of the Lord" appears throughout both the Old and the New Testaments and refers to a message that is divinely inspired by God. Sometimes the phrases mean "the commandment of the Lord"—something to be obeyed or disobeyed. Often the Bible speaks of the word of the Lord as coming to people. Here, Jesus speaks "the word of God" and everyone listens.

Master
a term of respect

Fish Finding

LUKE 5:4–7 *When He had stopped speaking, He said to Simon, "Launch out into the deep and let down your nets for a catch." But Simon answered and said to Him, "Master, we have toiled all night and caught nothing; nevertheless at Your word I will let down the net." And when they had done this, they caught a great number of fish, and their net was breaking. So they signaled to their partners in the other boat to come and help them. And they came and filled both the boats, so that they began to sink. (NKJV)*

When Jesus had finished his teaching, he told Simon to move the boat into deeper water and let down the freshly cleaned nets. This request was ridiculous to a veteran fisherman, for Jesus's instruction violated common knowledge that the time to fish was at night and the place to fish was in shallow water. But Simon obeyed, and to his amazement, the nets filled with so many fish they began to break. Another team of fishermen quickly came to help, but both boats began to sink as the men filled them with the miraculous catch.

If you were Simon, what would you have learned from this experience? Perhaps you would have learned that where previously there was death and nothingness, Jesus could bring life and good fortune. You might have learned that Jesus did not need to operate by conventional means; he had power from beyond this world. Maybe you would have learned that Jesus is trustworthy; when he asks you to do something, you can be confident he has a reason for it.

Peter's Blues

LUKE 5:8–11 *When Simon Peter saw it, he fell down at Jesus' knees, saying, "Depart from me, for I am a sinful man, O Lord!" For he and all who were with him were astonished at the catch of fish which they had taken; and so also were James and John, the sons of Zebedee, who were partners with Simon. And Jesus said to Simon, "Do not be afraid. From now on you will catch men." So when they had brought their boats to land, they forsook all and followed Him. (NKJV)*

Here Luke refers to Simon as Simon Peter. We learn from the other Gospels that Jesus was the one who assigned Simon the new name of Peter. If Luke's readers knew of this fisherman-turned-disciple, they probably would have known him as Peter or Simon Peter, so Luke may be consciously making the connection between Simon and Peter for the sake of his readers.

go to

reward
Luke 18:29–30

As the fish came in, Peter was overwhelmed. Something about listening to the teacher speak the "word of God" and watching him bring in two boatloads of fish brought Peter to new realizations—about Jesus and about himself. Suddenly it didn't matter whether they were able to haul all the fish on board. In the face of Jesus's grace and power, all Peter could do was hit the deck and beg Jesus to leave, proclaiming himself "a sinful man."

But Jesus responded quickly to replace Peter's fear with hope. Jesus knew about Peter's sin, of course, but that didn't matter—at least, it didn't prohibit Peter from being a vital part of Jesus's ministry. With Jesus's power Peter had caught fish. Soon with the same power he would capture people to follow Jesus.

The fishermen were so impressed by Jesus's miracle that they made a commitment to him. They left their huge haul of fish, their boats, and their nets to follow him. Jesus rewards our obedience by giving us a deeper understanding of who he is.

Luke records events that took place in the first century. What do these events have to do with us today? They are relevant in several ways. First, God notices whatever we make available to him (Peter made his boat available) and whatever we do for him (Peter pushed the boat from the shore as Jesus requested). He promises to <u>reward</u> us—in this life or when we see him face-to-face. Also, we learn from the fishermen that obedience opens the gate to Christ's power in our lives.

apply it

Whenever we become personally aware of who Jesus is, we cannot keep from feeling what Peter expressed to Jesus. Suddenly aware of our sinfulness, we shrink from being in the presence of the Son of God. But, as with Peter, Jesus reaches out to us with grace and promises to help us become what we could never become on our own—effective ambassadors for him.

When we truly believe that Jesus is calling us to follow him, we are willing to make a genuine commitment. This is true despite the fear of commitment that has become an epidemic in our generation.

Touch of Compassion

LUKE 5:12–16 *And it happened when He was in a certain city, that behold, a man who was full of leprosy saw Jesus; and he fell on his face and implored Him, saying, "Lord, if You are willing, You can make me clean." Then He put out His hand and touched him, saying, "I am willing; be cleansed." Immediately the leprosy left him. And He charged him to tell no one, "But go and show yourself to the priest, and make an offering for your cleansing, as a testimony to them, just as Moses commanded." However, the report went around concerning Him all the more; and great multitudes came together to hear, and to be healed by Him of their infirmities. So He Himself often withdrew into the wilderness and prayed. (NKJV)*

He ventured out of isolation—this man with leprosy who had been consigned to live outside his hometown. When he saw Jesus, he begged to be made clean of his disease.

Jesus responded with compassion. He defied the laws rigidly followed for generations and reached out to touch the man. Jesus healed him, cautioning him not to share his good news, but to go to the priest and fulfill the obligations of the law. Jesus may have been guarding himself against attention that would distract people from his teaching.

Still the news of Jesus's miracle spread so that people flocked to him. They begged to have Jesus touch them as he had touched the man with leprosy. They clamored to hear what he had to say and they wanted him to heal their sicknesses. But it was all for themselves. They were not acknowledging God, either in praise to him for Jesus's miracles or in hunger for God and his righteousness. Although the multitudes listened to Jesus's teaching, they kept God, the center of Jesus's life, on the outside. So Jesus often slipped away from the crowds to draw close to his Father in hours of prayer.

ritually unclean
Leviticus 13:1–14:32

Being a leper was a designation that consigned a person to the worst discrimination and hopelessness. In Bible times the only way to deal with the disease of leprosy was quarantine because it was highly contagious. God gave laws that required a person with leprosy to live alone or in a separate colony with other lepers. It's hard to imagine the inner pain of a person with leprosy. It would be bad enough to have a disease for which there was no cure. But it must have been a living death to be cut off from any gesture of compassion, any interaction with friends or family.

God's quarantine laws were given for the protection of others, but today discrimination against people with leprosy, which is now called Hansen's disease, is not warranted. Most forms of the disease are not contagious, and medication is available to greatly relieve the effects of the disease.

what others say

Philip Yancey

Mother Teresa, whose sisters in Calcutta run both a hospice and a clinic for leprosy patients, once said, "We have drugs for people with diseases like leprosy. But these drugs do not treat the main problem, the disease of being unwanted. That's what my sisters hope to provide." The sick and the poor, she said, suffer even more from rejection than material want.[3]

Michael Card

When Jesus felt alone, it was because His Father was so visibly absent in the world. Jesus sought his presence in lonely places.[4]

Jesus reached out to touch a man who was covered with leprosy. In doing so, Jesus violated a law and followed the rule of love and

apply it

compassion, which superseded it. Today Jesus calls us to reach out with compassion to people whom society has given up on. Because Jesus is not here in physical form, we are to be the hands of Jesus. No human condition is beyond Jesus's compassion and power to heal.

No Boundaries

LUKE 5:17–26 *Now it happened on a certain day, as He was teaching, that there were Pharisees and teachers of the law sitting by, who had come out of every town of Galilee, Judea, and Jerusalem. And the power of the Lord was present to heal them. Then behold, men brought on a bed a man who was paralyzed, whom they sought to bring in and lay before Him. And when they could not find how they might bring him in, because of the crowd, they went up on the housetop and let him down with his bed through the tiling into the midst before Jesus. When He saw their faith, He said to him, "Man, your sins are forgiven you." And the scribes and the Pharisees began to reason, saying, "Who is this who speaks blasphemies? Who can forgive sins but God alone?" But when Jesus perceived their thoughts, He answered and said to them, "Why are you reasoning in your hearts? Which is easier, to say, 'Your sins are forgiven you,' or to say, 'Rise up and walk'? But that you may know that the Son of Man has power on earth to forgive sins"—He said to the man who was paralyzed, "I say to you, arise, take up your bed, and go to your house." Immediately he rose up before them, took up what he had been lying on, and departed to his own house, glorifying God. And they were all amazed, and they glorified God and were filled with fear, saying, "We have seen strange things today!" (NKJV)*

Word spread that Jesus was not only a miracle worker, but also an amazing teacher. Instead of relying on the authority of ancient teachers, as was the custom of teachers, Jesus spoke with the assurance of one who was the authority. This drew the intellectuals from surrounding areas who came to hear him.

One day Jesus's teaching session was suddenly interrupted. Men who had tried to get their paralytic friend in to see Jesus had been refused admittance. Showing great ingenuity and determination, they removed some tiles in the roof and lowered their friend to Jesus. This must have amazed the people. Even more stunning was

Jesus's response. When he saw their faith, he looked at the paralytic and said, "Man, your sins are forgiven you" (Luke 5:20 NKJV).

The audience was shocked to the point of outrage. How could Jesus dare to forgive sin, something only God can do? This was **blasphemy**!

Then, to demonstrate his authority, Jesus told the man to get up, pick up his mat, and go home. In healing the man's paralysis, Jesus proved that he also had power to heal the man's deepest need: forgiveness of sin. Jesus's act of healing was proof that he had the authority to forgive sins.

blasphemy
Leviticus 24:10–16, 23

blasphemy
slanderous speech
directed toward
God, punishable by
death

what others say

William Barclay

We must remember that sin and suffering were in Palestine inextricably connected. It was implicitly believed that if a man was suffering he had sinned. . . . [The scribes and Pharisees] objected to Jesus claiming to extend forgiveness to the man. But on their own arguments and assumptions the man was ill because he had sinned; and if he was cured that was proof that his sins were forgiven. The complaint of the Pharisees recoiled on them and left them speechless.[5]

Philip Yancey

Jesus never met a disease he could not cure, a birth defect he could not reverse, a demon he could not exorcise. But he did meet skeptics he could not convince and sinners he could not convert. Forgiveness of sins requires an act of will on the receiver's part, and some who heard Jesus' strongest words about grace and forgiveness turned away unrepentant.[6]

Partying with Sinners

LUKE 5:27–30 *After these things He went out and saw a tax collector named Levi, sitting at the tax office. And He said to him, "Follow Me." So he left all, rose up, and followed Him. Then Levi gave Him a great feast in his own house. And there were a great number of tax collectors and others who sat down with them. And their scribes and the Pharisees complained against His disciples, saying, "Why do You eat and drink with tax collectors and sinners?" (NKJV)*

sinners
irreligious Jews, syn-
agogue dropouts

scribes
scholars, experts in
the law of Moses

As Levi collected duty on merchandise at his tollbooth, he was constantly aware that he belonged to a group that was despised by the Jews—on a par with robbers and murderers. He was a Jew who had signed up for employment by the hated Roman government. One day Jesus approached him, saying, "Follow Me." Immediately this hard-headed tax officer left everything and went with Jesus.

It may be that at this time Jesus changed his name from Levi to Matthew, which means "the gift of God."

To make public the decision he had made and to honor Jesus, Matthew invited his friends and colleagues to a banquet at his house. Tax collectors and **sinners** were among the many guests.

The **scribes** and Pharisees who were hostile to all at the gala affair were also extremely critical of Jesus. How could he enjoy eating with these outcasts? He was compromising the standards they followed of keeping separate from sinners. Instead, he was seeking them out—and enjoying himself!

The Doctor's Clientele: A Primer

LUKE 5:31–32 *Jesus answered and said to them, "Those who are well have no need of a physician, but those who are sick. I have not come to call the righteous, but sinners, to repentance." (NKJV)*

Jesus pointed out that the doctor's office is not full of healthy people but the sick whose ailments have driven them to seek help. Similarly, Jesus had not come to call the righteous, those who considered themselves so healthy that they did not need him, but to bring healing to sinners through repentance and turning to him in faith. Jesus came to save those who were willing to admit their need of him.

what others say

Max Anders

The Pharisees prided themselves in the fact that they never came in contact with sinners: They viewed it as evidence of their purity. Jesus, however, readily associated with sinners. This was a direct affront to religious leaders, and, by implication, exposed the bleakness of their lives.[7]

Everybody's Doing It!

LUKE 5:33–35 *Then they said to Him, "Why do the disciples of John fast often and make prayers, and likewise those of the Pharisees, but Yours eat and drink?" And He said to them, "Can you make the friends of the bridegroom fast while the bridegroom is with them? But the days will come when the bridegroom will be taken away from them; then they will fast in those days." (NKJV)*

On another occasion Jesus's critics pointed out how he and his disciples were different from John's disciples and those of the Pharisees.

While John's and the Pharisees' followers fasted and prayed, Jesus's disciples did not fast but enjoyed regular meals. The Pharisees and teachers of the law thought this proved they were not spiritual!

Jesus observed that it would be entirely inappropriate for a party of wedding guests to fast, as if the bridegroom were dead. Jesus went on to say that a time would come when the bridegroom (Jesus) would be "taken away from them" (Luke 5:35 NKJV). Then it would make sense for his followers to fast. Jesus seems to be referring to his own future death here. The idea behind Jesus's words may have been, "Don't worry, Pharisees. My followers will fast soon enough—when you kill me. But then they will not be doing ceremonial fasting, which you hold so precious; they will be doing the fasting that naturally follows the death of a loved one."

Garments and Goatskins

LUKE 5:36–39 *Then He spoke a parable to them: "No one puts a piece from a new garment on an old one; otherwise the new makes a tear, and also the piece that was taken out of the new does not match the old. And no one puts new wine into old wineskins; or else the new wine will burst the wineskins and be spilled, and the wineskins will be ruined. But new wine must be put into new wineskins, and both are preserved. And no one, having drunk old wine, immediately desires new; for he says, 'The old is better.'" (NKJV)*

In a parable Jesus used everyday items—garments and wineskins—to announce that he had come to bring something new. Nobody would take a piece from a new garment to patch a hole in an old garment—both would be ruined. Similarly, Jesus had not come to patch up the old religious forms of the law but to create something fresh and totally new.

Problems would come if new wine were poured into old wineskins, because as the wine fermented, it would burst the old wineskin (see Illustration #6). Not only would the new wine spill out, but the old wineskin would be ruined. People who are familiar with old things are content to stick with what they know and are unwilling to try the new. Similarly, the people in Jesus's day were familiar with the laws of Moses and the traditions that had grown through the years. Jesus came to bring something new. Like wine that would burst out of old containers, his salvation could not be delivered in Judaism. Further, his listeners were unwilling to try the new because they preferred to stick with what was familiar. Jesus came not to reform the old legalistic system but to replace it.

Jesus came as a teacher, but one who reached far beyond the expected norms. No one was outside his circle of influence. In this chapter alone Luke shows Jesus teaching crowds of common people, calling fishermen to be his close associates, and healing an outcast leper. He taught the Pharisees and teachers of the law—students whose view of him registered anywhere from critical to hostile. And he called Levi (Matthew)—a wealthy, influential tax collector regarded as a "sinner" by the law-abiding establishment—to be his disciple. What should we learn from this? That nobody is beyond the reach of Jesus!

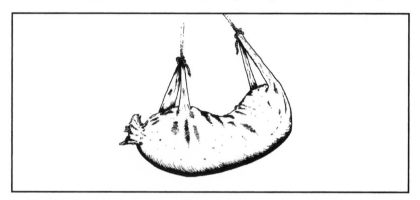

Illustration #6
Wineskin—Wine was kept in a goatskin bottle as shown here. New skin was supple but in time became dried, hard, and cracked.

Chapter Wrap-Up

- Jesus instructed Simon to go into deep water and cast his net. The huge catch that resulted was clearly a miracle. Recognizing Jesus's power, Peter fell at his feet and acknowledged that he was a sinner. Jesus reassured Peter not to be afraid but to be prepared to catch men. (Luke 5:1–11)

- Jesus touched a leper and healed him instantly. He told the man to show himself to the priest so he could be pronounced clean. (Luke 5:12–16)

- One day when Jesus was teaching the religious elite, four men opened the roof of the house and let the man down in front of Jesus. Noting their faith, Jesus told the man his sins were forgiven. The religious leaders silently accused Jesus of speaking blasphemy, since only God can forgive sins. Jesus healed the man, proving he had power both to heal and to forgive sins. (Luke 5:17–26)

- Jesus called Levi to follow him, though he was a tax collector on the payroll of the hated Roman government. When the religious leaders complained that Jesus socialized with outcasts, Jesus said he had come to call sinners who recognized their need of him. (Luke 5:27–32)

- Jesus's critics asked why his followers did not practice regular fasting and prayers, as they did and as John the Baptist's followers did. Jesus claimed that he had come to replace the old legalistic system with something new and better. (Luke 5:33–39)

Study Questions

1. Why did Jesus's instructions to Simon to cast for fish seem ridiculous? What were two results of Simon's obedience?

2. What did Jesus reveal of himself when he healed the leper?

3. What did Jesus prove to the religious leaders when he healed the paralyzed man?

4. How did Jesus upset common practice when he called Matthew to follow him?

5. What did Jesus want his critics to understand when he replied to their question about fasting?

Luke 6 Jesus, Ph.D.

Let's Get Started

Jesus had launched a mission that touched the lives of people from all over the land, but his outreach lacked the trappings of modern ministries. He had no assistants organizing his schedule, sending out press releases, or setting up photo opportunities. There were no direct-mail campaigns to solicit gifts or offer tickets to special healing events.

God's ways
Isaiah 55:8–9

Jesus concentrated on people—individuals who needed to know about his Father's love and care. Jesus helped them understand that <u>God's ways</u> were so different from their ways that he had come to turn their way of doing things upside down!

In this chapter we'll discover Jesus's concept of the Sabbath. We'll also be introduced to all twelve of Jesus's disciples. Most importantly, we'll learn about one of Jesus's most important sermons. Up until now we've heard that Jesus taught; in this chapter we'll learn what Jesus taught. So settle in behind your desk. Professor Jesus is about to enter the classroom.

Jesus and His Critics

LUKE 6:1–5 *Now it happened on the second Sabbath after the first that He went through the grainfields. And His disciples plucked the heads of grain and ate them, rubbing them in their hands. And some of the Pharisees said to them, "Why are you doing what is not lawful to do on the Sabbath?" But Jesus answering them said, "Have you not even read this, what David did when he was hungry, he and those who were with him: how he went into the house of God, took and ate the showbread, and also gave some to those with him, which is not lawful for any but the priests to eat?" And He said to them, "The Son of Man is also Lord of the Sabbath." (NKJV)*

grain
Leviticus 19:9–10;
Deuteronomy
23:4–25

David
1 Samuel 21:1–6

delight
Isaiah 58:13–14

Taking grain was not stealing. God had told farmers to leave some of their <u>grain</u> to provide for the needs of people who could not afford to buy it. The problem for the Pharisees was not in eating the grain but in the day on which the disciples did it. Rubbing heads of grain to release the kernels was considered threshing, and threshing was not allowed on the Sabbath according to Jewish tradition.

Jesus's reply set them back on their heels. He pointed out that King <u>David</u>, whom the Pharisees held in the highest esteem, had gone into the tabernacle and taken consecrated bread to eat. This was food that only priests could eat. Further, he gave some of the bread to his companions! This was a blatant disregard of the law. Jesus ended his argument with an exclamation point by telling the Pharisees that he himself was Lord of the Sabbath—the author of the whole idea of Sabbath and the person in charge of how it should be kept.

God set apart the Sabbath, the seventh day of the week (Saturday), as a reminder of his completion of Creation and as a day of rest for people. The Sabbath was designed to remind the Jews that they were God's people and that they had a special commitment to him. He specified that his people, their servants, and even their animals were to refrain from ordinary work so they could delight in this day set apart for him.

In time the people began to focus more on the no-work clause of God's commandment than on the rest-and-<u>delight</u>-in-the-Lord clauses. The religious leaders drew up long, detailed statements about what was "work" and what wasn't. One list gave thirty-nine activities that were prohibited on the Sabbath.

What are we to make of all this? Are we responsible for obeying the Sabbath laws, as the Pharisees demanded in Jesus's day? Obviously not, as Jesus didn't even follow the Pharisees' laws.

But are we to keep the Sabbath at all? Christians have different ideas about how to view the Sabbath, but this much we know: Jesus's first-century followers did not observe the Jewish Sabbath. They did, however, meet for worship on the first day of the week, which was Sunday. On this day they remembered that Jesus rose from the dead. Jesus confirmed that God gave the Sabbath for man's benefit.

Rotten Nasty Filthy Healing

LUKE 6:6–11 *Now it happened on another Sabbath, also, that He entered the synagogue and taught. And a man was there whose right hand was withered. So the scribes and Pharisees watched Him closely, whether He would heal on the Sabbath, that they might find an accusation against Him. But He knew their thoughts, and said to the man who had the withered hand, "Arise and stand here." And he arose and stood. Then Jesus said to them, "I will ask you one thing: Is it lawful on the Sabbath to do good or to do evil, to save life or to destroy?" And when He had looked around at them all, He said to the man, "Stretch out your hand." And he did so, and his hand was restored as whole as the other. But they were filled with rage, and discussed with one another what they might do to Jesus. (NKJV)*

Jesus's critics were aching to make an accusation against him. Would he dare to break the Sabbath law and perform a miracle of healing? Jesus knew how eager his critics were to accuse him, so he posed a question. Which is obeying the Sabbath law: Doing good or doing evil? Saving life or destroying it? The only reply was silence as Jesus looked around the room. Then he told a man to stretch out his atrophied hand, and right before their eyes, Jesus healed the hand. Without question, Jesus reflected his Father's heart when he put loving, caring human relationships over slavish adherence to man-made laws. The critics were almost crazy with anger at Jesus.

Matthew and Mark fill in the incident by recording that as the Pharisees made their exit from the synagogue that day, they plotted with the **Herodians** how they could have Jesus killed (Matthew 12:14; Mark 3:6).

gospel harmony

Twelve World Changers

> LUKE 6:12–16 *Now it came to pass in those days that He went out to the mountain to pray, and continued all night in prayer to God. And when it was day, He called His disciples to Himself; and from them He chose twelve whom He also named apostles: Simon, whom He also named Peter, and Andrew his brother; James and John; Philip and Bartholomew; Matthew and Thomas; James the son of Alphaeus, and Simon called the Zealot; Judas the son of James, and Judas Iscariot who also became a traitor.* (NKJV)

One day Jesus left the crowds and went to spend the night alone in conversation with his Father. He sought guidance. The next morning Jesus called his followers together and selected from them twelve men to be in his inner circle, both as disciples to follow him on earth and as apostles to continue his work after he returned to his Father.

Jesus the Son of God had laid aside his divine ability to know all, so he acknowledged his dependence on his Father for the wisdom he needed in choosing the twelve who would become his disciples. If Jesus needed to spend time with his Father seeking guidance, how much more do we need that time alone with God?

apply it

Herodians
political group, supporting Herod Antipas, who joined the Pharisees to oppose Jesus

The Jesus Team

Name	Nickname or Family Affiliation	Distinguishing Characteristics
Peter	Also called Simon, Cephas (Rock)	Fisherman; became one of three disciples closest to Jesus; wrote two New Testament books
Andrew	Peter's brother	Brought Peter to Jesus
James	Son of Zebedee and Salome	One of the three disciples closest to Jesus

The Smart Guide to the Bible

The Jesus Team (cont'd)

Name	Nickname or Family Affiliation	Distinguishing Characteristics
John	Brother of James	Known with James as Son of Thunder; one of the three disciples closest to Jesus; probably "the disciple Jesus loved"; wrote five New Testament books
Philip		Brought Nathanael to Jesus
Bartholomew	May be Nathanael, Philip's friend or brother	
Matthew	Also called Levi	Tax officer; hosted a banquet for Jesus; wrote one New Testament book
Thomas	Also called Didymus (the Twin)	Because of his hesitancy to believe that Jesus rose from the dead, became known as Doubting Thomas
James	Also called James the Younger; son of Alphaeus	
Simon	Also called the Zealot	May have been active in the movement committed to overthrow Roman rule
Judas	Also called Thaddaeus; son of James; also one of the Twelve	
Judas Iscariot		Treasurer of the group; betrayed Jesus

unschooled, ordinary
Acts 4:13

what others say

R. Kent Hughes

All except Judas Iscariot were Galileans, "country boys." Four were fishermen. One was a hated tax-gatherer. Not one of them was famous or rich or noble or well-connected. Not one of them was a scribe of a priest or an elder or a ruler of the people. They were, as their detractors labeled them, "unschooled, ordinary men." All were poor.[3]

The men who made up the Twelve were a diverse group. They seemed to have little in common, yet they became a tightly knit group that changed the world. What bound them together was their relationship to Jesus.

Jesus's Keynote Speech

LUKE 6:17–19 *And He came down with them and stood on a level place with a crowd of His disciples and a great multitude of people from all Judea and Jerusalem, and from the seacoast of Tyre and Sidon, who came to hear Him and be healed of their diseases, as well as those who were tormented with unclean spirits. And they were healed. And the whole multitude sought to touch Him, for power went out from Him and healed them all. (NKJV)*

Was there no escape? Crowds surrounded Jesus: the newly chosen Twelve, his friends, and a great number of hopefuls who had come from a wide radius. They all wanted to hear him teach what would later become known as the Sermon on the Plain, so called because of his location—"a level place." Many in the crowd had come because they were desperate for healing. Among them were some who were tormented with unclean spirits, and others with various diseases. The people pressed against Jesus, because they were healed if they only touched him.

The World According to Jesus

LUKE 6:20–26 *Then He lifted up His eyes toward His disciples, and said:*
"Blessed are you poor,
For yours is the kingdom of God.
Blessed are you who hunger now,
For you shall be filled.
Blessed are you who weep now,
For you shall laugh.
Blessed are you when men hate you,
And when they exclude you,
And revile you, and cast out your name as evil,
For the Son of Man's sake.
Rejoice in that day and leap for joy!
For indeed your reward is great in heaven,
For in like manner their fathers did to the prophets.
"But woe to you who are rich,
For you have received your consolation.
Woe to you who are full,
For you shall hunger.
Woe to you who laugh now,
For you shall mourn and weep.
Woe to you when all men speak well of you,
For so did their fathers to the false prophets. (NKJV)

Jesus began to teach his disciples, but the setting was not an enclosed classroom. Though Jesus was clearly showing his chosen disciples that they would be a people set apart from others, the crowd listened in.

Jesus gave a series of contrasts: blessings for some and woes for others. What he said went against conventional wisdom—it simply didn't make sense. The table below summarizes what Jesus said. As you read it, remember that the disciples were about to experience the conditions that Jesus talked about—poverty, hunger, mourning, and persecution—because of their loyalty to Jesus.

Jesus's Sermon Summarized

Blessing	Woe
Blessed are you if you're poor. You have the kingdom of God.	Woe to you if you're rich. You have all the benefits you're going to get.
Blessed are you if you're hungry. You'll be satisfied.	Woe to you if you are greedily filling your stomach now. You'll go hungry.
Blessed are you if you're crying. You will laugh again.	Woe to you who are laughing as if sorrow can't touch you. Some day you will mourn and weep.
Blessed are you when others hate you because of me. They will exclude you and reject you because of your loyalty to me.	Woe to you when everyone speaks well of you. Even the false prophets could win in a popularity contest.

what others say

Peter Kreeft

The point of our lives in this world is not comfort, security, or even happiness, but training; not fulfillment but preparation. It's a lousy home, but it's a fine gymnasium. . . . Jesus didn't make it into a rose garden when he came, though he could have. Rather, he wore the thorns from this world's gardens.[4]

John Piper

One way of rejoicing in suffering comes from fixing our minds firmly on the greatness of the reward that will come to us in the resurrection. The effect of this kind of focus is to make our present pain seem small by comparison to what is coming.[5]

Jesus showed deep compassion for the poor, the hungry, those who mourned, and those who were rejected. He offered them hope. In contrast, he did not offer hope to the wealthy, the well-fed, the merrymakers, and those who compromised in order to win the admiration of others. They had it all now! With which group of

people do we identify today? Are we among those Jesus labeled "blessed" or those to whom he said, "Woe to you"? Do we acknowledge the dignity and value of people whom the world ignores? Do we show compassion for people in need and seek to give relief in practical, self-sacrificing ways?

Habits Worth Having

LUKE 6:27–36 *"But I say to you who hear: Love your enemies, do good to those who hate you, bless those who curse you, and pray for those who spitefully use you. To him who strikes you on the one cheek, offer the other also. And from him who takes away your cloak, do not withhold your tunic either. Give to everyone who asks of you. And from him who takes away your goods do not ask them back. And just as you want men to do to you, you also do to them likewise. But if you love those who love you, what credit is that to you? For even sinners love those who love them. And if you do good to those who do good to you, what credit is that to you? For even sinners do the same. And if you lend to those from whom you hope to receive back, what credit is that to you? For even sinners lend to sinners to receive as much back. But love your enemies, do good, and lend, hoping for nothing in return; and your reward will be great, and you will be sons of the Most High. For He is kind to the unthankful and evil. Therefore be merciful, just as your Father also is merciful. (NKJV)*

Jesus went on to say his disciples should view other people in a radically different way than they were used to. They were to love their enemies, show acts of kindness to those who hated them, and share generously with those who made demands. They were to deal with others with the quality of love and generosity that Jesus's Father showed to people who were ungrateful and wicked. And the reward? Jesus promised that his disciples would be greatly rewarded—the more they loved with his supernatural love, the more they would become like his Father.

what others say

Marcus Borg

[Matthew 5:39] specifies that the person has been struck on the right cheek. . . . In that world, people did not use the left hand to strike people. It was reserved for "unseemly" uses. Thus, being struck on the right cheek meant that one had been backhanded with the right hand. Given the social customs of the day, a backhand blow was the way a superior hit an inferior, whereas one fought social equals with fists.

This means the saying presupposes a setting in which a superior is beating a peasant. What should the peasant do? "Turn the other cheek." What would be the effect? The only way the superior could continue the beating would be with an overhand blow with the fist—which would have meant treating the peasant as an equal.[6]

Father's character
Psalm 112:4–5

Darrell L. Bock

Jesus' disciples should love with an exceptional love, a love so different that the world can see it. Such love is rewarded because it marks out the presence of the children of God, who reflect the character of God. God himself is kind to the ungrateful and selfish. To be his child is to reveal the <u>Father's character</u>.[7]

Paul N. Benware

Disciples are to respond to evil with good and with love. Patience and not retaliation is to be the response of the follower of Christ. These are radical words, and they are also impossible to obey. They drive the serious disciple to his knees as he realizes that without the enablement and the grace of God such commands cannot be kept.[8]

The Boomerang

LUKE 6:37–38 *"Judge not, and you shall not be judged. Condemn not, and you shall not be condemned. Forgive, and you will be forgiven. Give, and it will be given to you: good measure, pressed down, shaken together, and running over will be put into your bosom. For with the same measure that you use, it will be measured back to you." (NKJV)*

Jesus does not tell his disciples to be gracious to others because it's the right thing to do, though of course it is. Instead, Jesus tells his disciples to be gracious to others because there are perks for doing so! What's in it for you if you avoid condemning others? You'll get the rich benefits of not being condemned. What will you get if you give things to people and forgive people? You'll be given things! You'll be forgiven!

what others say

John Piper

Jesus made it very clear that the key to our joy and our love in the midst of hard times is the deep, unshakable confidence that every loss on this earth in the service of love for the sake of the kingdom will be abundantly restored, "pressed down, shaken together, running over." The mandate is clear: let us devote ourselves to cultivating stronger faith in the "great reward" of future grace. This is the power to love.[9]

A Teaching About Teaching

LUKE 6:39–40 *And He spoke a parable to them: "Can the blind lead the blind? Will they not both fall into the ditch? A disciple is not above his teacher, but everyone who is perfectly trained will be like his teacher. (NKJV)*

In this passage Jesus gave basic truth about how education works, but it's unclear how he meant for his listeners to take it. Maybe Jesus was encouraging his disciples to know their place and keep it. Or perhaps he was informing any aspiring teachers in the crowd (including those among the disciples) that the title of "teacher" came with a big responsibility, that of being sure not to misguide people. Maybe he was letting the disciples know they could expect to see the same bad attitudes in the Pharisees' disciples as they were used to seeing in the Pharisees. It's possible Jesus meant all of these things and more.

Regardless of what Jesus wanted people to do with the information, the information he gave was clear: a student is not better than but rather becomes like his teacher.

Many of Jesus's teachings were uniquely relevant to his time and place, and certainly this "teaching about teaching" had implications that were peculiar to his listeners. But this teaching also has a universal quality about it, which invites us of the twenty-first century to explore its implications for our world. One point we can glean from the idea that students become like their teachers is that it is important for us to choose our teachers wisely. People often assume that the responsibility of a student is merely to do the work that a teacher sets before him or her, but this isn't true. It's also the student's responsibility to make sure he or she is being taught by a worthy teacher.

key point

Also, Jesus's teaching reminds us that when we witness people doing bad things or making bad decisions, we ought to be slow to judge them. Too often we call people names in our minds and quickly dismiss them. We ought to remember that every person has had influences in his or her life, and these influences are at least partly to blame for the wrongs people commit.

Jesus, the Stand-Up Comic

> **LUKE 6:41–42** *And why do you look at the speck in your brother's eye, but do not perceive the plank in your own eye? Or how can you say to your brother, 'Brother, let me remove the speck that is in your eye,' when you yourself do not see the plank that is in your own eye? Hypocrite! First remove the plank from your own eye, and then you will see clearly to remove the speck that is in your brother's eye. (NKJV)*

fruit
Galatians 5:22–23

Most people have heard this passage so often that it's lost its humor, but Jesus seems to be painting a word picture of hilarity here. Think of a librarian who yells at someone to keep his voice down, thus creating even more noise in the process, and hopefully you'll catch some of the humor Jesus intended. Don't increase sin by committing the sin of ignoring your own sin.

Filling and Filtering

> **LUKE 6:43–45** *"For a good tree does not bear bad fruit, nor does a bad tree bear good fruit. For every tree is known by its own fruit. For men do not gather figs from thorns, nor do they gather grapes from a bramble bush. A good man out of the good treasure of his heart brings forth good; and an evil man out of the evil treasure of his heart brings forth evil. For out of the abundance of the heart his mouth speaks. (NKJV)*

This passage is instructive in two ways. One is that it helps people to determine the extent to which they should trust people. Don't trust people whose lives are characterized by bad things—corruption, gossip, unnecessary complaining, dissension, and so on. Instead, trust people whose lives are full of "good fruit"—such as kindness, generosity, joy, and peace.

But this passage promotes more than filtering one's outside influences. It also calls for internal maintenance. Jesus is calling his listeners to be sure that they cultivate hearts that please God. An effort to do so, Jesus says, will result in "good treasure." Jesus seems to be likening people to sponges. People, like sponges, can release only that which has already been absorbed.

Jesus places special emphasis on what people say, linking what is in one's heart with that which proceeds from one's mouth. This link between the heart and mouth runs throughout Scripture. Just look:

- "The word [of God's commandment] is very near you, in your mouth and in your heart, that you may do it" (Deuteronomy 30:14 NKJV).

- "Acquaint yourself with [God], and be at peace; thereby good will come to you. Receive, please, instruction from His mouth, and lay up His words in your heart" (Job 22:21–22 NKJV).

- "My mouth shall speak wisdom, and the meditation of my heart shall give understanding" (Psalm 49:3 NKJV).

- "With the heart one believes unto righteousness, and with the mouth confession is made unto salvation" (Romans 10:10 NKJV).

One thing we can conclude, therefore, is that what we say is a fairly reliable indicator of who we are, of what lives in our hearts. If we find ourselves saying things that routinely have an ill effect on those around us, it's time for us to do some heart work—praying, reading Scripture, and seeking God.

Practice What I Preach

LUKE 6:46–49 *"But why do you call Me 'Lord, Lord,' and not do the things which I say? Whoever comes to Me, and hears My sayings and does them, I will show you whom he is like: He is like a man building a house, who dug deep and laid the foundation on the rock. And when the flood arose, the stream beat vehemently against that house, and could not shake it, for it was founded on the rock. But he who heard and did nothing is like a man who built a house on the earth without a foundation, against which the stream beat vehemently; and immediately it fell. And the ruin of that house was great." (NKJV)*

In this parable it's important to notice that both men have heard Jesus's words. The only thing different is that one man puts Christ's words into action and the other doesn't.

The message? Putting Jesus's words into practice makes them a part of you. Knowing God's Word is not enough; we need to obey it. This enables you to resist evil influences and say no to temptations that foreshadow destruction. If, however, you fail to apply Jesus's words to your everyday life, evil will have its way with you. You won't be able to stand up to temptation, and you'll experience the usual consequences of sin—pain, confusion, and devastation.

Rock
1 Corinthians 10:1–4

what others say

Oswald Chambers

If a man has built himself up in private by listening to the words of Jesus and obeying them, when the crisis comes it is not his strength of will that keeps him, but the tremendous power of God—"kept by the power of God." Go on building up yourself in the Word of God when no one is watching you, and when the crisis comes you will find you stand like a rock; but if you have not been building yourself up on the Word of God, you will go down no matter what your will is like.[10]

Dallas Willard

In actually doing what Jesus knows to be best for us, we build a life that is absolutely indestructible, "on the Rock." "And that Rock was Christ."[11]

Chapter Wrap-Up

- In contrast to following the Pharisees' long list of prohibitions to keep the Sabbath holy, Jesus demonstrated that the Sabbath was to be a day of rest (Luke 6:1–11).

- Jesus chose twelve men to be his disciples and taught them and others with his Sermon on the Plain (Luke 6:12–19).

- Jesus gave good news to his disciples, who were going to experience poverty, hunger, pain, and persecution because of their allegiance to him. He promised that they would be blessed (Luke 6:20–26).

- Jesus taught that his disciples should reflect his Father's love and mercy, not just to their friends, but to the most undeserving. Though they would pay a price for doing so, they would be rewarded (Luke 6:27–38).

- Jesus warned that the heart attitudes his disciples held would certainly be reflected in their actions—for the benefit of others or for their ill. Jesus taught that the only way to stand firm is to build on the firm foundation of obeying his words. (Luke 6:39–49)

Study Questions

1. How did Jesus differ from the religious leaders when it came to the Sabbath? What did this reveal about who Jesus was?

2. How many men did Jesus choose to be in his inner circle of disciples? What is the difference between a disciple and an apostle?

3. How would you characterize the differences between people Jesus pronounced as blessed and those he pronounced as under judgment?

4. What result comes to disciples who show God's love and generosity to the undeserving?

5. What is the key to having strength to stand firm in times of temptation?

Luke 7 Jesus, M.D.

Let's Get Started

This chapter has a lot to teach us about the relationship between people's faith and God's power. Jesus proved he is the Great Physician who is able to heal the diseased and raise the dead. He also proved he is the Great Physician of the soul, who knows people's hearts and forgives sins.

Read about a Roman soldier who went above and beyond the call of duty. Find out how to impress Jesus. Watch Jesus perform his first resurrection. Listen in on John the Baptist's interview with Jesus. And witness the extraordinary love of a "sinful" woman for her Lord.

A Gentile's Faith

LUKE 7:1–6a *Now when He concluded all His sayings in the hearing of the people, He entered Capernaum. And a certain centurion's servant, who was dear to him, was sick and ready to die. So when he heard about Jesus, he sent elders of the Jews to Him, pleading with Him to come and heal his servant. And when they came to Jesus, they begged Him earnestly, saying that the one for whom He should do this was deserving, "for he loves our nation, and has built us a synagogue." Then Jesus went with them.* (NKJV)

Centurion Goodness

The man spotlighted in this passage is a Gentile, a Roman centurion (see illustration below). While centurions were trained to be take-charge representatives of Rome, this one was a man with a warm and caring heart. When one of his slaves became deathly ill, the centurion sent for the community leaders. He asked them to contact Jesus and request that he come to heal this slave whom the centurion "valued highly." The centurion must have heard of or seen previous healings performed by Jesus.

Luke highlights the centurion's fondness for Jews, saying he built their synagogue. Remember that Luke was writing to Theo, a Greek Gentile. With this account of the centurion, Luke may be promoting kind interaction between Gentiles and Jews. He might also be giving his Gentile readers a model of faith that they can look up to without reservation. Luke may also be demonstrating that Christ's love was not limited to Jews, nor is God's power reserved for only one group of people.

Luke identified with the centurion. While a doctor's concern is for his patient, he cannot be indifferent to the pleas of the patient's loved ones who wring their hands and say, "Doctor, do something!" Families want desperately to see everything made right, but are helpless to do anything about it.

The Wisdom of a Military Man

LUKE 7:6b–8 *And when He was already not far from the house, the centurion sent friends to Him, saying to Him, "Lord, do not trouble Yourself, for I am not worthy that You should enter under my roof. Therefore I did not even think myself worthy to come to You. But say the word, and my servant will be healed. For I also am a man placed under authority, having soldiers under me. And I say to one, 'Go,' and he goes; and to another,*

'Come,' and he comes; and to my servant, 'Do this,' and he does it." (NKJV)

The elders carried out the centurion's request faithfully, and Jesus responded by making his way to the centurion's house. Before Jesus got there, the centurion sent friends to stop him from entering his house, saying, "Do not trouble Yourself . . ." This may be a reference to how long it would take Jesus to walk to the centurion's house, but it's more likely to be a reference to the ridicule Jesus would bring upon himself for entering a Gentile's home. The centurion obviously had a lot of respect for Jesus because he said he didn't deserve to have Jesus enter his house.

The soldier then made a fascinating analogy. In the same way that people beneath the centurion did what he said because he had the power of the Roman Empire backing him, so Jesus could issue orders that would be carried out because Jesus had the power of God behind him. The centurion demonstrated an outstanding comprehension of who Jesus was, whom he represented, and what he could do.

What Impresses Jesus

LUKE 7:9–10 *When Jesus heard these things, He marveled at him, and turned around and said to the crowd that followed Him, "I say to you, I have not found such great faith, not even in Israel!" And those who were sent, returning to the house, found the servant well who had been sick.* (NKJV)

Jesus was taken aback. This centurion, who was not one of God's covenant people, demonstrated more faith than Jesus had ever seen from anyone in Israel. In fact, Jesus yearned for his fellow Jews to have as much faith as this Gentile man. Needless to say, his servant was healed instantly.

Have you ever wanted to know how to impress Jesus? Here's the answer according to Luke. Practice a faith in God that goes beyond the accepted norm.

Matthew, in recording this same miracle, points out that Jesus marveled at the centurion's amazing faith because this was the kind of response he longed to see in Israel (Matthew 8:5–13).

While the Jews of Jesus's day thought they were guaranteed entrance into Christ's kingdom because they were Jews, Jesus demonstrated that one's ethnicity didn't matter. What mattered was faith.

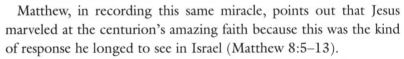

what others say

Warren W. Wiersbe

Twice in the Gospel record we are told that Jesus marveled. Here in Capernaum, he marveled at the faith of a Gentile; and in Nazareth, he marveled at the <u>unbelief</u> of the Jews.[2]

gospel harmony

go to

unbelief
Mark 6:6

Death Overturned

LUKE 7:11–17 *Now it happened, the day after, that He went into a city called Nain; and many of His disciples went with Him, and a large crowd. And when He came near the gate of the city, behold, a dead man was being carried out, the only son of his mother; and she was a widow. And a large crowd from the city was with her. When the Lord saw her, He had compassion on her and said to her, "Do not weep." Then He came and touched the open coffin, and those who carried him stood still. And He said, "Young man, I say to you, arise." So he who was dead sat up and began to speak. And He presented him to his mother. Then fear came upon all, and they glorified God, saying, "A great prophet has risen up among us"; and, "God has visited His people." And this report about Him went throughout all Judea and all the surrounding region. (NKJV)*

One day as Jesus traveled to Nain, a town about twenty-five miles from Capernaum (see map in appendix A), he saw a funeral procession—men carrying a stretcher with a cloth-covered body and a grieving widow whose only son had died just that day. Following her was a large crowd of sympathizers, including professional mourners whose wails and doleful flute playing added to the misery.

Jesus felt great compassion for the grieving woman. In the death of her son she had lost not only the one person who could support and protect her, but the one who could carry on her family name. Jesus approached her and said, "Do not weep." Though many have said those words in tragic circumstances, only Jesus had the power to give this woman reason to stop crying.

He went to the bier, touched it, and told the young man to get up! To the amazement of all, the dead man sat up and spoke. We can picture Jesus taking the young man to his mother and clasping their hands together. Everyone was filled with worshipful awe. They praised God and quickly spread the word about Jesus. He was the greatest physician they had ever encountered. No human doctor could raise patients from the dead!

In Jesus's day it was customary on the day of the death to wrap a dead body in cloth and carry it on a stretcher for immediate burial. A procession was formed, usually including musicians and professional wailers. Even the poorest family was expected to hire two flute players and one female mourner.

A doctor takes on a patient who is in critical condition, marshals all his skills in treating him, and finally when the patient is recovered, he dismisses him. Luke must have known some of the satisfaction a doctor experiences when he returns a patient to his family. He receives their expressions of joy and gratitude. As he recorded this incident of Jesus raising the son from death, he must have pictured the response of the grieving widow. Luke makes mention of three "only children" whom Jesus restored: the son of the widow of Nain, the <u>daughter</u> of Jairus, and the <u>boy</u> possessed by an evil spirit.

go to

daughter
Luke 8:40–56

boy
Luke 9:37–43

Are You Who I Think You Are?

LUKE 7:18–23 *Then the disciples of John reported to him concerning all these things. And John, calling two of his disciples to him, sent them to Jesus, saying, "Are You the Coming One, or do we look for another?" When the men had come to Him, they said, "John the Baptist has sent us to You, saying, 'Are You the Coming One, or do we look for another?'" And that very hour He cured many of infirmities, afflictions, and evil spirits; and to many blind He gave sight. Jesus answered and said to them, "Go and tell John the things you have seen and heard: that the blind see, the lame walk, the lepers are cleansed, the deaf hear,*

prison
Matthew 11:2

Isaiah
Luke 4:16–19;
Isaiah 61:1–2

the dead are raised, the poor have the gospel preached to them. And blessed is he who is not offended because of Me." (NKJV)

John paid a great price for being faithful. He was thrown in <u>prison</u> for confronting Herod about his sinful lifestyle. While in prison, John heard regularly from his disciples about the activities of Jesus. But events were not coming together as John thought they would. Perhaps he was expecting that by now Jesus would have taken action to overthrow the Roman occupation of their land.

Deeply troubled and acting like an investigative journalist, John sent two of his followers to ask Jesus a subtly accusing question: "Are You the Coming One, or do we look for another?" (Luke 7:20 NKJV).

Jesus dealt with the question, not behind closed doors, but out in the open where people watched him perform healings. He then told John's followers to go back and report what they had seen. They had watched the Great Physician in action.

Jesus was fulfilling the mission he had announced in Nazareth when he read and interpreted the passage from <u>Isaiah</u>. In other words, he counted on John to understand that he was fulfilling prophecy about the Messiah. Then Jesus added that there's a special blessing for John—and for all—who keep their trust in him in spite of difficulties that raise doubts in their minds. Jesus asks us to trust, even when we do not understand.

what others say

Darrell L. Bock

We sometimes think that the great saints never doubted. In doing so, we deny that they were normal human beings. The Scripture is honest and open about such struggles and doubts, just as the Christian community today should be.[3]

Charles R. Swindoll

Two words will help you cope when you run low on hope: *accept* and *trust*. *Accept* the mystery of hardship, suffering, misfortune, or mistreatment. Don't try to understand it or explain it. Accept it. Then, deliberately *trust* God to protect you by his power from this very moment to the dawning of eternity.[4]

God never abandons his suffering follower. He promises that when we pass through the <u>waters</u> of doubt, discouragement, pain, and suffering, he will be with us. He is a doctor not only of our bodies but also of our emotions and souls.

waters
Isaiah 43:1–3

A Recipe for True Success

LUKE 7:24–28 *When the messengers of John had departed, He began to speak to the multitudes concerning John: "What did you go out into the wilderness to see? A reed shaken by the wind? But what did you go out to see? A man clothed in soft garments? Indeed those who are gorgeously appareled and live in luxury are in kings' courts. But what did you go out to see? A prophet? Yes, I say to you, and more than a prophet. This is he of whom it is written:*

> *'Behold, I send My messenger before Your face,*
> *Who will prepare Your way before You.'*

"For I say to you, among those born of women there is not a greater prophet than John the Baptist; but he who is least in the kingdom of God is greater than he." (NKJV)

After John's disciples left, Jesus talked about him to the crowd. Was John a wimp that could be bent by the wind of opinion? Was he a sham dressed in the latest designer wear? No, he was a prophet who had fulfilled his mission. And, Jesus added, there was no greater prophet than John, for he had been privileged to announce the coming of the Messiah! However, anyone who enlisted for service in the kingdom of God, which Jesus was bringing, would enjoy blessings that John had only announced.

what others say

Leon Morris

Jesus' coming marked a watershed. He came to inaugurate the kingdom. And the least in that kingdom is greater than the greatest of men. This is a statement of historical fact. John belonged to the time of promise. The least in the kingdom is greater, not because of any personal qualities he may have, but because he belongs to the time of fulfilment.[5]

austere
rigorously
self-disciplined

Rejection Analysis

LUKE 7:29–35 *And when all the people heard Him, even the tax collectors justified God, having been baptized with the baptism of John. But the Pharisees and lawyers rejected the will of God for themselves, not having been baptized by him. And the Lord said, "To what then shall I liken the men of this generation, and what are they like? They are like children sitting in the marketplace and calling to one another, saying:*
  'We played the flute for you,
    And you did not dance;
  We mourned to you,
    And you did not weep.'
"For John the Baptist came neither eating bread nor drinking wine, and you say, 'He has a demon.' The Son of Man has come eating and drinking, and you say, 'Look, a glutton and a winebibber, a friend of tax collectors and sinners!' But wisdom is justified by all her children." (NKJV)

Jesus, having defended John, addressed the crowd and accused the unbelieving Pharisees and experts in the law. They would never be satisfied with the messenger of God because they did not want to believe the message of God. They had falsely accused John of being demon-possessed because they didn't like his **austere** lifestyle. On the other hand, they falsely accused Jesus of being too unrestrained—a glutton, a drunkard, and a friend of outcast sinners! Jesus said people could tell both his message and John's were valid because of the changes in their followers' lives.

Jesus pointed out that many people could not be pleased. They didn't like the way John preached the truth and they didn't like the way Jesus related to people on the "outside."

Today some people excuse their lack of response to the truth because they don't care for the mode in which it comes. They may be bored with traditional worship, for example, or turned off by contemporary worship. Jesus turns our focus away from the channels through which his message travels and toward the message itself. In many ways, Jesus is the message. Jesus warns us not to mix the style of the messenger with the substance of his message.

key point

Soul Doctor

LUKE 7:36–38 *Then one of the Pharisees asked Him to eat with him. And He went to the Pharisee's house, and sat down to eat. And behold, a woman in the city who was a sinner, when she knew that Jesus sat at the table in the Pharisee's house, brought an alabaster flask of fragrant oil, and stood at His feet behind Him weeping; and she began to wash His feet with her tears, and wiped them with the hair of her head; and she kissed His feet and anointed them with the fragrant oil.* (NKJV)

Simon, a Pharisee, invited Jesus to dinner. All the diners were reclining on couches (see Illustration #8) and enjoying a leisurely meal when a woman with a bad reputation entered through the open doorway, carrying an expensive jar of perfume. She approached Jesus and stood with her tears falling on his feet. She wiped them away with her hair, kissed his feet, and poured her perfume on them.

When we see Jesus for who he really is, we have to respond, either by turning and going our own way or by acknowledging him with humility and love. The woman had seen Jesus and believed that he could forgive her and turn her life around. She understood that Jesus had healed her soul. So great was her gratitude that she went to incredible lengths to express her love. Have we seen Jesus for who he really is? What is our response?

Illustration #8
Couches for Fine Dining—For a special meal, guests would recline comfortably on couches arranged around a table on which food was spread.

Jesus Teaches Accounting

LUKE 7:39–43 *Now when the Pharisee who had invited Him saw this, he spoke to himself, saying, "This Man, if He were a prophet, would know who and what manner of woman this is who is touching Him, for she is a sinner." And Jesus answered*

denarii
plural for denarius,
Roman coins repre-
senting a day's wage
for a workman

and said to him, "Simon, I have something to say to you." So he said, "Teacher, say it." "There was a certain creditor who had two debtors. One owed five hundred denarii, and the other fifty. And when they had nothing with which to repay, he freely forgave them both. Tell Me, therefore, which of them will love him more?" Simon answered and said, "I suppose the one whom he forgave more." And He said to him, "You have rightly judged." (NKJV)

Simon was far more critical of Jesus than he was of the woman. He thought that if Jesus were truly a prophet he would have known what an outcast this woman was and would refuse her gestures. Jesus, of course, knew Simon's thoughts and posed a situation to his host. Suppose two men owed money: one a small amount of fifty **denarii** and the other a greater amount of five hundred denarii. Since neither man could repay the debt, we can only imagine their relief and joy when the moneylender canceled their obligations. Which man, Jesus asked, would love the moneylender more? Simon gave the logical answer somewhat reluctantly. "I suppose," he answered, "the one whom he forgave more." Jesus was pointing out that this "sinful" woman obviously loved God more than Simon did.

Love's Expression

LUKE 7:44–50 *Then He turned to the woman and said to Simon, "Do you see this woman? I entered your house; you gave Me no water for My feet, but she has washed My feet with her tears and wiped them with the hair of her head. You gave Me no kiss, but this woman has not ceased to kiss My feet since the time I came in. You did not anoint My head with oil, but this woman has anointed My feet with fragrant oil. Therefore I say to you, her sins, which are many, are forgiven, for she loved much. But to whom little is forgiven, the same loves little." Then He said to her, "Your sins are forgiven." And those who sat at the table with Him began to say to themselves, "Who is this who even forgives sins?" Then He said to the woman, "Your faith has saved you. Go in peace." (NKJV)*

Jesus then pointed out to Simon that he had disregarded the common courtesies of a host. The woman had fulfilled these out of love for him. Jesus turned to the woman and pronounced her forgiven not on the basis of what she had done but on the basis of her faith.

There's no mention of Simon piping up after this (perhaps he'd been put in his place), but other guests did. They wondered about Jesus's identity. "Who is this?" was their question. "Who is this who even forgives sins?"

This is an interesting question because in New Testament times Jews did not necessarily expect their Messiah to be divine. They believed he would be a mighty king, but not God necessarily. The question that the guests ask in the above passage might indicate that they were willing to accept that Jesus was Messiah but wondered if they should go even further. Could it be that Jesus was a divine doctor of the soul? Was he God? All circumstances pointed toward that conclusion, but they struggled to believe.

Chapter Wrap-Up

- Even Jews who had been taught God's ways from their early years had not shown such understanding and faith as the Roman centurion. (Luke 7:1–10)

- Jesus feels compassion for the poor and for those who suffer and grieve. He still has compassion for all who are in need of his touch. (Luke 7:11–17)

- John wrestled with doubt that Jesus was the Messiah whose coming he had announced. Jesus's reply was proof that he was fulfilling Isaiah's prophecy of the Messiah. He had a special blessing for John if he kept trusting, in spite of his disappointment that Jesus had not yet established his kingdom. (Luke 7:18–35)

- The sinful woman lavishly expressed her love for Jesus and her longing for forgiveness. In contrast, Simon the Pharisee expressed no love because he had no longing to be forgiven. Jesus forgave the woman's sins on the basis of her faith. (Luke 7:36–50)

Study Questions

1. What caused Jesus to comment on the Roman centurion's faith?

2. In raising the widow's son from the dead, what did Jesus reveal about himself?

3. Suppose you were John the Baptist in prison. Would Jesus's answer satisfy your question? Why, or why not?

4. How would you explain that John was the greatest prophet, yet the "least" in the kingdom of God is greater?

5. Why would Jesus say that his unbelieving religious critics were behaving as spoiled children?

Luke 8 The Way of Jesus

Chapter Highlights:
- Jesus's Support Team
- A Tempestuous Trip
- Demons Begone
- Can Jesus Help Jairus?

Let's Get Started

To prepare the disciples to go out and minister, Jesus demonstrated his power both in the truth he taught and in the miracles he performed. Not everyone understood his message, and some refused what he said because, though they understood what he was saying, they did not want to accept it. Jesus's words were backed by deeds of love and compassion, and his demonstrations of power drew people from all over the surrounding area. They couldn't leave him alone!

Jesus's Support Team

LUKE 8:1–3 *Now it came to pass, afterward, that He went through every city and village, preaching and bringing the glad tidings of the kingdom of God. And the twelve were with Him, and certain women who had been healed of evil spirits and infirmities—Mary called Magdalene, out of whom had come seven demons, and Joanna the wife of Chuza, Herod's steward, and Susanna, and many others who provided for Him from their substance.* (NKJV)

As Jesus traveled from place to place, he was accompanied by his twelve disciples. In addition, Luke alone records, certain women followed him, quietly supporting him and his band. Much as the disciples had little in the way of education or position, these women had few credentials that would impress the religious leaders in Jerusalem. But Jesus had touched them and given them healing. Now they expressed their devotion to him by serving him and giving of their means.

Luke gives us the names of three of these women:

- Mary (called Magdalene) served from a heart that overflowed with gratitude. Jesus had cast seven demons out of her.

- Joanna, wife of Chuza, Herod's **steward**. Her presence on the team indicates that Jesus's influence had penetrated the palace.

devotion
Matthew 27:55–56;
Mark 15:40–41;
Luke 23:49

rich
2 Corinthians 8:9

servant
Philippians 2:6–8

duty to share
Galatians 6:6

steward
finance minister

• Susanna, of whom we know nothing beyond her name.

These women who came from very different backgrounds had one thing in common: their devotion to Jesus and their willingness to support him by using their money to provide food and other necessities. The depth of their <u>devotion</u> was proven when they stayed by Jesus during his crucifixion—even after his disciples had deserted him.

Through the years Mary has been portrayed as a former prostitute. Nowhere in Scripture is this supported. She was troubled by evil spirits, which Jesus cast out of her. This prompted her to follow Jesus so wholeheartedly that she helped support him and his band of twelve disciples.

> **what others say**
>
> **Sue and Larry Richards**
>
> [Mary] was healed of demon possession, and from that point on she never wavered in her commitment to Christ. Mary loved her Lord, not with a passion that would burn out, but with unceasing intensity.[1]

Jesus the Son of God was <u>rich</u> beyond our comprehension. He left the glories of heaven, stepping down and taking the role of a <u>servant</u>. As an itinerant teacher, Jesus led the Twelve from town to town and village to village with no visible income. Women willingly gave from their personal finances to fund Jesus's ministry. These women set an example for us, showing that it is our <u>duty to share</u> with those who feed us spiritually and enrich our lives.

A Tale of the Exceptionally Ordinary

LUKE 8:4–8 *And when a great multitude had gathered, and they had come to Him from every city, He spoke by a parable: "A sower went out to sow his seed. And as he sowed, some fell by the wayside; and it was trampled down, and the birds of the air devoured it. Some fell on rock; and as soon as it sprang up, it withered away because it lacked moisture. And some fell among thorns, and the thorns sprang up with it and choked it. But others fell on good ground, sprang up, and yielded a crop a hundredfold." When He had said these things He cried, "He who has ears to hear, let him hear!" (NKJV)*

Many people followed Jesus, swarming around him from all nearby towns. They heard him teach—but did they really listen? On the surface, there was nothing too special about his story. He spoke of what the people had seen again and again in the fields that lay outside their villages.

A farmer went out to sow (see illustration #9). As he tossed out the seed, some fell on the hardened path, where it made a meal for the birds. Some seeds fell on a thin layer of soil that covered stone. Because these seeds could not take root or find moisture, they sprouted, but soon withered and died. Some seed fell among thorns. Before long the weeds crowded them out. Finally, some seed was scattered on the good, tilled soil and yielded a bumper crop.

So what? The people must have wondered why Jesus told them the story. That's why he called out to them, asking if they really heard what he was saying.

James tells us that exposure to the Scriptures is like looking in a <u>mirror</u> that shows us what we look like. If we merely glance at it and go on our way, we lose out. Spiritual growth comes as we hear the Word with <u>spiritual understanding</u> and respond with active obedience.

go to

mirror
James 1:22–25

spiritual understanding
Romans 10:17

Illustration #9
Sowing—A farmer would carry seed in heavy cloth and scatter it by flinging it a handful at a time as shown here.

confused
Isaiah 6:9–10

devil
Satan

Jesus Does Some Unpacking

LUKE 8:9–15 *Then His disciples asked Him, saying, "What does this parable mean?" And He said, "To you it has been given to know the mysteries of the kingdom of God, but to the rest it is given in parables, that*

> *'Seeing they may not see,*
> *And hearing they may not understand.'*

"Now the parable is this: The seed is the word of God. Those by the wayside are the ones who hear; then the devil comes and takes away the word out of their hearts, lest they should believe and be saved. But the ones on the rock are those who, when they hear, receive the word with joy; and these have no root, who believe for a while and in time of temptation fall away. Now the ones that fell among thorns are those who, when they have heard, go out and are choked with cares, riches, and pleasures of life, and bring no fruit to maturity. But the ones that fell on the good ground are those who, having heard the word with a noble and good heart, keep it and bear fruit with patience. (NKJV)

When Jesus's disciples asked him what his story meant, he answered first by explaining why he had spoken in a parable form.

He wanted everyone to know the truth, but he knew many were not really open to hearing it. Those who were hungry for the truth would understand, while those who were only looking for a way to trip him up would be <u>confused</u> by the parable.

Then Jesus explained the story:

- The seed being scattered by the farmer is the "word of God" (Luke 8:11 NKJV). The Contemporary English Version of the Bible translates this as "God's message," which might make the meaning a little more clear. Today, when Christians hear the phrase "Word of God" or "God's Word," they immediately think of the Bible. But we need to remember that in Jesus's day, the New Testament did not exist, and back then there was some debate about what in our Old Testament was Scripture and what wasn't. Some scholars think Jesus used "word of God" to refer to himself.

- The packed-down path represents people with hard hearts who are not open to the truth. They listen with superficial interest. What they hear doesn't stick but is snatched away by the **devil**.

- The rocky soil represents people who accept the truth, but when they are tested, they easily reject what they claimed to have believed.

- The thorny soil represents people who put the affairs of this life ahead of spiritual growth. Their concerns and their many interests in comfort, career, and family crowd out what the Word of God is saying to them so that they do not bear spiritual fruit.
- The good soil represents people who receive the word with open, teachable hearts that put into practice what they hear, and thus bear fruit for God.

> **what others say**
>
> **Helmut Thielicke**
>
> [Jesus] says: Weed out the thorns; see to it that the seed does not fall on the path; be careful lest you be people so shallow that the Word cannot take root. Jesus says: Be good soil. And that means: Hold on to the Word in stillness, get rid of the hardness and callousness; don't squeeze God into a few cracks and crevices of your day's business, but give him a space of daily quiet.[2]

apply it

The four kinds of soil were represented in the listeners whenever Jesus taught—and they still are whenever God's Word is taught today. The preacher of the Word has a responsibility, and so do we, the hearers. The preacher needs to scatter the seed faithfully. We need to have prepared hearts that will receive the seed and allow it to take root and grow through our daily obedience to it.

> **what others say**
>
> **Max Lucado**
>
> If the ratio in the story is significant, three-fourths of the world isn't listening to God's voice. Whether the cause be hard hearts, shallow lives, or anxious minds, 75 percent of us are missing the message.
>
> It's not that we don't have ears; it's that we don't use them.[3]

The fruitfulness that resulted from the sowing of God's Word depended largely on the receptivity of the soil. We may make excuses when we do not grow spiritually, but the blame belongs to us. Are our hearts open to receive God's Word? Are we ready to allow God's Word to bear fruit in our lives? We bear spiritual fruit when we hear and heed God's Word.

A Light's Place

LUKE 8:16–18 *"No one, when he has lit a lamp, covers it with a vessel or puts it under a bed, but sets it on a lampstand, that those who enter may see the light. For nothing is secret that will not be revealed, nor anything hidden that will not be known and come to light. Therefore take heed how you hear. For whoever has, to him more will be given; and whoever does not have, even what he seems to have will be taken from him."* *(NKJV)*

When darkness falls we turn on a lamp so that we can see to move around. It would be ineffective, not to mention downright silly, to turn on a lamp and then cover it. Jesus used this parable to help people understand that he is the light of the world. When we receive his truth, we become lights to shine in a dark world. We are not to hide that light, but to place it on a stand so that others can be helped. When we hear God's Word, we become responsible to obey.

Further, the day is coming when God's light will shine on everything—even the secret thoughts and deeds that we have tried to hide. Our responsibility is to act in response to God's Word as we hear it. Then we do not need to fear exposure.

God will give more understanding to those who receive his initial message. Those who do not accept his initial message will forfeit their chance to hear more instruction.

Jesus's Family

LUKE 8:19–21 *Then His mother and brothers came to Him, and could not approach Him because of the crowd. And it was told Him by some, who said, "Your mother and Your brothers are standing outside, desiring to see You." But He answered and said to them, "My mother and My brothers are these who hear the word of God and do it."* *(NKJV)*

In this passage Jesus seems to dismiss his birth family as if they're of little concern to him. But just because Luke doesn't record anything Jesus said or did that would have shown more concern, this does not necessarily mean Jesus refrained from doing such things. Also, we should notice that Jesus certainly doesn't insult or belittle his birth family. Rather, he applauds those who hear and obey God's

Word. Here are just a few Scriptures that address how we should treat other people, including our families:

- "Honor your father and your mother, that your days may be long upon the land which the LORD your God is giving you" (Exodus 20:12 NKJV).

- "Be kindly affectionate to one another with brotherly love, in honor giving preference to one another" (Romans 12:10 NKJV).

- "Whatever you want men to do to you, do also to them, for this is the Law and the Prophets" (Matthew 7:12 NKJV).

Note Jesus's emphasis on putting God's Word into practice. More than once we've read that according to Jesus, it's not enough merely to hear God's Word. Doing no more than hearing God's Word is like building your house on sand, remember? Hours of praying and reading the Bible will not bring disobedient Christians as close to the Lord as doing his truth brings even the simplest believer.

It seems clear from other Gospel accounts that Jesus's relatives had not arrived to enjoy a family visit with him (see Matthew 12:24, 46–50; Mark 3:20–35). The Pharisees were accusing him of being empowered by **Beelzebub**. Opposition against him was growing. Jesus and his disciples were so busy ministering they did not have time to eat. So Jesus's family was fearful that he was wearing himself out or losing his mind; that's why they came to see him. Those who seek to obey God enjoy a close relationship with him.

Beelzebub
meaning "lord of flies" or "lord of filth"; Satan

A Tempestuous Trip

LUKE 8:22–25 *Now it happened, on a certain day, that He got into a boat with His disciples. And He said to them, "Let us cross over to the other side of the lake." And they launched out. But as they sailed He fell asleep. And a windstorm came down on the lake, and they were filling with water, and were in jeopardy. And they came to Him and awoke Him, saying, "Master, Master, we are perishing!" Then He arose and rebuked the wind and the raging of the water. And they ceased, and there was a calm. But He said to them, "Where is your faith?" And they were afraid, and marveled, saying to one another, "Who can this be? For He commands even the winds and water, and they obey Him!" (NKJV)*

Real seamen don't get scared in a storm, right? Well, maybe they don't panic in a normal storm, but when a violent squall swooped down, whipping up waves that threatened to swamp the boat, Jesus's disciples were terrified. They woke Jesus, crying, "We're going to drown!"

Jesus rebuked the wind and water and immediately the waters were calm. In the Old Testament God is the one who controls the sea, first in the creation story (Genesis 1:2) and then in the flood story (Genesis 7), so imagine what the disciples were thinking when they watched this man put a stop to the thrashing waves. Did this guy have the power of God? Luke says they were "afraid, and marveled" (Luke 8:25 NKJV).

what others say

William Barclay

He trusted his men; they were the fishermen of the lake and he was content to leave things to their skill and seamanship, and to relax. He trusted God; he knew that he was as near to God by sea as ever he was by land.[4]

Warren W. Wiersbe

The disciples failed this test of faith because they did not lay hold of his word that he was going to the other side. It has well been said that faith is not believing in spite of circumstances; it is obeying in spite of feelings and consequences. The disciples looked around and saw danger, and looked within and saw fear; but they failed to look up by faith and see God. Faith and Fear cannot dwell together in the same heart.[5]

Demons Begone

LUKE 8:26–31 *Then they sailed to the country of the Gadarenes, which is opposite Galilee. And when He stepped out on the land, there met Him a certain man from the city who had demons for a long time. And he wore no clothes, nor did he live in a house but in the tombs. When he saw Jesus, he cried out, fell down before Him, and with a loud voice said, "What have I to do with You, Jesus, Son of the Most High God? I beg You, do not torment me!" For He had commanded the unclean spirit to come out of the man. For it had often seized him, and he was kept under guard, bound with chains and shackles; and he broke the bonds and was driven by the demon into the wilderness. Jesus asked*

him, saying, "What is your name?" And he said, "Legion,"
because many demons had entered him. And they begged Him
that He would not command them to go out into the abyss. (NKJV)

Jesus arrived at the eastern shore of the Sea of Galilee, a Gentile
area, which shows Jesus's ministry extended beyond the Jews. Some
scholars think the storm in the previous passage was a demonic
attempt to prevent Jesus from liberating this man of the tombs.

As soon as Jesus stepped ashore, he was met with spine-chilling
howls and shouts. They came from a man who was inhabited by
demons. The demons gave him violent, superhuman strength. He
was a danger to himself and the nearby community.

Jesus spoke with authority, commanding the demons to come out
of the man. Amazingly, the demons recognized who Jesus was and
begged not to be tortured.

Jesus asked, "What is your name?" (Luke 8:30 NKJV), to which the
answer was **Legion**. The many demons begged Jesus again and again
not to order them to go into the **abyss**.

Matthew's account tells of two demon-possessed men, but Mark
and Luke single out the one who spoke. According to Matthew
8:28–34 the men were so violent that the locals did not dare come
near them. Mark 5:1–20 explains that day and night the man cried
out and cut himself with stones.

abyss
Revelation 20:1–3

Jesus Grants Demons' Request

LUKE 8:32–33 *Now a herd of many swine was feeding there on*
the mountain. So they begged Him that He would permit them
to enter them. And He permitted them. Then the demons went
out of the man and entered the swine, and the herd ran vio-
lently down the steep place into the lake and drowned. (NKJV)

It seems strange that Jesus would do the demons a favor, but in
this passage he does just that. It's difficult to say why, but we can be
sure Jesus didn't allow the demons to reenter this man. At long last
he was free.

Legion
unit in the Roman
army of three thou-
sand to six thousand
men

abyss
place where God will
send all evil spirits

go to

two thousand
Mark 5:13

lake of fire
Revelation 20:14–15;
Matthew 25:41

Note the symmetry between the storm and the pigs running off a cliff into the sea. The waves were not able to swallow up Jesus and his disciples, but they were able to swallow up this legion of demons. How large was this herd of pigs? We learn from Mark there were some <u>two thousand</u> of them.

The destruction of the pigs seems unwarranted until we stop to consider the value of the man who had been inhabited by the evil spirits. This man had been made in the image of God but had been robbed of this image by the evil spirits. In healing the tortured, demented man, Jesus restored him to the level of dignity that God had planned for humanity. While all of creation is important to God, the Bible consistently places the needs of humans above those of animals.

Demons were real in Jesus's day. People were painfully aware of their destructive influence on men and women. When Jesus proved his authority over them, he proved that he was indeed the Son of God. Jesus elevated the demon-tortured man as made in God's image when he commanded the demons to leave him.

key point

what others say

R. C. Sproul

Man is the crowning act of God's creation, he is given dominion over the world. The pig is the servant of the man, not the man the servant of the pig. If these demons must inhabit some place . . . it is nothing less than a totally redemptive act on Christ's part to release the man from this infestation of the demonic world, even at the cost of a herd of swine.[6]

Lawrence O. Richards

The New Testament portrays demons as living, malignant, conscious individual beings, subordinate to Satan and active in their allegiance to his kingdom. They will also share the fate of Satan, which is an eternity in what the Bible calls the "<u>lake of fire</u>."[7]

The Ungrateful Crowd

LUKE **8:34–37** *When those who fed them saw what had happened, they fled and told it in the city and in the country. Then they went out to see what had happened, and came to Jesus, and found the man from whom the demons had departed, sitting at the feet of Jesus, clothed and in his right mind. And they were* *afraid. They also who had seen it told them by what means he who had been demon-possessed was healed. Then the whole multitude of the surrounding region of the Gadarenes asked Him to depart from them, for they were seized with great fear. And He got into the boat and returned. (NKJV)*

fear
1 John 4:18

Word spread fast about what Jesus had done. Naturally, a crowd gathered to investigate the fuss. What they found was this man, whom everyone knew was a dangerous lunatic, sitting at Jesus's feet, "clothed and in his right mind" (Luke 8:35 NKJV). Luke tells us their response was that of <u>fear</u>—not joy, not astonishment, but fear. This doesn't mean joy and astonishment were entirely absent, but it does mean Luke wanted his readers to understand the people were fearful. Why were they afraid? Maybe they were scared Jesus would ruin more of their livestock, even though it wasn't really Jesus who did the ruining. All Jesus did was give the demons permission to enter the pigs. The demons were the ones who entered the pigs and then caused them to be drowned. Maybe the people were afraid of Jesus's power. If Jesus could make short order of the demons, what might he do to them?

Whereas the demons asked Jesus to let them enter the pigs so they could leave, the people asked Jesus to leave. And just as Jesus granted the demons' request, he granted the people theirs as well: "He got into the boat and returned" (Luke 8:37 NKJV).

Homework

LUKE 8:38–39 *Now the man from whom the demons had departed begged Him that he might be with Him. But Jesus sent him away, saying, "Return to your own house, and tell what great things God has done for you." And he went his way and proclaimed throughout the whole city what great things Jesus had done for him. (NKJV)*

As Jesus returned to the boat, the healed man begged to go with him. But Jesus sent him back home to tell everyone how much God had done for him. This is a reminder to us that God has different missions for different people. One mission is no less or more important than another.

go to

unclean
Leviticus 15:25–33

Can Jesus Help Jairus?

LUKE **8:40–44** *So it was, when Jesus returned, that the multitude welcomed Him, for they were all waiting for Him. And behold, there came a man named Jairus, and he was a ruler of the synagogue. And he fell down at Jesus' feet and begged Him to come to his house, for he had an only daughter about twelve years of age, and she was dying. But as He went, the multitudes thronged Him. Now a woman, having a flow of blood for twelve years, who had spent all her livelihood on physicians and could not be healed by any, came from behind and touched the border of His garment. And immediately her flow of blood stopped. (NKJV)*

The man who fell at Jesus's feet, Jairus, was a ruler of the synagogue. A prominent citizen, he was in charge of the synagogue building and all the services held there. Note that Jesus did not favor one group over another when it came to helping people. He ministered with equal compassion to both the community leaders and the riffraff, the rich and the poor, the sick and the healthy, the Jews and the Gentiles, the so-called sinners and the so-called righteous, men and women, adults and children.

Luke would not have said, "the multitudes thronged" (Luke 8:42 NKJV) Jesus, unless he wanted to emphasize just how much attention Jesus was getting. People literally threw themselves at Jesus, begging him to heal them. They really believed that this carpenter from the north country had the power to make all their problems go away. And it's no wonder. One touch of his cloak and a woman's bleeding problem was completely and instantly healed.

According to levitical law, this woman's condition would have made her and anything she sat or lay upon <u>unclean</u>. She would not have been allowed to participate in community worship. People would have kept their distance from her. She wouldn't have been invited to parties, family gatherings, or public feasts. She must have been desperate to be in this crowd looking for Jesus, because Jewish law and custom said she should not have been there.

The Human Healing Dispenser

LUKE **8:45–48** *And Jesus said, "Who touched Me?" When all denied it, Peter and those with him said, "Master, the multi-*

tudes throng and press You, and You say, 'Who touched Me?'"
But Jesus said, "Somebody touched Me, for I perceived power
going out from Me." Now when the woman saw that she was not
hidden, she came trembling; and falling down before Him, she
declared to Him in the presence of all the people the reason she
had touched Him and how she was healed immediately. And He
said to her, "Daughter, be of good cheer; your faith has made you
well. Go in peace." (NKJV)

Jesus stopped and asked, "Who touched Me?" The woman probably wanted to disappear into the crowd. The disciples, not knowing what had happened, thought Jesus's question was the most ridiculous thing they had ever heard. Peter said, "Look, Jesus, I hate to point this out to you, but lots of people are touching you. In fact, if you don't keep moving, they're apt to crush you!"

Not to be deterred, Jesus said he knew power had left him, and that's when the woman fell, trembling at his feet. Out came her sad history and her glad testimony that she had been healed the instant she touched his robe. Jesus knew power had gone out of him, but he may not have known where it went! In most of Jesus's healings, he first decided who to heal and then did it. In this case, God the Father may have given his healing power to someone without the Son knowing who the recipient was.

Everyone expected the unclean woman to contaminate Jesus because that was how things had worked for as long as anyone could remember. This time something different happened. Jesus purified the woman. And thus Jesus did a lot more than physically heal this woman. He gave her a new life; the hugs of friends and family, a dignified place in society, and community worship were just a few of the blessings that followed.

what others say

William Barclay

Almost everybody would have regarded the woman in the crowd as totally unimportant. For Jesus she was someone in need, and therefore he, as it were, withdrew from the crowd and gave himself to her. "God loves each one of us as if there was only one of us to love."[8]

go to

transfigured
Mark 9:2

transfigured
outwardly trans-
formed with a spiri-
tual brilliance

No-Cost Healing

> LUKE 8:49–50 *While He was still speaking, someone came from the ruler of the synagogue's house, saying to him, "Your daughter is dead. Do not trouble the Teacher." But when Jesus heard it, He answered him, saying, "Do not be afraid; only believe, and she will be made well." (NKJV)*

It looked as though healing the bleeding woman came with a cost. Because Jesus stopped to address her, he was delayed in seeing Jairus's daughter, who died in Jesus's absence. From the people's perspective, all was hopeless. Once death slammed the door on a human life, there was no opening it. They couldn't see the sense in asking Jesus to do something about it. Obviously, Jesus saw things differently.

It's interesting to step back and notice how different people responded to Jesus and his power in different ways. The centurion in Luke 7 believed Jesus could do a long-distance healing. The messenger from Jairus's house believed no such thing. Of course, the centurion's servant was only sick, while Jairus's daughter was dead, but the responses of these two men were fundamentally different. One was born of faith and hope; the other, of fear and despair. No situation is beyond the reach of Jesus's compassion and power.

Jairus must have been horrified to hear about his daughter's death, but Jesus immediately consoled him, saying, "Do not be afraid; only believe . . ." (Luke 8:50 NKJV). People may have expected Jesus to tell Jairus to increase the speed with which they were going to his home. Instead Jesus told him to increase his faith.

Jesus's View of Death

> LUKE 8:51–52 *When He came into the house, He permitted no one to go in except Peter, James, and John, and the father and mother of the girl. Now all wept and mourned for her; but He said, "Do not weep; she is not dead, but sleeping." (NKJV)*

At various points in Jesus's ministry he separated Peter, John, and James from the rest of the disciples, like when he led them up a mountain and was **transfigured**. Perhaps these three disciples were closer to Jesus than the other disciples, but if so, we know from other passages that these men were <u>far from perfect</u>. In other words, it was not because of their merit that Jesus was closer to them; it was because of Jesus's grace.

Why did Jesus choose to do this healing in relative privacy? No one is absolutely sure, but scholars have made a number of educated guesses. One is that Jesus was not interested in showboating. His concern was for the girl, not for becoming famous. Also, Jesus knew he had more work to do, so he may have been trying to avoid the extra attention that would have resulted from people calling him the Messiah.

Jesus and the three disciples entered the home to find friends and neighbors following the usual custom of loud mourning that preceded burial on the day of death. Jesus told the people who were present that the girl was not dead but asleep. As we shall see, only someone with the power of God would refer to this girl as asleep, because only God can raise the dead.

far from perfect
Mark 10:35–40;
John 18:10–11

The Day the Laughing Stopped

LUKE 8:53–56 *And they ridiculed Him, knowing that she was dead. But He put them all outside, took her by the hand and called, saying, "Little girl, arise." Then her spirit returned, and she arose immediately. And He commanded that she be given something to eat. And her parents were astonished, but He charged them to tell no one what had happened. (NKJV)*

If you or I had been one of the bystanders, we may have laughed too. But imagine how quickly the laughing ceased when the little girl's "spirit returned" and she stood up.

The phrase "spirit returned" means the girl was definitely dead before Jesus told her to get up. And this wasn't the only time Jesus brought a person back to life. You'll recall he did the same for the widow's son at Nain (Luke 7:11–15), and in John you can read about when he raised his dead friend Lazarus to life.

Jesus instructed those present to give the revived girl something to eat. In so doing, Jesus demonstrated that supernatural power and common sense go together. Sometimes we Christians use faith in God's power as an excuse for irresponsibility. We figure it's all in God's hands, so why should we try our best. But plain old common sense says otherwise. Of course we should ask God to bless the endeavors we undertake. But it's equally important for us to work hard at whatever task the Lord has set before us. To do less is to fail to use God's gifts—our minds and bodies—to his glory.

Luke must have listened with interest as he gathered the information for this chapter. He shines the spotlight on Jesus's power to do what was beyond the knowledge and skills of the medical profession of his day—and is still beyond modern science. Jesus had power

- to command forces of nature,
- to dismiss the powers of demons,
- to heal "hopeless" physical conditions, and
- to raise the dead.

what others say

Larry Richards

There are no "hopeless cases" with the Lord. And there are no "hopeless people" either. The power of Jesus Christ is great enough to meet every need, and to transform any sinner as well.[9]

Chapter Wrap-Up

- Women who had received Jesus's healing were especially devoted to him. They traveled with his group, sharing their personal finances to provide practical assistance to him. (Luke 8:1–3)

- Jesus told a parable in which the seed was the Word of God. The packed-down path represented people with hard hearts who are not open to the truth. The rocky soil represented those who accept God's message but reject it when they are tested. The thorny soil represented hearers who give more attention to this life than to eternal values. The good soil represented people who receive and obey God's Word. (Luke 8:4–15)

- Jesus is the light of the world. As believers we are like lamps, shining in a dark world. Jesus's light also shines within us, exposing our secret thoughts and actions. If we try to conceal them instead of confessing and forsaking them, He will expose them. We are responsible to act on the light we receive. (Luke 8:16–18)

- We become a close member of Jesus's family when we hear and heed God's Word. (Luke 8:19–21)

- Jesus wanted his disciples to trust him even when everything was in such chaos that death seemed certain. When Jesus demonstrated his authority to calm a tempest, they realized that Jesus was Lord of creation. (Luke 8:22–25)

- Jesus had authority to command demons to leave the man they had controlled. Though they could empower the man to break chains intended to restrain him, they had no power to resist Jesus. (Luke 8:26–39)

- A woman who had a twelve-year hemorrhage had faith that if she only touched Jesus's garment, she would be healed. Jairus, a ruler of the synagogue, appealed to Jesus for the healing of his dying daughter. Though she died before Jesus arrived at the home, Jesus raised her to life again. (Luke 8:40–56)

Study Questions

1. What motivated women to assume a special role in Jesus's ministry?

2. In the parable of the farmer sowing seeds, what did the seed represent? The packed-down path? The rocky soil? The thorny soil? The good soil?

3. In what ways should Jesus's use of the image of a lamp impact you?

4. How can you be a member of Jesus's family?

5. What did the disciples learn when Jesus calmed the storm?

6. Suppose you are a reporter writing about the event of the woman being healed from twelve years of hemorrhaging. What do you say about the woman? What about Jesus?

7. Though Jesus seemed to do too little too late for Jairus's daughter, how did Jesus prove his power?

Luke 9 Who Jesus Is

Let's Get Started

In this chapter Luke combines significant events. First, he relates how Jesus sent out the Twelve to do the work they would be commissioned to do after Jesus left the earth. The twelve disciples would become the world's first Christian missionaries. Their mission would be to move throughout the land and preach the Gospel. Luke then gives his account of Jesus feeding the five thousand, followed by Peter's amazing confession of Christ, the Transfiguration, and Jesus's teaching on God's kingdom. Want to find out how God's views on greatness, tolerance, and priorities are unique? Keep reading.

other people
Acts 13:6–10; 19:13

authority
the right to perform a task

On the Front Line

LUKE 9:1–6 *Then He called His twelve disciples together and gave them power and authority over all demons, and to cure diseases. He sent them to preach the kingdom of God and to heal the sick. And He said to them, "Take nothing for the journey, neither staffs nor bag nor bread nor money; and do not have two tunics apiece. Whatever house you enter, stay there, and from there depart. And whoever will not receive you, when you go out of that city, shake off the very dust from your feet as a testimony against them." So they departed and went through the towns, preaching the gospel and healing everywhere. (NKJV)*

Up until the above passage the disciples watched and learned from Jesus. Now Jesus sent them out to do some ministering of their own. He gave them both power and **authority**, perhaps to distinguish them from <u>other people</u> at the time who had power to do supernatural acts but were without God-given authority. Also note that the disciples were not given titles; they were given tasks.

Jesus's instructions would have forced the disciples to trust God for food and lodging. They did not have the option of relying on their own protection or comfort. They were to stay in one home in

heathen
not of God

Herod Antipas
Herod the Great's
son; ruler of Galilee
during Jesus's
ministry

each village, even if another home afforded better accommodations. This, many scholars argue, was a way of being polite. Hosts would have felt snubbed if the disciples moved from one house to another.

If a particular place rejected the disciples, they were to shake the dirt off their feet as they left and move on. Why? This act of shaking dirt off the feet was something Jews did as they left Gentile territory and entered Jewish territory. By shaking dirt off their feet the disciples made an outward declaration that the house they left was **heathen**.

what others say

Matthew Henry

The communicating of Christ's power to those who were sent forth in his name was an amazing and convincing proof of his being the Messiah. That he could not only work miracles himself, but empower others to work miracles too, spread his fame more than anything.[1]

R. Kent Hughes

The reason Jesus ordered them to travel light was to avoid looking like other false missionaries in the ancient world who made personal profit from their preaching.[2]

No Peace in the Palace

LUKE 9:7–9 *Now Herod the tetrarch heard of all that was done by Him; and he was perplexed, because it was said by some that John had risen from the dead, and by some that Elijah had appeared, and by others that one of the old prophets had risen again. Herod said, "John I have beheaded, but who is this of whom I hear such things?" So he sought to see Him.* (NKJV)

Jesus was so popular that Jerusalem became a hotbed of speculation. News of his activities even reached **Herod Antipas** in the palace. Excitement mounted as rumors spread that Jesus was actually John the Baptist raised from the dead. Other rumors were that Jesus was the prophet Elijah or another resurrected Old Testament prophet.

Herod's question, "Who is this?" is one the disciples asked after Jesus calmed the storm in 8:25 and one that Jesus will pick up in 9:18–20. Luke spotlights the question because he knows how important its answer is.

Luke does not include information about the execution of John the Baptist—facts that Matthew (14:3–12) and Mark (6:17–29) provide. Herod had arrested John and put him in prison because John had sternly rebuked him for marrying Herodias, his brother's wife. Herod would have killed him immediately, but did not dare because of John's popularity with the people. However, a year and a half later, Herod celebrated his birthday with a lavish party for the elite. As part of the entertainment, the daughter of Herodias danced and so pleased Herod that he rashly promised to give her anything she wanted. After she consulted with her mother, she presented her request: the head of John the Baptist.

Herod was in a bind. He had sworn by oath to give her what she asked and did not want to be made a fool in front of his guests. So he gave the order for John's execution.

Jesus Feeds Five Thousand

LUKE 9:10–17 *And the apostles, when they had returned, told Him all that they had done. Then He took them and went aside privately into a deserted place belonging to the city called Bethsaida. But when the multitudes knew it, they followed Him; and He received them and spoke to them about the kingdom of God, and healed those who had need of healing. When the day began to wear away, the twelve came and said to Him, "Send the multitude away, that they may go into the surrounding towns and country, and lodge and get provisions; for we are in a deserted place here." But He said to them, "You give them something to eat." And they said, "We have no more than five loaves and two fish, unless we go and buy food for all these people." For there were about five thousand men. Then He said to His disciples, "Make them sit down in groups of fifty." And they did so, and made them all sit down. Then He took the five loaves and the two fish, and looking up to heaven, He blessed and broke them, and gave them to the disciples to set before the multitude. So they all ate and were filled, and twelve baskets of the leftover fragments were taken up by them. (NKJV)*

The Twelve must have been aglow as they reported on their tour. Although they had a great time, they were exhausted. They hoped to get away from the crowds to rest and reflect. When the crowds came, Jesus did not hang up a "Do not disturb" sign. He welcomed them, teaching them "about the kingdom of God" and healing those who needed his touch.

In the late afternoon the Twelve suggested that it was time to send the people away to find food and lodging. They were astonished when Jesus challenged them to feed their uninvited guests. How could they? There were five thousand men there, plus women and children. And food? They had only five loaves of bread and two fish.

Jesus instructed the Twelve to seat the people in orderly groups. He took the little bit of available food, gave thanks for it, and began to hand it to the disciples to serve the hungry people. Again and again the food was multiplied, so that all the people ate until they were satisfied. Luke is careful to say that when the disciples picked up the leftovers, they filled twelve baskets.

This is the only miracle recorded in all four Gospels, which testifies to its importance. John (6:4–13) points out that the five loaves and two fish came from a boy. The loaves were not loaves of bread as we think of them, but more like buns or flat pitas. Once their stomachs were filled, the crowd wanted to take Jesus by force and make him king. The hope of more free meals would get their vote any day! (You can read the other accounts in Matthew 14:15–21 and Mark 6:35–44.)

gospel harmony

Peter's Words of Wisdom

> LUKE 9:18–20 *And it happened, as He was alone praying, that His disciples joined Him, and He asked them, saying, "Who do the crowds say that I am?" So they answered and said, "John the Baptist, but some say Elijah; and others say that one of the old prophets has risen again." He said to them, "But who do you say that I am?" Peter answered and said, "The Christ of God."* (NKJV)

Jesus and the disciples moved north from Bethsaida to Caesarea Philippi (see map in appendix A), named after Augustus Caesar and the tetrarch, Herod Philip 1. Here we have the privilege of "listening in" on one of Jesus's private discussions with his disciples. Earlier in this chapter we heard Herod ask, "Who is this?" in reference to Jesus. Now we hear Jesus ask, "Who do the crowds say that I am?" The disciples related to Jesus some of the rumors that were going around—the same rumors Herod heard. Some believed he was John the Baptist, others thought he was Elijah, and still others thought he was an Old Testament prophet.

Jesus is purposefully making a distinction between the crowds and the disciples, because his question to the latter begins with "But." It's as if Jesus is anticipating a different response from the disciples than he would expect from the crowds. This makes sense when you consider that the disciples were closer to Jesus than the crowds. The disciples spent private time with Jesus. He explained at least some of his parables to them, and they obeyed orders from Jesus.

Jesus's question to the disciples is one of the most profound in all of Scripture. "But who do you say that I am?" he asked. As if on cue, Peter answered by saying, "The Christ of God" (Luke 9:20 NKJV). "Christ" comes from the Greek word that referred to the Messiah; "of God" emphasizes Jesus's divinity.

Matthew 16:13–20 and Mark 8:27–30 provide additional information to Peter's identification of Jesus as the Christ. Jesus confirmed that Peter's response was not just off the top of his head, but was an insight that had been revealed by Jesus's Father in heaven. Jesus also added that he would build his church on Peter's correct understanding of who Jesus was.

gospel harmony

Mum's the Word

> **LUKE 9:21–22** *And He strictly warned and commanded them to tell this to no one, saying, "The Son of Man must suffer many things, and be rejected by the elders and chief priests and scribes, and be killed, and be raised the third day." (NKJV)*

Jesus told the disciples to button up about his being the Messiah. This is probably because he didn't want to start an uprising. The Jews expected the Messiah to start a revolution and lead them into power, but Jesus had no such agenda. Also, the people didn't think the Messiah should declare himself the Messiah. They believed the real Messiah would first do the acts of Messiah, and then others would proclaim him such. Incidentally, this is why Jesus lists in his

Transfiguration
supernatural change
of appearance in
which Jesus was
glorified

message to John the Baptist what he has done instead of flatly declaring himself the Messiah.

Jesus then makes his first prediction within Luke's Gospel that he will be persecuted and killed and raised to life on the third day.

Count the Cost

LUKE 9:23–27 *Then He said to them all, "If anyone desires to come after Me, let him deny himself, and take up his cross daily, and follow Me. For whoever desires to save his life will lose it, but whoever loses his life for My sake will save it. For what profit is it to a man if he gains the whole world, and is himself destroyed or lost? For whoever is ashamed of Me and My words, of him the Son of Man will be ashamed when He comes in His own glory, and in His Father's, and of the holy angels.*

"But I tell you truly, there are some standing here who shall not taste death till they see the kingdom of God." (NKJV)

This passage begins with "Then He said to them all." It is unclear whether "all" refers to all the disciples or the disciples plus a crowd of observers. In any case, if anybody had ideas of being swept into Camelot with Jesus as reigning king, he or she needed a wake-up call. Jesus spelled out clearly the cost of committing to him. What he said might be restated in this way: "Do you want to follow me? Don't look for recognition and praise. Instead, choose to deny yourself. Expect self-sacrifice and pain. Do you want to hang on to your life? You'll lose it! But if you lose your life for me, you'll save it. Do you want to gain the whole world? Aim for that and you'll lose your very self. Are you ashamed of me and my Word? I'll be ashamed of you when I come in glory."

Jesus ended his teaching by saying that some of the people listening to him would "see the kingdom of God" (Luke 9:27 NKJV) before dying. Scholars and theologians aren't exactly sure what Jesus meant by this, but he may have been referring to the **Transfiguration**, which is what Luke recounts next.

what others say

Jack Hayford

Jesus explains the paradox of discipleship. To lose life is to find it; to die is to live. To deny oneself is not to assume some false, external asceticism, but to put the interests of the king-

glory
Revelation 1:12–18

Jesus did not promise to award his disciples with the trappings of success that our society values today. Christ has special rewards for those who deny themselves, are willing to lose their lives in humble service for others, and set aside selfish ambition for the sake of Christ. The rewards? A clearer revelation of himself, a quiet undercurrent of joy even in times of struggles and difficulties, and a keen sense of his nearness.

The Ultimate in Mountaintop Experiences

LUKE 9:28–33 *Now it came to pass, about eight days after these sayings, that He took Peter, John, and James and went up on the mountain to pray. As He prayed, the appearance of His face was altered, and His robe became white and glistening. And behold, two men talked with Him, who were Moses and Elijah, who appeared in glory and spoke of His decease which He was about to accomplish at Jerusalem. But Peter and those with him were heavy with sleep; and when they were fully awake, they saw His glory and the two men who stood with Him. Then it happened, as they were parting from Him, that Peter said to Jesus, "Master, it is good for us to be here; and let us make three tabernacles: one for You, one for Moses, and one for Elijah"—not knowing what he said. (NKJV)*

Jesus took Peter, James, and John up onto a mountain, but which mountain? Bible scholars are not in agreement. Some think it was Mount Hermon, but others think it was Mount Tabor or Mount Meron.

After their long climb Jesus's friends grew drowsy in the cool night air while he talked with his Father. Suddenly they were aroused by a spectacular sight. In a simultaneous flash they saw the past and the future fused in one scene. They saw Jesus's face changed with an out-of-this-world glow and his clothes became dazzling bright. This was a preview of how Jesus will look in heaven's glory. Standing with Jesus were men from the past—Moses, who had been dead nearly 1,500 years, and Elijah, who had been swept from earth in a whirlwind some eight centuries before. They were talking with Jesus about his coming death.

The disciples were witnesses to what is called the Transfiguration and were in awe when they realized what they had seen. As Moses and Elijah left, Peter came up with what he considered a bright idea. In his excitement and enthusiasm he didn't sense how far off base he was. As Peter saw it, this was a majestic moment that should be honored. Why not build three memorials—one for Jesus, one for Moses, and one for Elijah?

A Voice from the Cloud

> LUKE 9:34–36 *While he was saying this, a cloud came and overshadowed them; and they were fearful as they entered the cloud. And a voice came out of the cloud, saying, "This is My beloved Son. Hear Him!" When the voice had ceased, Jesus was found alone. But they kept quiet, and told no one in those days any of the things they had seen.* (NKJV)

The God of heaven and earth had spoken from the cloud. What would be the appropriate response? Silence. What the disciples had seen and heard was so amazing it was beyond words. They didn't know what to make of what happened until much later. What made the Transfiguration an unforgettable experience?

- The three disciples were <u>eyewitnesses</u> to Jesus's glory as the Son of God.
- They recognized intuitively that <u>Moses</u> and <u>Elijah</u> came to talk about Jesus's <u>departure</u> (his death, resurrection, and return to heaven).
- They saw that glory lay ahead of suffering and death.
- They heard God's voice saying they should heed Jesus's teaching and follow him as disciples.

A Jew's View of Clouds

Clouds stirred up a number of thoughts and memories in the minds of Jews back then. Here is a list of what clouds meant to first-century Jews:

go to

eyewitnesses
John 1:14;
2 Peter 1:16–19

Moses
Deuteronomy 18:15

Elijah
Malachi 4:5

departure
John 16:28

- After the exodus from Egypt God led the Jews through the desert with a "pillar of cloud" (Exodus 13:21–22; 16:10; 24:16; 40:34–38).

- Clouds were linked with the future coming of the **"Son of Man"** (Daniel 7:13).

- Clouds were associated with the Second Coming of the Messiah (Isaiah 4:5).

- Most importantly, clouds represented the presence of God (Exodus 19:16).[4]

go to

power and authority
Luke 9:1, 6

faith
Matthew 17:19–20

Son of Man
how Daniel described the person he saw coming from heaven with divine power at the end of the world

consternation
dismay and confusion

Downhill . . . in More Ways Than One

LUKE 9:37–43a *Now it happened on the next day, when they had come down from the mountain, that a great multitude met Him. Suddenly a man from the multitude cried out, saying, "Teacher, I implore You, look on my son, for he is my only child. And behold, a spirit seizes him, and he suddenly cries out; it convulses him so that he foams at the mouth; and it departs from him with great difficulty, bruising him. So I implored Your disciples to cast it out, but they could not." Then Jesus answered and said, "O faithless and perverse generation, how long shall I be with you and bear with you? Bring your son here." And as he was still coming, the demon threw him down and convulsed him. Then Jesus rebuked the unclean spirit, healed the child, and gave him back to his father.*
And they were all amazed at the majesty of God. (NKJV)

Jesus and his three disciples came down from the mountain of transfiguration and found a scene of **consternation**. A father was wringing his hands in despair. He asked the disciples to heal his son, who was being tormented by an evil spirit. But they couldn't. Jesus was disappointed. He had given them power and authority to heal, and they had some success. Their failure was not because they lacked power but because they lacked faith. When Jesus healed the boy and gave him back to his father, all the people were amazed at God's greatness.

Luke's heart must have been tugged as he heard the report of the distressed father and his son who was suffering from an evil spirit. The boy's seizures often caused him to fall into the fire or into the water (Matthew 17:15). The boy would foam at the mouth, gnash his teeth, and become rigid (Mark 9:18). According to the father, the spirit was destroying his son by its persistent activity.

Even as the father brought his son to Jesus, the demon caused another violent convulsion. Jesus rebuked the evil spirit and handed the boy back to his father completely healed. Certainly if Luke had been on the scene he would have joined all who were amazed at the greatness of God!

Tough Times Are Coming

> LUKE 9:43b–45 *But while everyone marveled at all the things which Jesus did, He said to His disciples, "Let these words sink down into your ears, for the Son of Man is about to be betrayed into the hands of men." But they did not understand this saying, and it was hidden from them so that they did not perceive it; and they were afraid to ask Him about this saying. (NKJV)*

As usual, Jesus's attitude was very different from that of everyone around him. While everyone else was celebrating, Jesus warned his disciples that he would soon be betrayed into the hands of his enemies. They did not understand what he was saying partly because it was kept from them and partly because they were afraid to ask Jesus what he meant.

Luke emphasized their fear. Why were they afraid? Maybe they were afraid because they had just seen Jesus use the power of God to cast out yet another demon (this is Jesus's third demon exorcism in Luke). Maybe they were afraid because they couldn't bear the thought of people doing harm to him. Whatever the reason, they were too afraid to ask. So, Luke implied, they missed an opportunity to find out more about what was in store for Jesus and what was in store for them.

Puzzling Paradoxes

> LUKE 9:46–50 *Then a dispute arose among them as to which of them would be greatest. And Jesus, perceiving the thought of their heart, took a little child and set him by Him, and said to them, "Whoever receives this little child in My name receives Me; and whoever receives Me receives Him who sent Me. For he who is least among you all will be great."*

Now John answered and said, "Master, we saw someone casting out demons in Your name, and we forbade him because he does not follow with us." But Jesus said to him, "Do not forbid him, for he who is not against us is on our side." (NKJV)

By this point in Luke's account the disciples believed Jesus was the Messiah, so they assumed he would do what the Messiah was supposed to do—defeat the Jews' oppressors and lead God's people into power. But which individuals would be at the helm, the disciples wondered. Who would be the greatest, the highest in rank? This was the subject of the disciples' argument—an argument hardly worth having when moments earlier Jesus predicted his own betrayal. Obviously the disciples' focus was very different from Jesus's focus. Pride and envy lead to a breakdown in relationships with others and with Christ.

Earlier in Luke's Gospel the disciples dropped their nets to follow Jesus, asked him questions, and marveled at his miracles. But as Luke progresses we read about the disciples being afraid of Jesus, lacking the faith necessary to heal people, and getting into foolish arguments born of pride and ambition. As the climax of Jesus's ministry grew closer and closer, the disciples seemed to divert farther and farther from his agenda.

While the disciples bickered about who would be Jesus's right-hand man, Jesus quietly brought a child to his side. Jesus was saying, "You want to know who my right-hand man will be? I pick this child."

What a shock! In that culture children had no social status whatsoever, yet here one was, standing right beside the Messiah. Jesus's profound action was followed by profound words. "Stop worrying so much about yourselves and your precious positions," he might be paraphrased as saying. "Follow my example. Concern yourselves with the neglected and the rejected. This is how to have God within you."

John reported that when they had seen a man driving out demons in Jesus's name, they tried to stop him, thinking that they were earning Jesus's favor. But Jesus counseled him that if a person was not an enemy, they should treat him as a friend.

temple tax
Matthew 17:24–27

what others say

Warren W. Wiersbe

Perhaps this debate started because of envy (three of the disciples had been with Jesus on the mount), or because of pride (the other nine had failed to cast out the demon). Also, just before this, Jesus had paid Peter's <u>temple tax</u> for him; and this may have aroused some envy.[5]

Since the early chapters of Genesis, Scripture records human competition and a drive to come out on top and to be recognized as the greatest. Jesus used a child to teach that how we relate to children—and others who need our care and protection—will reveal how we relate to him. Do we want to be great by his measurement? Then we need to stoop to help those for whom Jesus has compassion.

How to Handle Rejection

LUKE 9:51–56 *Now it came to pass, when the time had come for Him to be received up, that He steadfastly set His face to go to Jerusalem, and sent messengers before His face. And as they went, they entered a village of the Samaritans, to prepare for Him. But they did not receive Him, because His face was set for the journey to Jerusalem. And when His disciples James and John saw this, they said, "Lord, do You want us to command fire to come down from heaven and consume them, just as Elijah did?" But He turned and rebuked them, and said, "You do not know what manner of spirit you are of. For the Son of Man did not come to destroy men's lives but to save them." And they went to another village. (NKJV)*

There was no Red Roof Inn down the road, so Jesus sent messengers ahead to a Samaritan village to announce his arrival. This was an amazing move, for Jews and Samaritans avoided one another. Jesus was offering to break down the prejudice and accept their offer of hospitality. But the Samaritans refused to welcome him. They knew he was going to Jerusalem, "which they refused to acknowledge as a valid center of worship."[6] James and John were furious and wanted to pray for fire to descend from heaven and destroy the whole village. But Jesus corrected their attitude and moved on to another village.

Omri
1 Kings 16:21–24

The Cost of Discipleship

LUKE 9:57–62 *Now it happened as they journeyed on the road, that someone said to Him, "Lord, I will follow You wherever You go." And Jesus said to him, "Foxes have holes and birds of the air have nests, but the Son of Man has nowhere to lay His head." Then He said to another, "Follow Me." But he said, "Lord, let me first go and bury my father." Jesus said to him, "Let the dead bury their own dead, but you go and preach the kingdom of God." And another also said, "Lord, I will follow You, but let me first go and bid them farewell who are at my house." But Jesus said to him, "No one, having put his hand to the plow, and looking back, is fit for the kingdom of God." (NKJV)*

Three men could have followed Jesus but did not. One wanted the security of a home. Another wanted to bury his father, and the third man had a divided heart and put his family ahead of Jesus. At first glance Jesus appears to be harsh and unfeeling. Caring for and loving our families is not wrong. But Jesus wanted to emphasize the radical requirements involved in following him. Those who say they will follow Jesus wherever he leads rarely understand the cost of doing so. They must be fully committed to him, not trying to live with one foot in both worlds as the third man was asking to do.

Some scholars disagree about whether the second man's father was dead. If the father was dead, scholars believe the man would not have been talking with Jesus. The man would have been home, consumed with duties and details of the funeral and the estate. These scholars believe the man was asking to stay home and care for his aged father until he died. This could have taken years, and Jesus was saying that working for him required immediate service.

Other scholars believe the man's father was literally dead. If so, Jesus's response was radical. To Jews the duties involved in a burial had a greater urgency than studying the law, going to the Temple, killing a Passover sacrifice, or having a child circumcised. Jesus was saying that the spiritual duties of his servants were more important than all these things—even burying the dead.

As a final illustration Jesus spoke of a farmer. Looking back is clearly not the way to plow a field. The rows get crooked if a farmer doesn't watch where he's going. Discipleship demands immediate and wholehearted commitment to Jesus Christ.

Jesus calls us to love him so deeply that we put responding to him ahead of everything else. There's no excuse for procrastination when Jesus calls us to follow him.

apply it

what others say

Jerry White

Ordinary people who make simple, spiritual commitments under the lordship of Jesus Christ make an extraordinary impact on their world. Education, gifts, and abilities do not make the difference. Commitment does.[8]

Chapter Wrap-Up

- Jesus gave the Twelve power and authority to go out preaching and healing. News of Jesus's ministry spread even to Herod's palace. (Luke 9:1–9)

- Jesus fed five thousand by multiplying a boy's lunch, showing the disciples firsthand that he was able to supply resources for them to serve others. (Luke 9:10–17)

- Jesus asked his disciples who they thought he was. Peter answered that Jesus was the Christ of God. Jesus warned his disciples not to share this truth, because he had yet to suffer rejection, death, and resurrection. He warned his disciples that they too would face rejection and persecution. (Luke 9:18–27)

- Jesus took Peter, James, and John with him to a mountain. As Jesus prayed he was changed so that his true glory shone brightly. Moses and Elijah appeared with him. (Luke 9:28–36)

- A distressed father brought his son to Jesus's disciples for healing, but they couldn't cast out the evil spirit. Jesus expressed his disappointment with the unbelieving disciples, and then healed the boy. (Luke 9:37–45)

- Jesus explained several paradoxes of his kingdom to his disciples. He who wants to be the greatest should be the servant of all. Christ's followers reach out to everyone and don't take revenge on those who don't welcome them. He who wants to save his life must first be willing to lose it. (Luke 9:46–62)

Study Questions

1. What did the Twelve learn from their preaching tour?

2. Peter identified Jesus as the Christ of God. How did he come to this insight? Why did Jesus tell his disciples not to talk about it?

3. Why did Jesus spell out the standards of being his disciple? In terms of living today, how do his four points apply?

4. What did the Transfiguration reveal about Jesus?

5. What did Jesus say is the way to greatness?

Luke 10 Significant Decisions

Chapter Highlights:
- On a Mission
- Keep the Focus
- Time Out for Praise
- Expert Lawyer Quiz
- Martha's Hospitality

Let's Get Started

Jesus had been ministering in Galilee and had sent the Twelve out to represent him in surrounding areas. Now he turned his attention to Judea and sent seventy-two disciples ahead to prepare the area for his coming. He grieved over the cities that heard the good news but rejected it. The seventy-two were elated over the success of their mission, but Jesus expressed joy at the salvation of individuals who truly believed in him.

An expert in the Old Testament tested Jesus by asking what he needed to do to inherit eternal life. Jesus answered by telling a story that illustrated the deepest and fullest meaning of the law—loving as our neighbor anyone who is in need.

Later, in the home of Mary and Martha, Jesus lovingly told Martha that listening to him pleased him more than laboring for him to the point of exasperation.

On a Mission

> LUKE 10:1–4 *After these things the Lord appointed seventy others also, and sent them two by two before His face into every city and place where He Himself was about to go. Then He said to them, "The harvest truly is great, but the laborers are few; therefore pray the Lord of the harvest to send out laborers into His harvest. Go your way; behold, I send you out as lambs among wolves. Carry neither money bag, knapsack, nor sandals; and greet no one along the road.* (NKJV)

Jesus's ministry in Galilee was complete. He now prepared to go to Judea to the south and eventually to Jerusalem where he would offer himself as sacrifice for the sins of the world. In the meantime, there was much to do, and time was short.

He selected seventy-two of his followers (not the Twelve) and sent them out in pairs to prepare the people for his coming. They were to go with a clear sense of mission, not only to preach but also to

kingdom of God
place where God
reigns as King

pray earnestly that those who listened to them would join them as workers in the spiritual harvest. They were to go with a sense of urgency, knowing they would not be welcomed by everyone.

what others say

Leon Morris

Lambs in the midst of wolves are in no enviable situation. The simile points both to danger and to helplessness. God's servants are always in some sense at the mercy of the world, and in their own strength they cannot cope with the situation in which they find themselves. They must look to God.[1]

Keep the Focus

LUKE 10:5–12 *But whatever house you enter, first say, 'Peace to this house.' And if a son of peace is there, your peace will rest on it; if not, it will return to you. And remain in the same house, eating and drinking such things as they give, for the laborer is worthy of his wages. Do not go from house to house. Whatever city you enter, and they receive you, eat such things as are set before you. And heal the sick there, and say to them, 'The kingdom of God has come near to you.' But whatever city you enter, and they do not receive you, go out into its streets and say, 'The very dust of your city which clings to us we wipe off against you. Nevertheless know this, that the kingdom of God has come near you.' But I say to you that it will be more tolerable in that Day for Sodom than for that city.* (NKJV)

Jesus gave specific instructions to the seventy-two. Their to-do list was similar to the instructions Jesus gave the Twelve when he sent them out. This was no pleasure excursion. There must be no wasting time! They were to enter a town, find a house that would welcome them, and then get down to the business of announcing the **kingdom of God** and healing the sick. No theatrics, no fundraising, no making themselves into stars. If a town would not welcome them and their message, they were to leave with a solemn warning that by refusing their message they were inviting severe judgment.

Nothing to Joke About

LUKE 10:13–16 *"Woe to you, Chorazin! Woe to you, Bethsaida! For if the mighty works which were done in you had been done in Tyre and Sidon, they would have repented long ago, sitting in sackcloth and ashes. But it will be more tolerable for Tyre and Sidon at the judgment than for you. And you, Capernaum, who are exalted to heaven, will be brought down to Hades. He who hears you hears Me, he who rejects you rejects Me, and he who rejects Me rejects Him who sent Me."* (NKJV)

Sodom
Genesis 19:24–29

Jesus spoke of Chorazin and Bethsaida, towns on the north side of the Sea of Galilee where he had ministered earlier (see map in Appendix A). He also mentioned Capernaum, his adopted hometown. People in those towns who refused his message were facing severe judgment—even more severe than the judgment awaiting those in the pagan cities of Tyre, Sidon, and <u>Sodom</u>, who had never heard the message of God's kingdom nor seen his miracles of compassion.

Sackcloth was a coarse material that was worn as a sign of sorrow. Ashes were a symbol of repentance. Jesus said even the residents of pagan towns would have had enough sense to repent and be sorry for their sins if they had heard Jesus's message. Things didn't look good for these Jewish towns.

The seventy-two were authorized representatives so that those who listened to their message were in reality listening to Jesus, and those who rejected their message were in reality rejecting Jesus and the Father who had sent him.

Matthew includes Jesus's condemnation of the three towns in Galilee that had refused his message (Matthew 11:20–30). Then Matthew adds Jesus's comforting invitation to all who are hesitant to respond to his message. "Come," he said to the weary and burdened. "Don't be afraid to identify with and obey me. If you learn my ways, I will give rest to your soul."

gospel harmony

Satan's Bungee Jump Without a Cord

LUKE 10:17–20 *Then the seventy returned with joy, saying, "Lord, even the demons are subject to us in Your name." And He said to them, "I saw Satan fall like lightning from heaven. Behold, I give you the authority to trample on serpents and scor-*

go to

Lamb's Book of Life
Revelation 3:5;
21:27

pions, and over all the power of the enemy, and nothing shall by any means hurt you. Nevertheless do not rejoice in this, that the spirits are subject to you, but rather rejoice because your names are written in heaven." (NKJV)

The seventy-two were elated as they returned from their short-term mission. They were excited to report that even demons were subject to their authoritative commands! By simply speaking they were able to do things that stumped the medical profession.

Jesus acknowledged that Satan's power had been broken at his command and that Satan had already been defeated. He had taken a giant bungee jump without a cord. But Jesus cautioned the seventy-two to rejoice more in their personal relationship with God than in their power and authority. We should be most joyful about our salvation.

We may measure our success as Christ's followers by the good things we can achieve. Jesus, however, reminds us that our joy should not lie in what we do but in what He has done for us in providing the way for our names to be recorded in heaven in the <u>Lamb's Book of Life</u>. Our personal relationship with God should be the source of our joy.

Time Out for Praise

LUKE 10:21–24 *In that hour Jesus rejoiced in the Spirit and said, "I thank You, Father, Lord of heaven and earth, that You have hidden these things from the wise and prudent and revealed them to babes. Even so, Father, for so it seemed good in Your sight. All things have been delivered to Me by My Father, and no one knows who the Son is except the Father, and who the Father is except the Son, and the one to whom the Son wills to reveal Him." Then He turned to His disciples and said privately, "Blessed are the eyes which see the things you see; for I tell you that many prophets and kings have desired to see what you see, and have not seen it, and to hear what you hear, and have not heard it." (NKJV)*

Jesus was so thrilled he lifted his heart in spontaneous praise to his Father. His gang was getting it! Though the intellectual elite refused his message and rejected him, the ordinary, unschooled "nobodies" who made up his disciples were accepting the truth as innocently as little children. They were receiving the truth as God revealed it to them, while that truth was hidden from the hearts and minds of the "wise."

Turning to his disciples, he said that what they were seeing first-hand was what believing Old Testament people had longed to see.

what others say

The Bible Knowledge Commentary

The three Persons of the Godhead are clearly seen: Jesus the Son was doing the Father's will in the power of the Holy Spirit. Each had a specific function.[2]

John Piper

What is being hidden and revealed is not just the presence of the kingdom, but the true personal identity and divine glory of the messianic King and his Father.[3]

God has truths in the Bible that he hides from certain people. Fact or fiction? It's a fact! People who boast of being wise and having it all together without the slightest need for God will not discover the truths of Scripture. They may have the facts but will miss the experience of knowing God. Jesus said that God reveals himself to those who come to the Scripture with childlike dependence on him.

key point

Expert Lawyer Quiz

LUKE 10:25–29 *And behold, a certain lawyer stood up and tested Him, saying, "Teacher, what shall I do to inherit eternal life?" He said to him, "What is written in the law? What is your reading of it?" So he answered and said, "'You shall love the LORD your God with all your heart, with all your soul, with all your strength, and with all your mind,' and 'your neighbor as yourself.'" And He said to him, "You have answered rightly; do this and you will live." But he, wanting to justify himself, said to Jesus, "And who is my neighbor?" (NKJV)*

Students sometimes ask tricky questions in an attempt to stump their teacher. An expert in Jewish law asked Jesus a question with a different motive. He wanted to get Jesus into trouble by tricking him into giving an answer that would be **heresy**! The question:

go to

love the LORD
Deuteronomy 6:5

your neighbor
Leviticus 19:18

ceremonially unclean
Leviticus 21:1

priest
middleman between
God and the Jews,
charged to offer
sacrifices

Levite
responsible to over-
see temple services

"What shall I do to inherit eternal life?" His question indicates that he thought eternal life could be earned.

Knowing that the man was insincere, Jesus answered with a question that any expert in the law would know. "What is written in the law? What is your reading of it?" (Luke 10:26 NKJV).

The expert answered smoothly, "'You shall <u>love the LORD</u> your God with all your heart, with all your soul, with all your strength, and with all your mind,' and '<u>your neighbor</u> as yourself'" (Luke 10:27 NKJV).

Jesus replied that he had answered the question correctly. His job was to put into practice what he already knew he should be doing. Knowing and doing are two different things.

The man squirmed, knowing he could not perfectly obey the law and that he was not willing to admit his shortcomings, especially in front of everyone. This test was not going the way he planned.

To raise his failing grade, the lawyer tried to limit his responsibilities by bringing up another question: "And who is my neighbor?" (Luke 10:29 NKJV).

Passing On

LUKE 10:30–32 *Then Jesus answered and said: "A certain man went down from Jerusalem to Jericho, and fell among thieves, who stripped him of his clothing, wounded him, and departed, leaving him half dead. Now by chance a certain priest came down that road. And when he saw him, he passed by on the other side. Likewise a Levite, when he arrived at the place, came and looked, and passed by on the other side.* (NKJV)

Jesus answered the lawyer with a dramatic story. In his cast of characters he chose a Jew who was assaulted by robbers and left half dead on the side of the road. Next, he chose a **priest** who came along and avoided the injured man because he was fearful of becoming <u>ceremonially unclean</u> by any slight contact with him. Jesus also included a respected **Levite** who also avoided the man.

Will the Real Neighbor Please Stand Up!

LUKE 10:33–37 *But a certain Samaritan, as he journeyed, came where he was. And when he saw him, he had compassion.*

So he went to him and bandaged his wounds, pouring on oil and wine; and he set him on his own animal, brought him to an inn, and took care of him. On the next day, when he departed, he took out two denarii, gave them to the innkeeper, and said to him, 'Take care of him; and whatever more you spend, when I come again, I will repay you.' So which of these three do you think was neighbor to him who fell among the thieves?" And he said, "He who showed mercy on him." Then Jesus said to him, "Go and do likewise." (NKJV)

Samaritan
despised mixed-race descendant of Israel following a corrupt form of Moses's laws

lackeys
menial servants

Jesus rounded out his cast of characters with a despised **Samaritan** who helped the hurt man. To Jewish minds there was no such thing as a good Samaritan—until Jesus invented this story. The Samaritan's heart was filled with concern and sympathy that moved him to take immediate action. He stopped and applied first aid, probably using his own wine as disinfectant and his own clothing as bandages. Then he placed the man on his donkey and took him to an inn where he personally cared for the man. The next day he gave the innkeeper two denarii—enough to feed the patient for three weeks—and promised to reimburse the innkeeper for any additional expenses.

Jesus cut the story off with a penetrating question. "Which of these three do you think was neighbor to him who fell among the thieves?" (Luke 10:36 NKJV).

The answer was obvious, though it must have stuck in the throat of the self-righteous expert. He answered, "He who showed mercy on him" (verse 37 NKJV).

Love is shown by doing loving deeds, not by a strict following of law, as the Jews were fond of thinking. Love is costly. It requires great sacrifices of us. It calls us out of our comfort zone. Loving like God loves makes us dependent on Christ for strength.

apply it

what others say

John Piper

Another way of asking the lawyer's question would be, "Teacher, whom do I not have to love? Which groups in our society are exceptions to this commandment? Surely the Romans, oppressors of God's chosen people; and their despicable lackeys, the tax collectors; and those half-breed Samaritans—surely all these are not included in the term

love God
Matthew 25:31–46

'neighbor.' Tell me just who my neighbor is, Teacher, that as I examine various candidates for my love, I will be sure to choose him alone."[4]

Loving others sounds so simple until we are confronted by the needs of someone we hate. When Jesus said, "Go and do likewise," he set a high standard that he knew could be only reached when his followers used his power and love. The lawyer did not love God totally and therefore he could not possibly love others whose only claim to his acts of pity and mercy was their desperate need. Those who do not <u>love God</u> will not fully be able to love their fellow humans and vice versa. How we relate to hurting people who are not like us demonstrates how we relate to Christ.

what others say

Dallas Willard

Of course the words good Samaritan do not occur in the story. For those listening to Jesus, that phrase would have been what we call an "oxymoron": a combination of words that makes no sense. For the Jews generally, at that time, we could say that "the only good Samaritan was a dead Samaritan."[5]

Gary A. Haugen

Christians of mature faith know that love is both a deeply mystical and a profoundly practical calling. In some mysterious way, when we feed the hungry, visit the sick and clothe the naked, we do it for him also (Matthew 25). Jesus' model for love, a nameless Samaritan, messed up his clothes and his schedule by picking up a stranger who lay wounded and naked in the ditch (Luke 10). Acts of love like this are so important to God that when the Israelites couldn't be bothered with the workaday practicalities of what it takes "to loose the chains of injustice" and "to set the oppressed free," God stopped listening to their prayers (Isaiah 58:1–6).[6]

Martha's Hospitality

LUKE 10:38–42 *Now it happened as they went that He entered a certain village; and a certain woman named Martha welcomed Him into her house. And she had a sister called Mary, who also sat at Jesus' feet and heard His word. But Martha was distracted with much serving, and she approached Him and said, "Lord, do You not care that my sister has left me to serve alone? Therefore tell her to help me." And Jesus answered and said to her, "Martha, Martha, you are worried and troubled about many things. But one thing is needed, and Mary has chosen that good part, which will not be taken away from her."* (NKJV)

One day Jesus stopped by the home of Martha. She and her sister, Mary, and brother, Lazarus, lived in Bethany and were some of Jesus's best buddies. Both Martha and Mary loved Jesus and welcomed him whenever he visited them.

Martha began preparations for a meal that was appropriate for honoring their special guest and his disciples. She wanted to dish up a good spread. If all twelve disciples were there, she was preparing to serve a meal to at least sixteen people. She whipped up her favorite dishes and didn't dream of "cheating" on the old family recipes. Without the conveniences of four burners, a family-size oven, a microwave, a refrigerator and freezer, she had taken on a large task.

Nearby Mary sat at Jesus's feet, hanging on his every word. She should have known how hard Martha was working, but if she did, she made no indication. She had committed herself to the role of a disciple, a learner. This role had been reserved by the religious leaders for men alone, so Mary was something of a feminist.

Martha was feeling overloaded. So she walked up to Jesus and scolded him. Didn't he notice or care that Mary had abandoned her duties and left Martha to slave away in the kitchen? He should tell Mary to get to work!

But Jesus responded differently. He understood that Martha was stressed out about the many details she was handling. A lavish meal was not needed, especially when doing so took Martha away from spending time with him. With all that Jesus was facing as he proceeded to Jerusalem, he needed a peaceful environment and the support of loving, understanding friends. There was only one essential and Mary had chosen it—listening to him. Food and lodging were temporary. What Mary had chosen would last forever and never be taken away from her. Followers of Christ need to have proper priorities.

As a doctor, even without meeting Martha personally, Luke could immediately detect that she was a Type A personality. She was com-

serving
Romans 12:13;
1 Peter 4:10

listening
Luke 8:15

contemplative
capable of considering thoroughly and thinking deeply

petitive, perfectionistic, and verbal. She pushed herself with a distinct sense of urgency.

Both Martha and Mary made choices—one to work her fingers to the bone <u>serving</u> Jesus as a gracious hostess, while inwardly fuming, and the other to sit at his feet <u>listening</u> to him. Do we have to choose one or the other? It's possible to be Mary and Martha in one: doing much service and enjoying close fellowship with Jesus at the same time. But if a choice is required, then we need to set priorities and remember that Jesus said Mary made the better choice.

Some people see Martha and Mary as having very different temperaments. Martha was the zealous put-faith-in-action type and Mary was the easygoing, docile, **contemplative** type. But consider this: Martha accused Mary of having left her. This would indicate that Mary had served acceptably in the kitchen. Her work was missed! Consider also that Jesus said that Mary had chosen to spend time with him. Martha could have made the same choice.

> ## what others say
>
> ### Lawrence O. Richards
> Jesus' rebuke might be paraphrased, "Just a casserole, Martha, not a smorgasbord." Love for God is expressed best in listening and responding to Jesus' words, not in busily doing "for" him.[7]

Chapter Wrap-Up

- Jesus appointed seventy-two followers to go ahead of him into the towns of Judea. They returned from their mission rejoicing that even the demons had submitted to them. (Luke 10:1–20)

- Jesus rejoiced that God had chosen to reveal the truths of Scripture not to the wise but to the childlike—those who were humble and dependent on God. The disciples received the truth and acted on it with childlike trust. (Luke 10:21–24)

- An expert in the law posed a question to Jesus, hoping to trap him. Jesus, in turn, asked the expert to quote from Old Testament Scripture what God had said—to love him supremely and to love one's neighbor. (Luke 10:25–29)

- Jesus told a story in which a despised Samaritan was neighborly to a wounded Jew who had been bypassed by a priest and a Levite. The point was that love is shown by actions, not by a strict following of law. (Luke 10:30–37)

- While visiting the home of Martha and Mary, Jesus explained that loving, personal devotion to him was better than acts of service. (Luke 10:38–42)

Study Questions

1. Why did Jesus send out seventy-two followers to Judea, and what happened?

2. To whom does God choose to reveal the truths of Scripture? Why?

3. What purpose did the expert in the law have in asking Jesus what he must do in order to inherit eternal life? What did he learn from Jesus's response?

4. If the Samaritan was neighbor to the half-dead Jew, to whom should the expert in the law be a neighbor? To whom should you be a neighbor?

5. In what different ways did Martha and Mary show their love for Jesus? Which way is better? In what ways are you like Martha and Mary?

Luke 11 Candid Conversations

Chapter Highlights:
- Prayer Powwow
- Power in Persistence
- Demon Power?
- Tense Moment
- Painful Pronouncements

Let's Get Started

It became increasingly impossible for people to be neutral as they heard Jesus teach and watched him perform miracles. The disciples, observing his close relationship with his Father in heaven, asked Jesus to teach them to pray. Then when Jesus cast out a demon, the crowd recognized his power. Some were amazed, some accused him of being in league with Satan, and others demanded an even greater miracle—a sign from heaven.

In his candid conversations Jesus stressed that our heart attitudes enable us to receive the truth or prevent us from recognizing the truth when it is presented to us. The Pharisees and experts in the law were highly respected for their adherence to the Scripture but were missing the point of that Scripture because they had closed hearts.

Prayer Powwow

LUKE 11:1–4 *Now it came to pass, as He was praying in a certain place, when He ceased, that one of His disciples said to Him, "Lord, teach us to pray, as John also taught his disciples."*
So He said to them, "When you pray, say:
Our Father in heaven,
Hallowed be Your name.
Your kingdom come.
Your will be done
On earth as it is in heaven.
Give us day by day our daily bread.
And forgive us our sins,
For we also forgive everyone who is indebted to us.
And do not lead us into temptation,
But deliver us from the evil one." (NKJV)

Again and again the disciples had seen Jesus step aside from them to spend time talking to his Father in prayer, but sometimes he

Father
Romans 8:15–1

octogenarian
a person in his or
her eighties

prayed in their presence. Remembering that John the Baptist had given his followers instruction in prayer, the disciples asked Jesus to give them lessons on prayer.

In response, Jesus gave a prayer pattern that can be followed by every culture and every person from a child to an **octogenarian** and beyond. First, approach God as your Father. God loves you as a perfect <u>Father</u> who cares for you and wants to give you what is best for you.

Then, make these requests:

- *May your name be honored.* By your words and actions demonstrate your desire that the name and character of God your Father will be lovingly reverenced.

- *May your kingdom come.* Live each day under Christ's kingdom rule—doing his will, obeying him, and working to extend his kingdom throughout the earth.

- *Provide us daily food.* Depend on your Father to provide for your everyday needs.

- *Forgive our sins.* Trust God to forgive your sins even as you keep an open heart to forgive others.

- *Keep us from being tempted.* Aware of your weakness, ask God to keep you from yielding to temptation.

Jesus did not give a prayer to be recited mindlessly, but a pattern to be adapted in the words of our hearts.

what others say

Richard J. Foster

Jesus' relationship with God the Father is, of course, absolutely unique, but experientially we are invited into the same intimacy with Father God that he knew while here in the flesh. We are encouraged to crawl into the Father's lap and receive his love and comfort and healing and strength. We can laugh, and we can weep, freely and openly. We can be hugged and find comfort in his arms. And we can worship deep within our spirit.[1]

Dallas Willard

I believe the most adequate description of prayer is simply, "Talking to God about what we are doing together."[2]

Jesus gives us permission to do what no Old Testament saint would have dared to do. We can approach God as a child comes to his or her earthly father—trustfully, lovingly, respectfully—and address him as *Abba*—Daddy!

Matthew gives us what is called the Lord's Prayer, which is slightly longer than Luke's version, but is essentially the same.

Abba
"Daddy" in Aramaic, the language Jesus spoke

The Lord's Prayer in Matthew and Luke

Matthew 6:9–13	Luke 11:2–4
Our Father in heaven,	Our Father in heaven,
Hallowed be Your name.	Hallowed be Your name.
Your kingdom come.	Your kingdom come.
Your will be done On earth as it is in heaven.	Your will be done On earth as it is in heaven.
Give us this day our daily bread.	Give us day by day our daily bread.
And forgive us our debts, As we forgive our debtors.	And forgive us our sins, For we also forgive everyone who is indebted to us.
And do not lead us into temptation, But deliver us from the evil one. For Yours is the kingdom and the power and the glory forever. Amen. (NKJV)	And do not lead us into temptation, But deliver us from the evil one. (NKJV)

Power in Persistence

LUKE 11:5–8 *And He said to them, "Which of you shall have a friend, and go to him at midnight and say to him, 'Friend, lend me three loaves; for a friend of mine has come to me on his journey, and I have nothing to set before him'; and he will answer from within and say, 'Do not trouble me; the door is now shut, and my children are with me in bed; I cannot rise and give to you'? I say to you, though he will not rise and give to him because he is his friend, yet because of his persistence he will rise and give him as many as he needs. (NKJV)*

Jesus told a story to encourage his disciples to bring their needs to God in prayer. Luke is the only Gospel writer to share it.

In Bible times homes often had only one room. People slept on mats spread out on the floor. To get up in the middle of the night to answer the door meant that the father would have to step over (and probably fall on) his sleeping children to reach the door. Then he'd have to slide back the heavy bolt that kept the door shut. By

go to

pray
1 Thessalonians 5:17

this time everyone in the family would be awake—and not too happy! You can understand why he told his friend to go away and not bother him.

But his friend was desperate. Hosts in the first century were expected to welcome their guests regardless of when they arrived. Guests couldn't go to the local motel or sleep in their cars until morning. There were no coffee shops open all night long. This host was in a bind and he knew his friend could help. The host persisted without embarrassment. Finally, the friend gave in and handed over the bread—not because the host was his friend but because he was so boldly persistent!

> **what others say**
>
> **Darryl DelHousaye**
>
> Isn't prayer simply talking to your heavenly Father? Why is something appearing to be so simple so difficult?
>
> The theology of prayer continues to be a mystery. How does praying effect the sovereign hand of God? Isn't He going to do what He's going to do anyway?
>
> Jesus doesn't talk about the mystery of the theology of prayer here. He takes a pragmatic approach.
>
> Do it![3]

Prayer isn't something we impose on God, like the uninvited telephone solicitors who annoy us. God welcomes us, even encouraging us to <u>pray</u> without interruption.

No Side Orders of Scorpions or Snakes

LUKE 11:9–13 *"So I say to you, ask, and it will be given to you; seek, and you will find; knock, and it will be opened to you. For everyone who asks receives, and he who seeks finds, and to him who knocks it will be opened. If a son asks for bread from any father among you, will he give him a stone? Or if he asks for a fish, will he give him a serpent instead of a fish? Or if he asks for an egg, will he offer him a scorpion? If you then, being evil, know how to give good gifts to your children, how much more will your heavenly Father give the Holy Spirit to those who ask Him!"* (NKJV)

To reinforce the point of his story, Jesus gave more examples. An earthly father would never respond to his son's request for food with something hurtful. Jesus encourages us to count on our Father's kindness and willingness to meet our needs. Keep two points in mind. First, God is our heavenly Father and will do nothing less than what an earthly father would do for his children. Second, God is perfect. He will do much more than what earthly, sinful fathers would do. God never loses his patience with us. And he will give us only <u>good gifts</u>—even fulfilling our request for the Holy Spirit. We can come to God as our loving heavenly Father, trusting him to give us only what he knows is best for us.

good gifts
Matthew 7:11

Beelzebub
meaning "lord of flies" or "lord of filth"; Satan

Demon Power?

> LUKE 11:14–16 *And He was casting out a demon, and it was mute. So it was, when the demon had gone out, that the mute spoke; and the multitudes marveled. But some of them said, "He casts out demons by Beelzebub, the ruler of the demons." Others, testing Him, sought from Him a sign from heaven.* (NKJV)

A hush came over the crowd. They pressed forward to watch as Jesus performed yet another miracle. He healed a man who had never been able to speak because he had been under the control of a demon. Suddenly, to the astonishment of the crowd, the man was released from both his disability and the demon that had oppressed him.

Mixed with the amazement of the onlookers, though, were other reactions. Some made a wicked accusation that Jesus could drive out demons only because he was in league with **Beelzebub**. Others taunted, "This miracle was good, but show us something better. Let's have a sign from heaven."

Right Reason

> LUKE 11:17–20 *But He, knowing their thoughts, said to them: "Every kingdom divided against itself is brought to desolation, and a house divided against a house falls. If Satan also is divided against himself, how will his kingdom stand? Because you say I cast out demons by Beelzebub. And if I cast out demons by Beelzebub, by whom do your sons cast them out? Therefore they will be your judges. But if I cast out demons with the finger of God, surely the kingdom of God has come upon you.* (NKJV)

go to

finger of God
Exodus 8:19

finger of God
the Holy Spirit

Jesus had every right to flare out in anger. Their accusation was outrageous; their unbelief, inexcusable. Instead, Jesus chose to reason with them, to give them yet another opportunity to believe in him and the One who sent him.

It would be self-defeating, he argued, for Satan to weaken his kingdom by driving out his demons. Further, their followers credited God's power when they drove out demons. Therefore, if the **finger of God** was Jesus's power, then it must indicate that the kingdom of God had come.

Let Me Illustrate My Point

> LUKE 11:21–26 *When a strong man, fully armed, guards his own palace, his goods are in peace. But when a stronger than he comes upon him and overcomes him, he takes from him all his armor in which he trusted, and divides his spoils. He who is not with Me is against Me, and he who does not gather with Me scatters.*
>
> *"When an unclean spirit goes out of a man, he goes through dry places, seeking rest; and finding none, he says, 'I will return to my house from which I came.' And when he comes, he finds it swept and put in order. Then he goes and takes with him seven other spirits more wicked than himself, and they enter and dwell there; and the last state of that man is worse than the first."* (NKJV)

Jesus told a brief parable to illustrate his point. A strong man (Satan) keeps his house secure until a stronger man (Jesus) overpowers him and takes all. Some of what he takes, obviously, would include those formerly possessed by demons whom Jesus had released from Satan's oppression.

Obviously, no one can be neutral in the contest between God and Satan. Each in the crowd listening to Jesus that day had to make a choice. Those who believed that Jesus was empowered by Beelzebub to cast out demons were actively against him.

And this was serious business. If the man who had been healed joined Jesus's accusers in crediting Satan for his healing, his condition would become far worse than it was before Jesus healed him.

Tense Moment

LUKE 11:27–28 *And it happened, as He spoke these things, that a certain woman from the crowd raised her voice and said to Him, "Blessed is the womb that bore You, and the breasts which nursed You!" But He said, "More than that, blessed are those who hear the word of God and keep it!" (NKJV)*

The atmosphere was so tense it was seconds away from exploding. Suddenly a woman spoke out clearly from the crowd. She blessed Jesus's mother for bringing him into the world.

Jesus didn't disagree, but he expanded her blessing to include all who hear God's Word and obey it. His words were an encouragement to the woman—and to all who are on his side.

Jesus's words were a real encouragement to this nameless woman. She risked derision and censure for standing by him. Maybe she spoke out of a surge of emotion as a member of his fan club, or maybe she spoke out of deep conviction. Whatever, he gave her a blessing, and his blessing extends to us today. Yes, Mary had a special privilege in being chosen to be the mother of Jesus. Truly she was blessed, but he said, "More than that, blessed are . . ." (Luke 11:28 NKJV), and that includes us. We are blessed rather when we hear God's Word and follow through with practical obedience in our everyday lives.

One Down, One to Go

LUKE 11:29–32 *And while the crowds were thickly gathered together, He began to say, "This is an evil generation. It seeks a sign, and no sign will be given to it except the sign of Jonah the prophet. For as Jonah became a sign to the Ninevites, so also the Son of Man will be to this generation. The queen of the South will rise up in the judgment with the men of this generation and condemn them, for she came from the ends of the earth to*

Jonah
Jonah 3

Queen of Sheba
1 Kings 10

hear the wisdom of Solomon; and indeed a greater than Solomon is here. The men of Nineveh will rise up in the judgment with this generation and condemn it, for they repented at the preaching of Jonah; and indeed a greater than Jonah is here. (NKJV)

Jesus's attackers had accused him of healing the demon-possessed man by Satan's power. He had just answered that. Now he spoke to those who wanted a sign from heaven to prove the source of his power.

Jesus would give them the same sign <u>Jonah</u> gave the people of Nineveh—his presence and his message. Jonah was a prophet of old who was called to preach to the people of Nineveh. Instead of obeying, Jonah ran away. But his flight was cut short when he was the cause of a terrible storm at sea, was thrown overboard, and was swallowed by a large fish. Inside the fish for three days, Jonah repented. God gave him a second chance by having the fish deposit him on land remarkably close to Nineveh. This time Jonah obeyed and preached to the Ninevites.

Both Jesus and Jonah preached repentance. Jesus, like Jonah, would be buried for three days and then be made alive again. The people of Nineveh responded in droves and God withheld his judgment. Too bad the same couldn't be said of Jesus's attackers.

Jesus also spoke of the <u>Queen of Sheba</u>, who traveled from a great distance to hear the wisdom of Solomon. Now, in the person of the Son of God, the people hearing Jesus had the opportunity to hear someone infinitely greater than Solomon. Would they open their hearts to listen, as she did?

Jesus was grieved by the crowds who followed him because they hoped to see a great miracle performed. Their hearts were not hungry for the truth that would have brought a greater miracle—change of their hearts toward God.

Today we may be tempted to search for unusual signs of God's blessing on a ministry and get on board because it is exciting. While we do that, however, we may miss what God wants to do in our hearts if we would just listen and obey!

Burning Light

LUKE 11:33–36 *"No one, when he has lit a lamp, puts it in a secret place or under a basket, but on a lampstand, that those who come in may see the light. The lamp of the body is the eye. Therefore, when your eye is good, your whole body also is full of light. But when your eye is bad, your body also is full of darkness. Therefore take heed that the light which is in you is not darkness. If then your whole body is full of light, having no part dark, the whole body will be full of light, as when the bright shining of a lamp gives you light."* (NKJV)

light
John 3:19

Jesus pictured his preaching of the truth as a lamp that was lit and placed where all could see its bright light. If the people could not see the light it was because their eyes were bad. Those who had good eyes could receive the light and their whole bodies would be flooded with it.

The bad eye Jesus referred to was not a physical disability. It was a heart attitude that was closed to the truth, not wanting its sin to be exposed by the light. In contrast, the good eye was a sincere openness to truth, a desire to have sin exposed and removed, and a willingness to allow the truth of Jesus to transform a person's life.

We are not condemned because of doing wrong. We are condemned because God has provided <u>light</u> and we refuse to come to it in order to have our wrongdoings exposed and removed.

Painful Pronouncements

LUKE 11:37–41 *And as He spoke, a certain Pharisee asked Him to dine with him. So He went in and sat down to eat. When the Pharisee saw it, he marveled that He had not first washed before dinner. Then the Lord said to him, "Now you Pharisees make the outside of the cup and dish clean, but your inward part is full of greed and wickedness. Foolish ones! Did not He who made the outside make the inside also? But rather give alms of such things as you have; then indeed all things are clean to you.* (NKJV)

As soon as Jesus finished speaking, a Pharisee invited him to his home for dinner. This was a dinner with a purpose. The host hoped to roast Jesus as the main course. Jesus, however, turned out to be the one doing the roasting.

go to

justice and mercy
Micah 6:8

generously
Deuteronomy
15:10–11

love
Deuteronomy 6:5

tithes
one tenth of one's
income

Before the meal, the Pharisee completed an elaborate ritual of washing his hands, as was his custom. Just as pointedly, Jesus declined to observe the ritual. When the Pharisee expressed his surprise, Jesus made his point. Pharisees were like dishes that were clean on the outside, but inside, where cleanliness really mattered, the dishes were dirty. Pharisees followed all the rules on the outside, but inside they were full of greed and evil. To become clean, they needed to get rid of their greed and give generously to the poor.

> **what others say**
>
> **Max Anders**
>
> While Jesus was very patient, understanding, and compassionate with those with weaknesses, he was very direct with those who were stubbornly unbelieving. Many times the Bible says that the religious leaders did not believe in Jesus because they were jealous of him. He challenged their pride of position and prestige over the people. Jesus was not patient with these leaders and was very forthright in his responses to them.[5]

Triple Whammy of Woes, Round One

LUKE 11:42–44 But woe to you Pharisees! For you tithe mint and rue and all manner of herbs, and pass by justice and the love of God. These you ought to have done, without leaving the others undone. Woe to you Pharisees! For you love the best seats in the synagogues and greetings in the marketplaces. Woe to you, scribes and Pharisees, hypocrites! For you are like graves which are not seen, and the men who walk over them are not aware of them." (NKJV)

Jesus pronounced the Pharisees guilty on three counts.

First, they were meticulous in giving their **tithes** while they neglected the poor. There's nothing wrong with donating to good causes, but these Pharisees took it too far. They counted the herbs picked from their gardens and gave one-tenth to God. They were so busy being spiritual they didn't have time to help the poor. The Old Testament Scriptures said God's people were to show <u>justice and mercy</u> for their fellows, giving <u>generously</u> out of <u>love</u> for God.

Second, far from being humble, the Pharisees paraded their self-righteousness. Dressed in their religious costumes as they attended the synagogue, they sought to sit in the seats reserved for the honored. In the marketplace they loved to be greeted as persons of great importance.

Third, Jesus said that the Pharisees were like unmarked graves.

God's law declared that a person who stepped on a grave had been <u>defiled</u>. For this reason graves were always marked in some way.

For example, <u>whitewashing</u> was common. The meaning here was clear. By their influence, these Pharisees defiled people by actually spreading false teaching and unbelief and keeping others from the truth.

go to

defiled
Numbers 19:11

whitewashing
Matthew 23:27

what others say

Max Anders

Today, it would be considered impolite and going overboard to speak in this way to any religious leader, and perhaps so. But Jesus being God saw the true nature of their hearts and had the moral authority to speak so directly. He was not one to trifle with if you were deliberately cooperating with sin.[6]

Triple Whammy of Woes, Round Two

LUKE 11:45–52 *Then one of the lawyers answered and said to Him, "Teacher, by saying these things You reproach us also." And He said, "Woe to you also, lawyers! For you load men with burdens hard to bear, and you yourselves do not touch the burdens with one of your fingers. Woe to you! For you build the tombs of the prophets, and your fathers killed them. In fact, you bear witness that you approve the deeds of your fathers; for they indeed killed them, and you build their tombs. Therefore the wisdom of God also said, 'I will send them prophets and apostles, and some of them they will kill and persecute,' that the blood of all the prophets which was shed from the foundation of the world may be required of this generation, from the blood of Abel to the blood of Zechariah who perished between the altar and the temple. Yes, I say to you, it shall be required of this generation. Woe to you lawyers! For you have taken away the key of knowledge. You did not enter in yourselves, and those who were entering in you hindered." (NKJV)*

A lawyer in the audience was becoming increasingly uncomfortable. Finally, he spoke up, protesting that when Jesus condemned the Pharisees he was also insulting the experts in the law. Right on! Jesus responded with three jabs especially suited to the lawyers.

First, they had made it their business to formulate excessive laws—some six thousand of them—which they piled on top of the laws God had given through Moses. It was not enough that they kept the laws themselves, but they burdened the people with them. Jesus faulted them not for making the laws but for making life miserable for the people they should have been helping.

Second, with brilliant discernment Jesus took aim at their project of building beautiful tombs to honor the prophets who had delivered God's Word to his people—while at the same time they were demonstrating the very attitude of those who had killed the prophets.

Third, Jesus accused the experts in the law of removing the key to knowledge—the truth of the Scriptures. Not only did they not want the truth for themselves but, with their preoccupation with rule keeping, they were preventing the common people from having the truth of Scripture.

The men Jesus addressed at the dinner were among the most respected in the land. They majored on being righteous. They followed religious rules with zeal. But Jesus pointed out that they had completely missed the point. They were majoring on minors. We would never be guilty of that—or would we? Take this test to see how you measure up.

- I am more concerned about my inner attitude of compassion for people in need than I am about an outward show of my faith.
- I am more concerned about justice for others and love for God than I am about letting people know how much I give to worthy causes.
- I am content to know I have God's praise and I don't seek the applause of others.
- Instead of being judgmental of others, I seek to encourage them.
- I listen to God's messengers with a humble, teachable attitude.

- I portray God as lovingly beckoning sinners rather than imposing a view of God as a hard-hearted judge.

When we focus all our attention on our behavior with the view of impressing others, we neglect what Christ says is most important. When we let Christ transform our hearts, however, our actions will become those that please him and others.

The Darkening Cloud

LUKE 11:53–54 *And as He said these things to them, the scribes and the Pharisees began to assail Him vehemently, and to cross-examine Him about many things, lying in wait for Him, and seeking to catch Him in something He might say, that they might accuse Him.* (NKJV)

The meal in the Pharisee's house ended with the Pharisees and experts in the law in a state of rage. The air was tense as they rolled out their heavy artillery of accusations and questions designed to catch Jesus in a false statement. The ominous cloud of hateful opposition gained strength.

Chapter Wrap-Up

- Jesus gave his disciples a pattern for prayer that showed God as a loving heavenly Father. (Luke 11:1–13)

- When Jesus cast out the demon from the man who was mute, some in the crowd accused him of getting his power from Satan and others asked for a sign from heaven. Jesus answered his critics by pointing out that Satan would not weaken his kingdom by working against himself. Jesus said his presence was the sign they sought. (Luke 11:14–33)

- Jesus said those who were open to his message would be able to see the light of his truth. (Luke 11:33–36)

- At a dinner Jesus condemned the Pharisees and experts in the law for their lack of interest in righteous attitudes. He said their meticulous adherence to man-made laws was worthless if they overlooked their inner heart attitudes toward God and man. (Luke 11:37–52)

- After Jesus pronounced three woes on the Pharisees and experts in the law, they became furious and sought ways to trap him. (Luke 11:53–54)

Study Questions

1. What elements did Jesus include in the pattern for prayer he gave the disciples?

2. How did Jesus answer those who accused him of being empowered by Satan?

3. How did Jesus answer the woman who said Mary was blessed for being the mother of Jesus?

4. How did Jesus answer those who demanded a sign from heaven?

5. What three traits did Jesus condemn in the Pharisees?

6. What three traits did Jesus condemn in the experts in the law?

Luke 12 Wise Words

Chapter Highlights:
- A Word for the Greedy
- A Word for the
  Watchful
- A Word for the
  Unprepared

Let's Get Started

Luke 12 is a series of warnings and promises that Jesus gave. Some were for his disciples. Others were for the crowds who followed him, some who were seeking truth, perhaps, but more who were hoping to see a spectacular miracle.

Throughout his warnings to those who crowded around him, Jesus gave words that we would do well to heed today. We need to pay special attention, because what he had to say is contrary to all that society offers as answers to our needs. We, as well as Jesus's listeners, have to make a choice.

The contents of Luke 12 are scattered in parts of the Gospels of Matthew and Mark. This leads many Bible experts to believe that here Luke is compiling some of Jesus's teachings given on a number of different occasions.

leaven
fermenting agent allowing dough to rise, symbol of evil

hypocrisy
acting a part, masking one's true self charade: pretense, deception

transparency
being open, concealing nothing in order to create a good impression

gospel harmony

A Word for the Inner Circle

> LUKE 12:1–3 *In the meantime, when an innumerable multitude of people had gathered together, so that they trampled one another, He began to say to His disciples first of all, "Beware of the leaven of the Pharisees, which is hypocrisy. For there is nothing covered that will not be revealed, nor hidden that will not be known. Therefore whatever you have spoken in the dark will be heard in the light, and what you have spoken in the ear in inner rooms will be proclaimed on the housetops.* (NKJV)

Jesus was like a reporter on *60 Minutes* exposing a scam. He warned his disciples about the **leaven** of the Pharisees—something he labeled **hypocrisy**. The Pharisees made rules, talked about following those rules, and then made a charade of keeping the rules while their hearts remained in opposition to God.

The word *hypocrite* was used originally by the Greeks to mean an actor, a person who used a mask and acted and spoke behind that facade. Jesus warned against hypocrisy and called for **transparency**.

omniscience
ability to know all

Though his disciples might be tempted to follow the ways of the Pharisees and even seem to succeed with spiritual role-playing, the truth would be exposed some day. You can fool people, but you can't fool God. Christ does not expect perfection but transparency.

what others say

R. Kent Hughes

Full disclosure will come on Judgment Day. Everything will be revealed, and the disclosure will be ruthless. The things whispered invisibly in the dark will be shouted in full light from the rooftops. The limitless capacities of divine **omniscience** assure perfect exposure of hypocrisy.[1]

Bad Fear, Good Fear

LUKE 12:4–7 *"And I say to you, My friends, do not be afraid of those who kill the body, and after that have no more that they can do. But I will show you whom you should fear: Fear Him who, after He has killed, has power to cast into hell; yes, I say to you, fear Him! Are not five sparrows sold for two copper coins? And not one of them is forgotten before God. But the very hairs of your head are all numbered. Do not fear therefore; you are of more value than many sparrows. (NKJV)*

As the disciples saw the growing hostility of the religious leaders against Jesus, they were probably afraid that they too would become the targets of wrath. But Jesus pointed out that whatever these leaders did, they could hurt the disciples only temporarily here on earth. If they were going to be afraid, the disciples should fear God, who has power over them on earth and in eternity!

But God is not a big meanie in the sky. Jesus hastened to remind them that God, who cares for the throwaway sparrows, cares for his own so intimately that he keeps count of the hairs on their heads. Surely, they can rely on his love and care for them now—and for eternity. If we fear God, we need not fear men.

what others say

R. C. Sproul

A healthy fear and respect for God should always be balanced by our confidence that in God's sight we are of exceedingly great value. Yes, God knows us intimately, knows the secrets that we harbor in our hearts, yet we should not allow our fear of divine disclosure to drive us to despair. Rather it should drive us to embrace the redemption that is ours in Christ.[2]

I'll Stand by You

LUKE 12:8–10 *"Also I say to you, whoever confesses Me before men, him the Son of Man also will confess before the angels of God. But he who denies Me before men will be denied before the angels of God. And anyone who speaks a word against the Son of Man, it will be forgiven him; but to him who blasphemes against the Holy Spirit, it will not be forgiven. (NKJV)*

When faced with opposition, Jesus's followers might be tempted to deny their allegiance to him. For this, Jesus had strong words: If people are faithful to me, I will stand by them and in heaven will acknowledge them as my own. But heavenly hosts will note it if they are ashamed of me and deny their association with me.

From Luke's account it is hard to understand the meaning of "blaspheme," sometimes called the "unpardonable sin." Matthew 12:25–36 and Mark 3:23–30 show that blaspheming the Holy Spirit is giving Satan credit for God's works. We may sin against God in attitudes and actions and be forgiven. We may even reject Christ at one point in life and, by God's grace, change our minds later in life. But total, complete, sustained denial of God the Father, Jesus the Son, and the Holy Spirit results in eternal damnation. That sin is unforgivable.

Jesus's warning points out the importance of making good choices on earth because those choices determine where we spend eternity. Most of us today are not in a position in which our lives are at risk because we acknowledge Jesus. We can deny Jesus as the Son of God, however, when we fail to obey all that the Bible teaches. If we pick and choose only what is convenient or easy to believe and obey, we deny Christ. Jesus says that some day we will stand in God's presence and our sinful attitudes will be exposed. The choice is ours: Will we acknowledge Jesus Christ as the Son of God?

Don't Worry About This Test

LUKE 12:11–12 *Now when they bring you to the synagogues and magistrates and authorities, do not worry about how or*

never leave
Hebrews 13:5–6

what you should answer, or what you should say. For the Holy Spirit will teach you in that very hour what you ought to say." (NKJV)

Some form of persecution would be unavoidable if the disciples remained loyal to Jesus, and Jesus assured them not to worry. True believers don't speak against the Holy Spirit. And better yet, when they are persecuted, they will discover that the Holy Spirit gives them words to say. When under pressure of his enemies, God would guide their speech.

God will not leave his faithful follower to deal with persecution alone. He promises that he will <u>never leave</u> his own. That's why the disciple can face even cruel and unjust mistreatment without fear.

A Word for the Greedy

> LUKE 12:13–15 *Then one from the crowd said to Him, "Teacher, tell my brother to divide the inheritance with me." But He said to him, "Man, who made Me a judge or an arbitrator over you?" And He said to them, "Take heed and beware of covetousness, for one's life does not consist in the abundance of the things he possesses." (NKJV)*

Because it was common for rabbis to offer judgment on matters of dispute, a man felt free to bring up a personal concern to Jesus. Jesus did not take part in the dispute but not because he didn't have advice or because he didn't care. Rather, he spoke to something over which no one else had authority—attitudes or motives. Jesus could read minds and hearts. Everyone in the audience faced a loss caused by greed. Jesus said that getting wrapped up in material things blinds us to the only significant values.

Jesus made a statement that would rock today's society back on its heels when he said that what makes us persons of significance does not depend on what we have, even when we have an abundance of possessions.

Boss Man

> LUKE 12:16–21 *Then He spoke a parable to them, saying: "The ground of a certain rich man yielded plentifully. And he thought within himself, saying, 'What shall I do, since I have no*

room to store my crops?' So he said, 'I will do this: I will pull down my barns and build greater, and there I will store all my crops and my goods. And I will say to my soul, "Soul, you have many goods laid up for many years; take your ease; eat, drink, and be merry."' But God said to him, 'Fool! This night your soul will be required of you; then whose will those things be which you have provided?' So is he who lays up treasure for himself, and is not rich toward God." (NKJV)

To make his point, Jesus told a parable that probed the heart of each listener. A rich farmer hauled in bumper crops and patted himself on the back not only for having a great harvest but also for what he thought was wise storage and estate planning. He thought he had it made.

Notice how selfish he was. In a few short sentences the farmer used the words *I* or *my* eleven times. He wasn't concerned about the needs of the poor or even about passing on an inheritance to his relatives. He wanted to indulge in a life of luxury and ease. God showed him who was boss. Possessions stored away cannot predict the future or save a person from death and eternal judgment. When a person who is rich in this world dies, he or she can suddenly discover he or she is poor in God's eyes. Jesus's parable about the rich farmer points out the fiction in any promise that wealth brings contentment or security.

key point

We may wonder what crossed Luke's mind as he heard about the story Jesus told. Any doctor knows there is a price to be paid for luxury living—laziness and indulgence with no concern for anything beyond eating, drinking, and partying. Since the body pays a price, what about the soul?

what others say

Warren W. Wiersbe

Wealth cannot keep us alive when our time comes to die, nor can it buy back the opportunities we missed while we were thinking of ourselves and ignoring God and others.[3]

Perspective Is Everything

LUKE 12:22–26 *Then He said to His disciples, "Therefore I say to you, do not worry about your life, what you will eat; nor about the body, what you will put on. Life is more than food, and*

go to

ravens
Leviticus 11:13–15;
Deuteronomy
14:11–14

Solomon
2 Chronicles
9:13–21

lilies
scarlet poppies and
anemones, which
bloom for a day
then die

Solomon
Israel's richest,
wisest king

the body is more than clothing. Consider the ravens, for they neither sow nor reap, which have neither storehouse nor barn; and God feeds them. Of how much more value are you than the birds? And which of you by worrying can add one cubit to his stature? If you then are not able to do the least, why are you anxious for the rest? (NKJV)

Jesus's disciples did not share the rich farmer's problem of over-abundance. They had given up everything to follow him, and most of them didn't have many material things to give up. They had no guaranteed provision for the next day, let alone their future. Jesus quickly put their concerns to rest. God provides even for ugly <u>ravens</u> or crows. How much more lovingly he would provide them with the food they needed!

As for worry—what good does it do? Since worrying can't add a single hour to life or an inch to height, why indulge in something so useless when they could trust their loving Father? Worry doesn't work. Let God supply your needs.

what others say

Leon Morris

From the sins of greed and selfishness Jesus turns to that of worry, which in a way is connected with the other two.
"Greed can never get enough, worry is afraid it may not have enough" (Arndt).[4]

Proper Priorities

LUKE 12:27–31 *Consider the lilies, how they grow: they neither toil nor spin; and yet I say to you, even Solomon in all his glory was not arrayed like one of these. If then God so clothes the grass, which today is in the field and tomorrow is thrown into the oven, how much more will He clothe you, O you of little faith? And do not seek what you should eat or what you should drink, nor have an anxious mind. For all these things the nations of the world seek after, and your Father knows that you need these things. But seek the kingdom of God, and all these things shall be added to you. (NKJV)*

In assuring his disciples that God would provide for them, Jesus gave them a visual reminder of his care—the **lilies** that grew wild in the fields. King <u>**Solomon**</u> in all his royal robes was not dressed as elegantly as these common flowers. Knowing this, Jesus's disciples did not need to focus on their need for food and clothing. God had already promised to care for these. Instead, they should put their hearts and minds on one thing—seeking God's kingdom on earth. As they did, God would provide all that they needed.

Treasures Guaranteed

LUKE 12:32–34 *Do not fear, little flock, for it is your Father's good pleasure to give you the kingdom. Sell what you have and give alms; provide yourselves money bags which do not grow old, a treasure in the heavens that does not fail, where no thief approaches nor moth destroys. For where your treasure is, there your heart will be also.* (NKJV)

Jesus promised his disciples that if they trusted all to him, they would enjoy a prosperity that the world could never provide. Their heavenly Father would give them the kingdom—plus, as they shared their earthly provisions with the poor, they would be storing treasure away in heaven. This meant not only guaranteed praise and reward from God in the future but also abundance now in terms of proper perspectives, knowing that nothing could destroy their treasures because they were secure in God. Keep first things first. Seek God's kingdom.

Doctors are concerned with the needs of their patients. How appropriate that Luke includes Jesus's calling his disciples "little flock." This is the only use of this form of address in the New Testament. It implies that the disciples and all believers are to expect God to care for them just as a shepherd cares for his helpless sheep.

Do we sometimes think that our gifts to care for the physical needs of the poor are less spiritual than gifts for building churches and publishing Bibles? Jesus made no such distinction. He consistently showed his heart of compassion for those in humble circumstances.

A Word for the Watchful

LUKE 12:35–40 *"Let your waist be girded and your lamps burning; and you yourselves be like men who wait for their master, when he will return from the wedding, that when he comes and knocks they may open to him immediately. Blessed are those servants whom the master, when he comes, will find watching. Assuredly, I say to you that he will gird himself and have them sit down to eat, and will come and serve them. And if he should come in the second watch, or come in the third watch, and find them so, blessed are those servants. But know this, that if the master of the house had known what hour the thief would come, he would have watched and not allowed his house to be broken into. Therefore you also be ready, for the Son of Man is coming at an hour you do not expect." (NKJV)*

Worry-free living does not mean careless living. "Let your waist be girded" in the first century meant that the person tucked his outer robe up into his belt to get it out of the way, allowing free movement. He was then ready for hard work, vigorous travel, or dangerous battle. Likewise, Jesus's followers have strenuous duties. Jesus told his disciples that they were to live on alert—watching and waiting for his return.

For a while they would not see him, but when he returned he expected them to be ready, as servants would be ready for their master to return from a wedding ceremony bringing his bride with him. Much as a thief breaks in when a homeowner least expects him, Jesus will return at an unexpected hour. Disciples need to be looking for him in an attitude of tiptoed expectancy.

Employees on Trial

LUKE 12:41–46 *Then Peter said to Him, "Lord, do You speak this parable only to us, or to all people?" And the Lord said, "Who then is that faithful and wise steward, whom his master will make ruler over his household, to give them their portion of food in due season? Blessed is that servant whom his master will find so doing when he comes. Truly, I say to you that he will make him ruler over all that he has. But if that servant says in his heart, 'My master is delaying his coming,' and begins to beat the male and female servants, and to eat and drink and be drunk, the master of that servant will come on a day when he is not looking for him, and at an hour when he is not aware, and will cut him in two and appoint him his portion with the unbelievers. (NKJV)*

Peter, spokesman for the group, asked about responsibility. Jesus answered with a question and a parable that showed the disciples had a special responsibility.

A boss needed to leave for an extended time. He put a manager in charge, gave specific work assignments, provided for the needs of all workers, and promised to return. What should he find when he returned? If the workers had been negligent, they would be punished in proportion to the responsibilities and resources they had been given. Serve with faithfulness, knowing that someday you will be evaluated.

Earned Degrees

LUKE 12:47–48 *And that servant who knew his master's will, and did not prepare himself or do according to his will, shall be beaten with many stripes. But he who did not know, yet committed things deserving of stripes, shall be beaten with few. For everyone to whom much is given, from him much will be required; and to whom much has been committed, of him they will ask the more. (NKJV)*

This parable illustrated the idea of degrees of punishment. The ignorant workers were judged because they should have made it their responsibility to find out what the boss wanted. While everyone was responsible for his or her actions, the workers who knew what the boss wanted but did not obey were told to expect harsher treatment than those who were ignorant of the boss's instructions. Both groups were punished according to their level of responsibility.

In Bible times business travelers did not enjoy the convenience of instant contact with the home office. An executive would prepare his staff as best he could before leaving, but once he was gone he would have to trust the faithfulness of his staff to carry on until he returned.

reveal
1 Corinthians 4:5

Though we have technology for communication that was undreamed of in Bible days, we have the kind of responsibility Jesus spoke of in this parable. He, like the business executive, is gone for an extended time. We are to be faithful in conducting his business. When he returns, there will be an accounting.

First, he will <u>reveal</u> actions and motives that we have concealed from others. Then, if we have been faithful even in the hidden things, he will praise us for fulfilling the duties he assigned us.

A Word for the Uncommitted

> LUKE 12:49–53 *"I came to send fire on the earth, and how I wish it were already kindled! But I have a baptism to be baptized with, and how distressed I am till it is accomplished! Do you suppose that I came to give peace on earth? I tell you, not at all, but rather division. For from now on five in one house will be divided: three against two, and two against three. Father will be divided against son and son against father, mother against daughter and daughter against mother, mother-in-law against her daughter-in-law and daughter-in-law against her mother-in-law."* (NKJV)

Jesus had a warning for the uncommitted. If they were expecting a smooth ride into his kingdom, they needed to stop and count the cost. Commitment to him carries a price. Much as people were split in their acceptance of him, so people would be split in their acceptance of his followers. Families would be divided, often bitterly, between those who followed Jesus and those who rejected him.

When Jesus was born, God sent angelic messengers to announce peace, but now we have Jesus declaring that he was bringing division, not peace.

The angel announced peace on earth at Jesus's birth. Jesus gives inner peace to those <u>who trust</u> him, but sometimes their loyalty to Jesus causes <u>division</u> and opposition with family and friends. But even if we do not find peace on earth among earth-dwellers, we have Jesus's promise of peace <u>in heaven</u> throughout eternity.

A Word for the Unprepared

> LUKE 12:54–59 *Then He also said to the multitudes, "Whenever you see a cloud rising out of the west, immediately you say, 'A*

shower is coming'; and so it is. And when you see the south wind blow, you say, 'There will be hot weather'; and there is. Hypocrites! You can discern the face of the sky and of the earth, but how is it you do not discern this time?

"Yes, and why, even of yourselves, do you not judge what is right? When you go with your adversary to the magistrate, make every effort along the way to settle with him, lest he drag you to the judge, the judge deliver you to the officer, and the officer throw you into prison. I tell you, you shall not depart from there till you have paid the very last mite." (NKJV)

Jesus had stern words for those who could use clues from the sky and wind to predict weather, but who were blind to the overwhelming evidence that he was the promised Messiah. They could prepare for changes in the weather but were not prepared to heed his warnings for repentance. He could warn, but he could not spare them the judgment that lay ahead if they continued to reject him.

who trust
Romans 5:1

division
John 7:12, 43; 9:16; 10:19

in heaven
Luke 19:38

Chapter Wrap-Up

- Jesus warned against the leaven of the Pharisees, which he identified as hypocrisy. (Luke 12:1–3)

- Jesus taught that his followers should not fear those who can hurt the body but fear God, who has power over this life and the next. (Luke 12:4–12)

- Jesus warned against greed, which blinds us to God's desire for us to share with others who have needs and keeps us from building treasure in heaven. (Luke 12:13–21)

- Jesus gave clear guidelines about our attitude toward "things." Since God will provide for our needs we should not worry. Rather we should focus on doing his will. (Luke 12:22–34)

- Jesus challenged his disciples to be faithful to the assignments he gave them—even when he would be absent from them. (Luke 12:35–48)

- Jesus warned that belief in him would disrupt family relationships because allegiance to him must come before allegiance to family members. (Luke 12:49–53)

- We are alert enough to pay attention to signs of weather change, but need to be even more alert and responsive to what Jesus teaches that impacts our lives now—and forever. (Luke 12:54–59)

Study Questions

1. What spiritual danger did Jesus identify as yeast of the Pharisees? How could this be a danger for his disciples?

2. According to Jesus, why is greed such a destructive sin?

3. What did Jesus say should be our attitude toward "things"?

4. What was the point of Jesus's parable about the servants who awaited their master's return from his wedding? How does this impact us today?

5. In what way does Jesus disrupt family relationships?

Luke 13 Going Against the Grain

Let's Get Started

Sometimes love has to be tough. Sometimes the truth has to be spoken even if it offends. A warning has to hurt before it can be heeded.

Jesus moved toward Jerusalem where his ministry would climax in his death. While he didn't step back from his compassionate work of healing and teaching the common people, he stepped up his confrontation with the religious leaders, calling on them to turn from their pride and hypocrisy and to believe his teaching. His mission had consistently disturbed and angered the unbelieving leaders, and the time had come for him to openly state his claim as Messiah.

Repentance Required

LUKE 13:1–5 *There were present at that season some who told Him about the Galileans whose blood Pilate had mingled with their sacrifices. And Jesus answered and said to them, "Do you suppose that these Galileans were worse sinners than all other Galileans, because they suffered such things? I tell you, no; but unless you repent you will all likewise perish. Or those eighteen on whom the tower in Siloam fell and killed them, do you think that they were worse sinners than all other men who dwelt in Jerusalem? I tell you, no; but unless you repent you will all likewise perish." (NKJV)*

Jesus spoke of two events with which his audience was familiar. First, he responded to a horrible report that some Galileans had been killed by Pilate's soldiers while they were at the Temple to offer sacrifices. In another unfortunate event, eighteen people died when a tower fell on them. In Bible times people generally accepted the idea that anyone who died tragically had been punished by God. Jesus differed. He said that those who died were not "worse sinners" than others. In fact, unless all those listening to him repented, they would also perish. This meant changing their hearts and minds about Jesus.

A person going through a series of misfortunes asks, "What did I do to deserve this?" Compounding the problem, onlookers conclude, "He must have done something bad because this happened." Jesus clearly says that troubles and death are common to all. Calamities happen without regard to individual guilt. Every person is sinful. What is truly individual is each person's attitude about Jesus and the need to **repent**. The need for individual repentance brings everyone down to the same level.

Upsetting the Fruit Basket

LUKE 13:6–9 *He also spoke this parable: "A certain man had a fig tree planted in his vineyard, and he came seeking fruit on it and found none. Then he said to the keeper of his vineyard, 'Look, for three years I have come seeking fruit on this fig tree and find none. Cut it down; why does it use up the ground?' But he answered and said to him, 'Sir, let it alone this year also, until I dig around it and fertilize it. And if it bears fruit, well. But if not, after that you can cut it down.'"* (NKJV)

Jesus told a parable to help his listeners apply his point. He had told them that they needed to repent (verses 3 and 5). Now he said that if their lives did not show spiritual vitality, then repentance was not present and judgment would surely come for them. The parable dealt with planting a fig tree. For three years the owner looked in vain for the tree to bear fruit. Disgusted, he directed that it should be cut down to make room for another planting. The caretaker pleaded for the unproductive tree, asking for one more year. He would give it every possible advantage and if it still did not bear fruit, he would cut it down.

The point? For three years Jesus had been proclaiming the truth about himself. Would the people believe him? If so, their lives would have indications of spiritual fruit. If there was no fruit, then judgment was sure to come. God patiently waits for fruit.

what others say

Charles C. Ryrie

Every Christian will bear spiritual fruit. Somewhere, sometime, somehow. Otherwise that person is not a believer. Every born-again individual will be fruitful. Not to be fruitful is to be faithless, without faith, and therefore without salvation.[1]

Hypocrisy Exposed

Job's boils
Job 2:7

Paul's thorn
2 Corinthians 12:7–9

Luke 13:10–13 Now He was teaching in one of the synagogues on the Sabbath. And behold, there was a woman who had a spirit of infirmity eighteen years, and was bent over and could in no way raise herself up. But when Jesus saw her, He called her to Him and said to her, "Woman, you are loosed from your infirmity." And He laid His hands on her, and immediately she was made straight, and glorified God. (NKJV)

In a synagogue one Sabbath Jesus used an opportunity to make his claims even more clear. Seeing a woman who had been crippled for eighteen years, he called her to step forward and said words she must have yearned to hear: "Woman, you are set free from your infirmity." He reached out to put his hands on her, and immediately she was relieved of her problem and able to stand up straight and move about. Her instant response was praise to God.

Even doctors can be taken by surprise. Luke the physician reports the details of this miracle. The woman was bent over so severely that she could not even look upward. For eighteen years she had been unable to straighten her back. That she made it to the synagogue was no small undertaking! When Jesus spoke to her, freeing her of the restraints that prevented her movement, she was able to stand up and move uninhibited. No medication was prescribed, no surgery, no physical therapy—just instant healing!

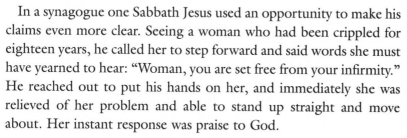

what others say

William MacDonald

The curvature of the spine was caused by Satan. We know from other parts of the Bible that some sicknesses are the result of Satanic activity. Job's boils were inflicted by Satan. Paul's thorn in the flesh was a messenger of Satan to buffet him. The devil is not allowed to do this on a believer, however, without the Lord's permission. And God overrules any such sickness or suffering for His own glory.[2]

Critical Response

Luke 13:14–17 But the ruler of the synagogue answered with indignation, because Jesus had healed on the Sabbath; and he said to the crowd, "There are six days on which men ought to work; therefore come and be healed on them, and not on the

go to

mustard
Matthew 13:31;
17:20;
Mark 4:31;
Luke 17:6

mustard
plant grown for its
aromatic, oily seeds;
could get ten to fif-
teen feet high; its
seeds attracted
birds

Sabbath day." The Lord then answered him and said, "Hypocrite! Does not each one of you on the Sabbath loose his ox or donkey from the stall, and lead it away to water it? So ought not this woman, being a daughter of Abraham, whom Satan has bound—think of it—for eighteen years, be loosed from this bond on the Sabbath?" And when He said these things, all His adversaries were put to shame; and all the multitude rejoiced for all the glorious things that were done by Him. (NKJV)

In contrast to the woman's reaction of praise, the instant response of the synagogue ruler was indignation. Rather than speaking to Jesus directly, he lashed out at the innocent people, saying they had no business seeking miracles on the Sabbath. He insisted that Jesus's healing clinic be closed on the Sabbath.

Jesus spoke up, pointing out the hypocrisy of having Sabbath rules that allowed care for animals but not for humans. Jesus ignored man-made rules to bring healing.

He made his point. His opponents were humiliated.

Human Standards Challenged

LUKE 13:18–21 Then He said, "What is the kingdom of God like? And to what shall I compare it? It is like a mustard seed, which a man took and put in his garden; and it grew and became a large tree, and the birds of the air nested in its branches." And again He said, "To what shall I liken the kingdom of God? It is like leaven, which a woman took and hid in three measures of meal till it was all leavened." (NKJV)

Luke placed two illustrations here to teach more about the kingdom of God. The Jewish religious system had added thousands of rules to God's laws; yet it was powerless to bring about heart changes. Jesus contrasted that massive system with the seemingly insignificant kingdom of God. His kingdom was like a tiny **mustard** seed, which grows gradually so that it takes over the garden, providing a lush environment for birds to enjoy. His kingdom could bring about true change and it would do so gradually. His kingdom was also like a little leaven that slowly changes flour so that it rises to make bread. The power of both the seed and the leaven is inherent or built in. Both work quietly from the inside out. Likewise, the power of the kingdom of God is built in, and it works quietly from the inside out to change people's hearts and lives.

The Jews were looking for a kingdom that would burst onto the world political scene with power and majesty. Instead, the kingdom Jesus proclaimed seemed insignificant. Beyond the miracles he performed, there was almost no evidence of what the Old Testament prophets had promised.

But quietly throughout the centuries the kingdom has spread to cover the whole earth. Much as a mustard seed grows to cover a garden or a pinch of leaven moves throughout a large quantity of dough, Jesus's kingdom is advancing through the church now and in his reign to come.

Sincerity Sought

LUKE 13:22–27 *And He went through the cities and villages, teaching, and journeying toward Jerusalem. Then one said to Him, "Lord, are there few who are saved?" And He said to them, "Strive to enter through the narrow gate, for many, I say to you, will seek to enter and will not be able. When once the Master of the house has risen up and shut the door, and you begin to stand outside and knock at the door, saying, 'Lord, Lord, open for us,' and He will answer and say to you, 'I do not know you, where you are from,' then you will begin to say, 'We ate and drank in Your presence, and You taught in our streets.' But He will say, 'I tell you I do not know you, where you are from. Depart from Me, all you workers of iniquity.' (NKJV)*

Jesus's teaching was so revolutionary that listeners scratched their heads. If the religious leaders were not on the right track, what hope was there for the common people to be saved? Jesus must be saying heaven will be sparsely populated. So someone asked, "Lord, are there few who are saved?"

Jesus did not answer the question numerically, but dealt rather with who would be saved. Only those who make the personal choice to enter through the narrow gate will be in heaven.

This was a shock to his listeners. As descendants of Abraham, Isaac, and Jacob, the listeners assumed they would have automatic entrance into the kingdom. But Jesus said, "Not so!"

The invitation is for everyone, but only those who make the personal choice to enter will be included in God's kingdom. Those who do not make that decision will someday find that it is too late.

key point

The word *strive* can also be translated "make every effort." It means wholehearted action like an athlete training for the Olympics. Halfhearted attempts to gain access to God's kingdom will not work, but any genuine efforts will be rewarded. No matter how people have outwardly identified with God's followers, only those who have made the inner choice to follow him will be included in the kingdom.

We enter this world alone. We leave it alone. And somewhere in between we make our decision about Jesus alone. No one can make it for us.

Outside Looking In

LUKE 13:28–30 *There will be weeping and gnashing of teeth, when you see Abraham and Isaac and Jacob and all the prophets in the kingdom of God, and yourselves thrust out. They will come from the east and the west, from the north and the south, and sit down in the kingdom of God. And indeed there are last who will be first, and there are first who will be last." (NKJV)*

Some people we expect to see in heaven will not be there. Others we expect not to see will be there. Jesus told the Jews that if they weren't careful to accept his teachings they would find themselves on the wrong side of the door of heaven. They thought they were God's privileged people, guaranteed a spot at the banquet with the Messiah. Jesus said the Gentiles would be sitting at places of honor around the table, while the Jews would be on the outside looking in.

rejecting
2 Kings 21:16;
Jeremiah 26:20–23

Duty Calls

> LUKE 13:31–33 *On that very day some Pharisees came, saying to Him, "Get out and depart from here, for Herod wants to kill You." And He said to them, "Go, tell that fox, 'Behold, I cast out demons and perform cures today and tomorrow, and the third day I shall be perfected.' Nevertheless I must journey today, tomorrow, and the day following; for it cannot be that a prophet should perish outside of Jerusalem. (NKJV)*

Some Pharisees came to Jesus with a warning—"Get out of here because Herod is after you!"

Jesus's reply must have mystified the messengers. He would continue his ministry until he reached Jerusalem, and he would do this with a deep sense of his mission. Luke emphasizes Jesus's strong sense of duty by using the words "must," "today," and "perfected." Jesus knew he was to die on the cross.

Sorry City

> LUKE 13:34–35 *"O Jerusalem, Jerusalem, the one who kills the prophets and stones those who are sent to her! How often I wanted to gather your children together, as a hen gathers her brood under her wings, but you were not willing! See! Your house is left to you desolate; and assuredly, I say to you, you shall not see Me until the time comes when you say, 'Blessed is He who comes in the name of the LORD!'" (NKJV)*

Jesus turned then to express his deep sorrow for Jerusalem and for the whole Jewish nation who had not believed him and was about to reject him by killing him. Jesus was deeply concerned about the city and the Jewish people. Although they had a history of <u>rejecting</u> God's messengers, Jesus had not rejected them. He still cared about them.

gospel harmony

Matthew includes Jesus's prayer for Jerusalem with its poignant reference to a hen caring for her chicks (Matthew 23:37–39). This tender image came from God to his people during their long journey from slavery in Egypt to the land of promise and was picked up in other Old Testament books (see Deuteronomy 32:11; Ruth 2:12; Psalms 17:8; 91:4). His care and protection came as the overflow of his love, and Jesus longed to spare them the consequences of their wrongdoing.

Chapter Wrap-Up

- People assumed that tragedy was punishment from God. Jesus said that wasn't true and that each person was responsible to repent and avoid eternal judgment. (Luke 13:1–5)

- In the parable of the fig tree, Jesus taught that genuine repentance leads to spiritual life and fruit. (Luke 13:6–9)

- On a Sabbath Jesus healed a woman who had been severely disabled for eighteen years. In responding to the synagogue ruler's indignation over his violation of Sabbath laws, Jesus pointed out that the rules showed more compassion for an animal than for a human. (Luke 13:10–17)

- Jesus said his kingdom was like a tiny mustard seed and like a small amount of leaven. Both seem insignificant but in time grow and provide nourishment for many. (Luke 13:18–21)

- Jews assumed they would be in God's kingdom simply because they were descendants of Abraham. Jesus pointed out that unless they had personal faith in him, they would be left outside looking in. (Luke 13:22–30)

- Jesus sorrowed over Jerusalem because the Jews had rejected him and would bear terrible consequences for their rejection. (Luke 13:31–35)

Study Questions

1. How did Jesus turn the generally accepted interpretation of two news events into something that had personal implications?

2. After Jesus healed the woman, how did Jesus expose the hypocrisy of the synagogue ruler?

3. In what way is the kingdom of God like a tiny mustard seed and a pinch of leaven?

4. What was the point of Jesus's warning about the narrow door? What application does it have for us today?

5. What prompted Jesus's expression of deep sorrow over Jerusalem?

Luke 14 Relating to People

Let's Get Started

Luke gives a series of Jesus's teachings that involve relating to others. First, Jesus was tested one Sabbath in the home of a prominent Pharisee. Would Jesus heal a man suffering from dropsy? Jesus healed him and said that his accusers valued an ox more than a suffering human.

Then Jesus pointed out the Pharisees' habit of self-seeking as they tried to outdo each other in taking places of honor at the dinner. Jesus advised his host to stop inviting only those guests who could pay him back with similar meals and to include those who could not do so. In showing generosity to them he would be sure of God's reward.

To illustrate, Jesus told a parable that exposed self-centeredness. The Jews claimed exclusive rights to God's kingdom, but when Jesus came to invite them to his banquet they were too occupied with their own interests to respond.

Finally, Jesus clearly outlined the cost of discipleship. Of all relationships people sought, their relationship with him was costly but paramount.

Valuing People

LUKE **14:1–6** *Now it happened, as He went into the house of one of the rulers of the Pharisees to eat bread on the Sabbath, that they watched Him closely. And behold, there was a certain man before Him who had dropsy. And Jesus, answering, spoke to the lawyers and Pharisees, saying, "Is it lawful to heal on the Sabbath?" But they kept silent. And He took him and healed him, and let him go. Then He answered them, saying, "Which of you, having a donkey or an ox that has fallen into a pit, will not immediately pull him out on the Sabbath day?" And they could not answer Him regarding these things. (NKJV)*

On a Sabbath day Jesus accepted an invitation for dinner in the home of a well-known Pharisee. Rather than being a gracious gesture on the part of the host, it was a trap. The seating around the table was not haphazard, for the Pharisee had placed in front of Jesus a man who was obviously afflicted with **dropsy**.

The trap was set. While everyone in the room watched to see what Jesus would do, Jesus turned the trap on the Pharisees by asking if it was lawful to heal on the Sabbath.

The Pharisees and experts in the law chose not to answer. If they said it was lawful, they would be violating one of their man-made Sabbath laws and could not complain if Jesus healed him. If they said it was unlawful, they would be showing callous indifference to the afflicted man. Their silence spoke volumes.

Jesus reached out and touched the man, healed him, and sent him home. Then he turned to his accusers and asked if any of them would rescue a donkey or an ox that fell into a well on the Sabbath day. Again they were trapped, so had to remain silent.

Luke the physician probably took great interest in the report of Jesus's healing. The man with dropsy was obviously retaining fluid, caused by kidney, heart, or liver trouble. He was very ill and the medical profession could offer little to relieve his discomfort.

Jesus showed compassion in sending the healed man away so that he would not have to hear the question he would raise with those who were eager to accuse him for performing the miracle of healing on the Sabbath.

what others say

Lawrence O. Richards

It must have been frustrating, to be an opponent of Jesus. Whenever they attempted to act against him, they simply injured themselves!

As long as we live in the spirit of Jesus, maintaining his compassion for others, any who criticize us will also expose only their own hardness of heart.[1]

Humble Etiquette

LUKE 14:7–11 *So He told a parable to those who were invited, when He noted how they chose the best places, saying to them: "When you are invited by anyone to a wedding feast, do not sit down in the best place, lest one more honorable than you be invited by him; and he who invited you and him come and say to you, 'Give place to this man,' and then you begin with shame to take the lowest place. But when you are invited, go and sit down in the lowest place, so that when he who invited you comes he may say to you, 'Friend, go up higher.' Then you will have glory in the presence of those who sit at the table with you. For whoever exalts himself will be humbled, and he who humbles himself will be exalted." (NKJV)*

knocked down
Proverbs 18:12

example
Philippians 2:5–11

Jesus noted that the guests at the Pharisee's home scrambled for places of honor next to the host. He pointed out their self-seeking in a parable about a wedding feast. He warned, "Don't assume you are the most important guest and assign yourself a place of honor at the table. Imagine your humiliation when the host asks you to move down in order to make room for someone who has been invited to take that place next to the host. Instead, come with a humble attitude. Take a low place. Then the host will invite you to move up to a place of honor."

Jesus then gave a principle that has implications for all our interactions with others. If we puff up ourselves as important, we will be <u>knocked down</u>. But if we sincerely humble ourselves following Jesus's <u>example</u>, God will see that we are exalted.

Jesus has a special word for people who are humble and are not self-seeking. They value God's approval more than the admiration of their peers. God, who sees the heart, will reveal himself to those who are humble.

Dinner Round Robin

LUKE 14:12–14 *Then He also said to him who invited Him, "When you give a dinner or a supper, do not ask your friends, your brothers, your relatives, nor rich neighbors, lest they also invite you back, and you be repaid. But when you give a feast, invite the poor, the maimed, the lame, the blind. And you will be blessed, because they cannot repay you; for you shall be repaid at the resurrection of the just." (NKJV)*

The host at the dinner had followed the prevailing custom of the day. He invited friends and relatives who could repay him with an invitation to their homes. It was a social game of ping-pong. This

from men
John 12:42–43

was no problem for the "in" group. In fact, it was a self-serving system. They could count on a steady flow of return invitations. Jesus's concern was for the "out" group—the poor and people with disabilities—who were never included on the guest list.

Granted, these people could not reciprocate, but Jesus promised that such acts of kindness and generosity would be rewarded, not with notes in the social columns of the newspaper, but with God himself in the resurrection.

what others say

Dallas Willard

[Jesus] . . . is . . . telling us to provide for more than our little circle of mutual appreciation, and thus to place ourselves in the larger context of heaven's rule where we have a different kind of mind and heart regardless of who we do or do not have over for dinner.[2]

Human nature has not changed through the centuries. Some leaders actually believed in Jesus, but, because they valued their reputations, did not dare to let that be known. They yearned for praise <u>from men</u> more than praise from God. Today many people place great emphasis on networking and name-dropping, all in an effort to impress others with their status.

Jesus cuts through all that kind of motivation as he points out that we should value all people, not just the individuals who help elevate our status.

Excuses, Excuses

LUKE **14:15–20** *Now when one of those who sat at the table with Him heard these things, he said to Him, "Blessed is he who shall eat bread in the kingdom of God!" Then He said to him, "A certain man gave a great supper and invited many, and sent his servant at supper time to say to those who were invited, 'Come, for all things are now ready.' But they all with one accord began to make excuses. The first said to him, 'I have bought a piece of ground, and I must go and see it. I ask you to have me excused.' And another said, 'I have bought five yoke of oxen, and I am going to test them. I ask you to have me excused.' Still another said, 'I have married a wife, and therefore I cannot come.'* (NKJV)

Someone broke into the conversation to express his anticipation of eating at the feast in God's kingdom. It was a self-righteous statement and possibly implied that while he and the other law-abiding Jews at the Pharisee's Sabbath dinner would be blessed in God's kingdom, Jesus would not!

Jesus answered with a parable about a man who planned a banquet and whose invited guests did not come. The guests had accepted the advance invitations, but now they insulted their gracious host by giving flimsy excuses for not coming.

The Pharisees could not miss the point of Jesus's parable. They assumed that as law-abiding Jews they would have a secure place in God's kingdom. However, when Jesus came to invite them to commit themselves to him, they made excuses. God sees our actions, but he also sees our motives in our interactions with others.

In Jesus's parable people had accepted the invitation to the banquet, but at the last minute they made excuses for not attending. Their desire for pleasure and financial security was too important to them. What kinds of things keep us from being committed to God's kingdom?

Invitations for Outcasts

LUKE 14:21–24 *So that servant came and reported these things to his master. Then the master of the house, being angry, said to his servant, 'Go out quickly into the streets and lanes of the city, and bring in here the poor and the maimed and the lame and the blind.' And the servant said, 'Master, it is done as you commanded, and still there is room.' Then the master said to the servant, 'Go out into the highways and hedges, and compel them to*

Jerusalem
Luke 13:33

come in, that my house may be filled. For I say to you that none of those men who were invited shall taste my supper.'" (NKJV)

The host sent his servant to comb the streets and back alleys and urge the riffraff and outcasts to come to the party. When this was accomplished and there was still room in the banquet hall, the host sent the servant to go outside the town and persuade even more such people to come.

And the men who had been invited in the first place? They would not be allowed even one bite of the sumptuous food! Since they rejected him, God welcomed those whom the Pharisees considered inferior and unworthy: the man with dropsy, the poor, crippled, lame, and blind. Further, God welcomed the Gentiles into his kingdom.

Discipleship Dilemmas

> LUKE 14:25–27 *Now great multitudes went with Him. And He turned and said to them, "If anyone comes to Me and does not hate his father and mother, wife and children, brothers and sisters, yes, and his own life also, he cannot be My disciple. And whoever does not bear his cross and come after Me cannot be My disciple.* (NKJV)

Crowds gathered around Jesus wherever he went. As he moved toward Jerusalem where he would give his life, he gave his would-be followers a sudden eye-opener. Anyone who wanted to follow him as a disciple must be so committed to Jesus that he would put Jesus first in everything. Every other relationship—good and worthy as it may be—must take second place. Further, the would-be follower must be willing to pay the price of loyalty to Jesus. This would mean suffering and even death.

what others say

R. Kent Hughes

What Jesus was saying paradoxically was that our love for him must be so great and so pervasive that our natural love of self and family pales in comparison. We are to subordinate everything, even our own being, to our love and commitment to Christ. He is to be our first loyalty.[4]

Jesus was not saying that his followers must harbor ill will toward family and friends. The reality is that the closer a disciple is to Jesus the more loving he or she becomes to others. In fact, Jesus commanded his disciples to <u>love</u> one another and said that the badge that identified his true disciples would be their love. But if a follower of Christ ever had to choose between Christ or family, he must choose Christ.

A Commitment to Completion

> LUKE 14:28–30 *For which of you, intending to build a tower, does not sit down first and count the cost, whether he has enough to finish it—lest, after he has laid the foundation, and is not able to finish, all who see it begin to mock him, saying, 'This man began to build and was not able to finish.'* (NKJV)

Many a town has an incomplete building or road, and the townspeople don't fail to mock the city "planners." Before even marking out the place for the foundation, the builder needs to work on his budget. Does he have enough money to complete the tower? If not, he will become the butt of many a joke.

A Commitment to Confrontation

> LUKE 14:31–33 *Or what king, going to make war against another king, does not sit down first and consider whether he is able with ten thousand to meet him who comes against him with twenty thousand? Or else, while the other is still a great way off, he sends a delegation and asks conditions of peace. So likewise, whoever of you does not forsake all that he has cannot be My disciple.* (NKJV)

Jesus then spoke of a king who is suddenly threatened by an enemy. He needs to weigh his options. He has an army of ten thousand. His enemy is approaching with an army of twenty thousand. If he is not willing to risk confronting the enemy, he would do well to send a delegation to negotiate a peaceful settlement to their dispute. But if he decides to risk the confrontation, he must be willing to give it his all. With Jesus, halfway commitment is not real commitment.

love
John 13:34–35

A Disciple Worth His Salt

LUKE 14:34–35 *"Salt is good; but if the salt has lost its flavor, how shall it be seasoned? It is neither fit for the land nor for the dunghill, but men throw it out. He who has ears to hear, let him hear!"* (NKJV)

Salt was essential to everyday living. It was used to add zest to food. It was also needed to preserve food and to be a cleansing agent. But if it became mixed with impurities, it would lose its value. Similarly, a disciple is unworthy if he or she comes with mixed motives and a less-than-sober renunciation of everything other than Christ.

Chapter Wrap-Up

- The Pharisees set a trap for Jesus at a Sabbath meal by putting a man with dropsy in front of him. Jesus healed the man and silenced the Pharisees. (Luke 14:1–6)

- Guests of the Pharisee elbowed their way to the seats of honor next to the host. Jesus said they should be humble and generous toward others. (Luke 14:7–14)

- The Pharisees understood that the reference to the feast related to their standing in God's kingdom. Jesus told a parable about a host whose guests made flimsy excuses not to come to his banquet. The host invited the poor and outcasts and they came. (Luke 14:15–24)

- Jesus told his followers that if they wanted to be his disciples they needed to count the cost and be totally committed to him. (Luke 14:25–35)

Study Questions

1. What attitude did Jesus expose in the Pharisees when he healed the man with dropsy?

2. What false attitudes did Jesus expose in the way (a) men chose seats at the dinner and (b) the host had chosen his guests?

3. In Jesus's parable of the great banquet, what was the significance to the Jewish people of the banquet? Who did the host invite in place of the guests who refused to come?

4. What standards did Jesus give for his disciples?

Luke 15 Lost and Found

Chapter Highlights:
- Saved Sheep
- Coined Celebration
- No Giving Up
- Race for Love
- Count Me Out!

Let's Get Started

Luke gives us a chapter that glows like a ring set with precious stones, for here Jesus tells three parables that give a sparkling revelation of his Father's heart of love. In each story something highly valued is lost, and the joy when it is recovered becomes a picture of the rejoicing in heaven when a lost person is found by the loving Father.

Jesus told his stories to a mixed audience. A large group of social outcasts gathered around him. On the outer edge stood Pharisees and experts in religion who not only despised the outcasts as sinners but also considered themselves superior to Jesus. Jesus's parables had a strong message to each listener—and to each of us today.

Saved Sheep

LUKE 15:1–2 *Then all the tax collectors and the sinners drew near to Him to hear Him. And the Pharisees and scribes complained, saying, "This Man receives sinners and eats with them." (NKJV)*

Pharisees and teachers of the law looked on with extreme distaste as they observed tax collectors and "sinners" flocking to Jesus and listening intently to his teaching. The Pharisees and teachers of the law had spent their lives observing every law and keeping separate from anything designated as unclean. They were horrified that Jesus mingled with the very people they considered to be both social and religious outcasts. They fumed as they watched him mingling with them and actually eating with them as if he enjoyed their company.

Jesus knew the complaints of his critics. Instead of judging them as they were judging him, Jesus told three parables that revealed his love and compassion for those who were despised—and for those who did the despising. How he longed for them to see that they too were lost and in need of being found by the Savior!

go to

love
1 Corinthians 13:7

sheep
Psalm 95:7; 100:3

lost
Isaiah 53:6

shepherd
Ezekiel 34:31

carried
Isaiah 46:3–4

Fall
Adam and Eve's first
disobedience to
God that plunged
all humankind into
sin

what others say

Gilbert Bilezikian

Because God is love, he created human life out of love. <u>Love</u>
bears all things, endures all things, and never ends. Therefore,
as horrible as it was, the **Fall** could not make God stop loving
the beings he had created in his image.[1]

Searching for Blacky

LUKE 15:3–7 *So He spoke this parable to them, saying: "What
man of you, having a hundred sheep, if he loses one of them, does
not leave the ninety-nine in the wilderness, and go after the one
which is lost until he finds it? And when he has found it, he lays
it on his shoulders, rejoicing. And when he comes home, he calls
together his friends and neighbors, saying to them, 'Rejoice with
me, for I have found my sheep which was lost!' I say to you that
likewise there will be more joy in heaven over one sinner who
repents than over ninety-nine just persons who need no repentance.* (NKJV)

Jesus used a common scenario to illustrate truth about God. A
shepherd led his flock to the sheepfold where they were protected as
they rested for the night (see Illustration #10). One hundred was a
common-sized flock. When the shepherd noticed he was missing
one sheep, he didn't say, "Oh well, ninety-nine is close enough." He
set out to find the lost sheep, leaving the ninety-nine secure in the
sheepfold, perhaps under the watch of a neighbor.

In case his listeners missed the point, Jesus made it clear. All who
heard the story were <u>sheep</u>. The <u>lost</u> sheep pictured a sinner who
repented because he knew he was lost. The <u>shepherd</u> was the Savior
who searched for him, gently lifted him on his strong shoulders, and
<u>carried</u> him to safety.

Notice that in this analogy Jesus initiated the search for the lost.
The idea is that God actively seeks sinners and wants to bring them
into relationship with him. And when he does, he throws a party to
celebrate. God is jubilant when the lost are saved. In heaven there is
more celebration over one sinner who repents than over ninety-nine
law-abiding "righteous" people who feel no need to be rescued by
the Savior.

key point

Luke understood the shepherd's unhesitating decision to search for the one missing sheep. What physician has not extended himself to relieve someone who was suffering, no matter what personal cost was involved? Luke identified with Jesus's compassion for the missing, who may not even be aware that he or she was missing, and the joy when that one was found and brought home.

Matthew 18:1–14 includes Jesus's parable in a different context. Jesus speaks of the loving concern his followers should have for young children. Children are significant to God—so much so that their angelic beings are constantly in his presence in heaven. The trust that children have, their unhesitating response to Jesus's love, is a quality that Jesus looks for in adult hearts. He warns of the consequences of leading children to sin. Then he tells the parable of the lost sheep to show that all his followers should be tireless in their efforts to seek and restore any little one who strays.

gospel harmony

what others say

Phyllis Kilbourn

Our heavenly Father fully understands the pain and fear of the world's suffering children, whatever difficult circumstances engulf them. I am convinced that his deepest heart-longing is to stir us, his people, to reach out with God-given compassion toward them—the youngest members of our world-wide family. We have the responsibility to bring them the message of God's redeeming love, holistic healing and hope.[2]

Coined Celebration

LUKE 15:8–10 *"Or what woman, having ten silver coins, if she loses one coin, does not light a lamp, sweep the house, and search carefully until she finds it? And when she has found it, she calls her friends and neighbors together, saying, 'Rejoice with me, for I have found the piece which I lost!' Likewise, I say to you, there is joy in the presence of the angels of God over one sinner who repents."* (NKJV)

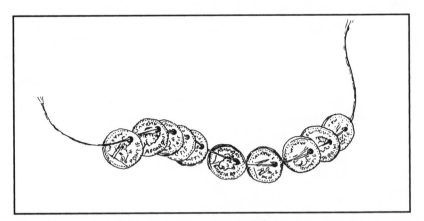

In Jesus's second parable, a woman had ten silver coins, each worth far more than their monetary value of a day's wage. These coins probably were her **dowry**, worn on her headdress (see Illustration #11). How much the woman valued her lost coin is reflected in her aggressive search.

Her house was dark with only a small window to allow light, so she lit a lamp, seized her broom, and carefully swept her house. She didn't stop for a coffee break or for a friendly chat with her neighbors. She swept and swept, turning over furniture and shaking out every cloth covering. She dropped to her knees and felt around the floor with her hands, all the time looking for a glint of light reflecting from the coin or listening for a whisper of its movement across the dirt floor. She did not give up until she found it! She had not recruited her friends to help her find it, but kept the loss to herself. Now her joy simply had to be expressed. A celebration was in order. She called her friends and neighbors to join her in marking the occasion of her great find.

No Giving Up

Jesus's parable made two points that must have astonished his listeners. First, God doesn't merely tolerate sinners and let them go their own way. He seeks to rescue them. Then, he doesn't give up when they do not respond to him. He keeps pursuing them. This was contrary to the Israelites' view of Jehovah the Lawgiver.

go to

estate
Deuteronomy
21:15–17

> **what others say**
>
> **Lawrence O. Richards**
>
> To God, people are a prize! We are important and valued, and the transformation of a single sinner brings joy, not only to God, but also to all who share his heart of love.[3]

Jesus calls his followers to be like the shepherd who went out to search for the lost sheep and to be like the woman who searched until she found her lost coin. Today he still asks his followers to care for all who need the Father's love and are willing to come to the Savior.

Homecoming

LUKE 15:11–16 *Then He said: "A certain man had two sons. And the younger of them said to his father, 'Father, give me the portion of goods that falls to me.' So he divided to them his livelihood. And not many days after, the younger son gathered all together, journeyed to a far country, and there wasted his possessions with prodigal living. But when he had spent all, there arose a severe famine in that land, and he began to be in want. Then he went and joined himself to a citizen of that country, and he sent him into his fields to feed swine. And he would gladly have filled his stomach with the pods that the swine ate, and no one gave him anything.* (NKJV)

In Jesus's third parable, what was lost was not an animal or a valued coin but a son who deliberately chose to be lost. He made a callous decision to ask his father to give him the part of the estate that he would receive when his father died. The father divided his estate in the way custom demanded. As soon as the younger son got his hands on the money, he took off, probably for the bright lights of the city.

go to

pigs
Leviticus 11:7;
Deuteronomy 14:8

pods
from a carob tree,
which, when ripe,
are filled with a
sweet syrup

Once there, he lived it up, and before long he had wasted all his money and was in need. Food was hard to find because the country was in the grip of a famine, and jobs were so scarce he had to feed pigs. Evidently a food allowance was not part of his employment contract. He was so hungry that he wished he could eat the **pods** that made up the pigs' diet.

Without question, the younger son had gone from riches to rags. As a Jew, having any contact with pigs was detestable. He had hit bottom.

what others say

The Bible Knowledge Commentary

The hearers immediately would have understood the point of the story. Jesus had been criticized for associating with sinners. The sinners were considered people who were far away from God, squandering their lives in riotous living. In contrast with the younger son, the older son continued to remain with the father and did not engage in such practices.[4]

Is McDad Hiring?

LUKE 15:17–20a *But when he came to himself, he said, 'How many of my father's hired servants have bread enough and to spare, and I perish with hunger! I will arise and go to my father, and will say to him, "Father, I have sinned against heaven and before you, and I am no longer worthy to be called your son. Make me like one of your hired servants."' And he arose and came to his father.* (NKJV)

The younger son was at the end of his rope and in despair. "He came to himself" implies repentance. He knew he had no right to be treated as a son, but he reasoned that being a servant in his father's household would be better than living where he was. The servants in his father's house had more than enough to eat.

As the son traveled toward home, he rehearsed the words he would say to his father. He was courageous enough to admit that he had sinned and to request a chance to come home and be treated like a hired man. The son assumed he could not be forgiven, but hoped to be tolerated.

stoned
Deuteronomy
21:18–21

> ## what others say
>
> ### Henri J. M. Nouwen
>
> The prodigal's return is full of ambiguities. He is traveling in the right direction, but what confusion! He admits that he was unable to make it on his own and confesses that he would get better treatment as a slave in his father's home than as an outcast in a foreign land, but he is still far from trusting his father's love. . . . There is repentance, but not a repentance in the light of the immense love of a forgiving God. It is a self-serving repentance that offers the possibility of survival.[5]

Race for Love

LUKE 15:20b *But when he was still a great way off, his father saw him and had compassion, and ran and fell on his neck and kissed him. (NKJV)*

What a beautiful picture! The father was waiting, looking for his son, and recognized him while he was still at a distance. According to the Old Testament law, the son should have been <u>stoned</u> to death because of the disgrace he had brought on the family and the community. However, with a heart overflowing with compassion for his boy, the father ran up to his son, embraced him and kissed him.

> ## what others say
>
> ### John Piper
>
> Well-to-do, dignified, aristocratic, aging men don't run, they walk. They keep their composure. They show that they are on top of their emotions. But not in Jesus's story about God's joy over his people.[6]

Party Hearty!

LUKE 15:21–24 *And the son said to him, 'Father, I have sinned against heaven and in your sight, and am no longer worthy to be called your son.' But the father said to his servants, 'Bring out the best robe and put it on him, and put a ring on his hand and sandals on his feet. And bring the fatted calf here and kill it, and let us eat and be merry; for this my son was dead and is alive again; he was lost and is found.' And they began to be merry. (NKJV)*

Before the son could spill his whole speech, the father interrupted. He could not contain himself. He called to his servants to make

go to

grace
Ephesians 2:1–10

grace
God's action taken
to meet human
need

preparations for a grand celebration. First, he called for the robe, the ring, and sandals for his son—all designed to confirm his status as son. The robe was a ceremonial garment reserved for honored guests. The ring may have been a signet ring, which meant the wearer had authority. Since only slaves went barefoot, the shoes marked the son as a freeman.

Then, the father called for the fattened calf to be killed. Such a calf was kept for special occasions, and the father showed by this action that he felt his lost son's return was worthy of its use.

His son had been as good as dead and now was alive. He was lost, and now was found. The father's joy spread throughout the household as the celebration began.

> **what others say**
>
> **Max Lucado**
>
> <u>Grace</u> is created by God and given to man. . . . On the basis of this point alone, Christianity is set apart from any other religion in the world. [John Stott says,] "No other system, ideology or religion proclaims a free forgiveness and a new life to those who have done nothing to deserve it but deserve judgment instead."[7]

God, the loving heavenly Father, never gives up waiting for lost ones to come home. He waits to welcome each repentant sinner with open arms.

Mysterious Music

LUKE 15:25–27 *Now his older son was in the field. And as he came and drew near to the house, he heard music and dancing. So he called one of the servants and asked what these things meant. And he said to him, 'Your brother has come, and because he has received him safe and sound, your father has killed the fatted calf.'* (NKJV)

The older brother had been out working in the field and was unaware of what had happened. As he approached the house, he heard music and dancing performed by entertainers hired for the party. He asked a servant, "What's up with the music?"

The servant relayed the news in a straightforward style, saying the younger brother was safe and sound.

Count Me Out!

> LUKE 15:28–30 *But he was angry and would not go in. Therefore his father came out and pleaded with him. So he answered and said to his father, 'Lo, these many years I have been serving you; I never transgressed your commandment at any time; and yet you never gave me a young goat, that I might make merry with my friends. But as soon as this son of yours came, who has devoured your livelihood with harlots, you killed the fatted calf for him.'* (NKJV)

The older brother was so angry he refused to join the merrymakers. His father left the party to reason with him. But all the father heard in response were scathing complaints against both himself and his son.

"It's not fair!" the older son said. "For all these years I have done the backbreaking work and have never once disobeyed you. Yet you never once gave even a little party for me and my friends. Yet now this deadbeat brother comes home having squandered all your money and disgraced our family, and you have the nerve to put on this big celebration. You should be ashamed of yourself. It isn't fair to me, and I won't go in."

The older brother's remarks show a slew of bad attitudes—self-righteousness, pride, disrespect toward his father, discontent, and unforgiveness.

---

what others say

Henri J. M. Nouwen

Outwardly, the elder son was faultless. But when confronted by his father's joy at the return of his younger brother, a dark power erupts in him and boils to the surface. Suddenly, there becomes glaringly visible a resentful, proud, unkind, selfish person, one that had remained deeply hidden, even though it had been growing stronger and more powerful over the years.[8]

Don't Worry, Be Happy

> LUKE 15:31–32 *And he said to him, 'Son, you are always with me, and all that I have is yours. It was right that we should make merry and be glad, for your brother was dead and is alive again, and was lost and is found.'"* (NKJV)

love
John 5:1–2

The father tried to point out that the issue wasn't how hard his older son had worked nor how wrong his younger son had been to waste the money—the issue was love and belonging. The older son had his father's love. He had the security of knowing that his father's resources were available to him. In other words, he had it all. Unfortunately, he did not value it for himself and did not want his wayward younger brother to have it either.

The Pharisees couldn't miss that the wayward son was like the publicans and sinners they so despised. They must have been astonished at the father's joy when the son returned even to the point of welcoming him into the family as an honored member.

But that was not the end of the story. Jesus went on to tell about the older brother, giving an amazingly accurate picture of those Pharisees. They worked hard to please God, obeying most of his laws and many others that they had added. They were critical of Jesus for associating with the lost and did not want to have anything to do with those who became converted.

The Pharisees had great pride in their strict adherence to the laws that governed every part of their lives. They abhorred sinners and wanted to stay as far away from them as they could. Through his parables Jesus showed that God's heart overflows with joy when anyone comes to him, and all heaven joins him in celebration.

The implications are clear for us today. As individuals we may share the attitude of the Pharisees as we discount certain people and discriminate against them in subtle or even overt ways. If we take Jesus's parables to heart, we cannot be indifferent to people whose lifestyles offend us, who are locked into poverty and hopelessness, who are chained by addictions, and who are labeled as dropouts or criminals. Nor can we look down on the self-righteous who sense no need of a Savior. Jesus seeks and welcomes each person—and so should we.

God tells us that when we truly <u>love</u> him, we will love and welcome each sinner who repents. In fact, we can measure our love for God by the love we have for the "least" in his kingdom and by the commitment in our hearts to obey his Word.

Chapter Wrap-Up

- The Pharisees were critical of Jesus for associating with "sinners," whom they despised. (Luke 15:1–2)

- Jesus told parables about a shepherd who searched for one lost sheep and about a woman who searched for a lost coin. Both stories showed how God rejoiced when sinners entered his kingdom. (Luke 15:3–10)

- Jesus's parable about a son who wasted his inheritance, repented, and returned home illustrated how God welcomed sinners who came to him. (Luke 15:11–27)

- The older brother's anger at his father's celebration upon the younger brother's return paralleled the Pharisees' contempt for sinners and Jesus's love for them. (Luke 15:28–32)

Study Questions

1. What prompted Jesus to give his three parables about the sheep, coin, and son?

2. What do we learn about God from Jesus's portrayal of the shepherd?

3. What does the woman's feeling about the lost coin tell us about God's attitude toward lost people?

4. In what ways are we like the younger son?

5. In what ways may we be like the older brother?

6. What do we learn about God from Jesus's portrayal of the father?

Luke 16 Money Matters

Let's Get Started

Money—or the lack of it—seems to influence every aspect of the world—whether at the gas pump or in the stock market. Jesus gives another perspective. Money—how we view it and how we use it—has direct bearing on what we will face in eternity. After death we cannot come back and make amends for bad choices. Therefore, Jesus said, we should use our money today to make deposits in our heavenly bank account.

Jesus addressed the disciples in the first part of chapter 16. They had left secure jobs and a stable future to follow him. Still, their attitude toward money needed some tweaking. In the second part of the chapter, Jesus included the Pharisees, who sneered at his no-spin warnings about their love of money.

Get Forever Friends

LUKE 16:1–4 *He also said to His disciples: "There was a certain rich man who had a steward, and an accusation was brought to him that this man was wasting his goods. So he called him and said to him, 'What is this I hear about you? Give an account of your stewardship, for you can no longer be steward.' Then the steward said within himself, 'What shall I do? For my master is taking the stewardship away from me. I cannot dig; I am ashamed to beg. I have resolved what to do, that when I am put out of the stewardship, they may receive me into their houses.'* (NKJV)

Jesus told of a manager who had been entrusted with the affairs of a rich man. His duty was to watch over the accounts so that they would make a profit. Instead, he carelessly wasted the money. When the rich man learned of his manager's mismanagement, he called for an audit and gave him a pink slip. Knowing he was in trouble, the manager decided on a crisis scheme that would provide him with friends who could help him out when he was unemployed.

How to Win Friends

> LUKE 16:5–7 *So he called every one of his master's debtors to him, and said to the first, 'How much do you owe my master?' And he said, 'A hundred measures of oil.' So he said to him, 'Take your bill, and sit down quickly and write fifty.' Then he said to another, 'And how much do you owe?' So he said, 'A hundred measures of wheat.' And he said to him, 'Take your bill, and write eighty.'* (NKJV)

The manager had to work quickly and secretly while he still had his job. Employer loyalty, ethics, and honesty were thrown out the window. One by one he called in each person who owed his master and authorized a significant reduction in each one's debt. In a matter of hours he gained friends who would remember him long after he was relieved of his responsibilities as manager.

what others say

William Barclay

[The steward] falsified the entries in the books so that the debtors were debited with far less than they owed. This would have two effects. First, the debtors would be grateful to him; and second, and much more effective, he had involved the debtors in his own misdemeanors, and, if the worst came to the worst, he was now in a strong position to exercise a little judicious blackmail![1]

You Got Me

> LUKE 16:8–9 *So the master commended the unjust steward because he had dealt shrewdly. For the sons of this world are more shrewd in their generation than the sons of light. And I say to you, make friends for yourselves by unrighteous mammon, that when you fail, they may receive you into an everlasting home.* (NKJV)

The manager had probably mismanaged the rich man's wealth in other ways before he reduced people's debts. Nowhere in the passage does it say that the manager was dishonest by reducing the debts. It's possible that the debts may have been questionable in the first place. Jews were not supposed to charge interest to fellow Jews. But "smart" businessmen on the street reasoned their way around this by saying the law's intent was to protect the poor. If a borrower had a little wheat or oil, he was not destitute and therefore could be charged interest, payable in wheat and oil.

When the manager canceled the debts, he put the owner in a tough spot. If the owner protested the loss of income from interest, he would appear to be acting unlawfully. The best thing the owner could do was put on a fake smile and congratulate the manager who had outsmarted him. The manager had made a quick decision in a time of crisis and used money to help himself and others!

The people <u>of the light</u> could learn a lesson from the people of this world. The dishonest manager worked cleverly to gain friends for his own benefit. People of the light, who have all eternity ahead, should use their gifts and resources to gain friends who will enjoy eternity with them.

How tirelessly do we work to ensure that a host of friends will be in heaven because we have thoughtfully and generously invested our resources in relieving the distress of poverty and disease and in spreading the gospel message around the world?

of the light
Ephesians 5:8–10

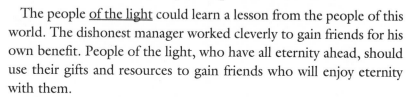

> **what others say**
>
> **Charles R. Swindoll**
>
> Examine your heart. Nobody but you can do this. Open that private vault and ask several hard questions, like:
>   Is my giving proportionate to my income?
>   Am I motivated by guilt . . . or by contagious joy?
>   If someone else knew the level of my giving to God's work, would I be a model to follow?
>   Have I prayed about giving . . . or am I just an impulsive responder?[2]

Put God First

LUKE 16:10–12 *He who is faithful in what is least is faithful also in much; and he who is unjust in what is least is unjust also in much. Therefore if you have not been faithful in the unrighteous mammon, who will commit to your trust the true riches? And if you have not been faithful in what is another man's, who will give you what is your own? (NKJV)*

Jesus has a word for us all. Whatever we have, whether it is little or much, must be handled with faithfulness. If we are not faithful in handling matters of this life, who will trust us with spiritual wealth?

And if we are not faithful in handling the affairs of another, who will trust us with our own wealth? Never forget, we are accountable to the one we serve.

Craving money lies at the bottom of all kinds of temptation and wrong actions. God gives us his perspective on money, both the good and the bad:

key point

- We should be careful not to love money but to be content with what we have. God's presence in our lives is of far greater value than a big bank account (see Hebrews 13:5–6).

- Money is a gift from God for our enjoyment and generous sharing, which lays up treasure in the life to come (see 1 Timothy 6:17–19).

- We should handle money as a trust for which we will need to give an account (see 1 Corinthians 4:2).

- Having money allows us to do good to all people, especially to believers (see Galatians 6:9–10).

- God's love and generosity to us is a model for us to express self-sacrificing generosity to people who have needs (see 1 John 3:15–18).

- God loves us when we give cheerfully and enables us to be generous so that he receives praise (see 2 Corinthians 9:6–15).

<u>One Boss Is Enough</u>

LUKE 16:13–15 No servant can serve two masters; for either he will hate the one and love the other, or else he will be loyal to the one and despise the other. You cannot serve God and mammon."

Now the Pharisees, who were lovers of money, also heard all these things, and they derided Him. And He said to them, "You are those who justify yourselves before men, but God knows your hearts. For what is highly esteemed among men is an abomination in the sight of God. (NKJV)

Jesus pointed out to the Pharisees that they were attempting something impossible. They were trying to serve both God and money—which was pulling them in opposite directions. They hated to hear this. They had a reputation to keep up. They had convinced themselves and the common people that their wealth proved they had God's stamp of approval. They worked hard for the admiration of people, but in their hearts they loved the power and prestige of money. Jesus saw through them and said plainly that God detested their attitudes.

God will never reject anyone who works hard to please him. The Pharisees would claim this to be a fact. But Jesus did not agree. Humans cannot set up the standard for what pleases God. Only he can do so, and Jesus spelled this out clearly.

No Divorce over Dinner

> LUKE 16:16–18 *The law and the prophets were until John. Since that time the kingdom of God has been preached, and everyone is pressing into it. And it is easier for heaven and earth to pass away than for one tittle of the law to fail. Whoever divorces his wife and marries another commits adultery; and whoever marries her who is divorced from her husband commits adultery.* (NKJV)

Although the Pharisees sneered at Jesus, he went right on with his verbal attack. Jesus said the Law and the Prophets (longhand for the Old Testament) were faithfully proclaimed until John the Baptist came to announce the good news of the kingdom of God. However, Jesus consistently claimed that the Old Testament would be <u>fulfilled</u> and that the gospel of the kingdom of God did not **negate** the Old Testament. Jesus said his coming did not do away with the Old Testament.

While the Pharisees claimed to stand firmly on the Old Testament law, they broke it regularly. Jesus gave an example of laws they broke that carried over into the new kingdom of God. They were lax about applying the Old Testament laws about divorce because they wanted the approval of the people. Some rabbis taught that a man could divorce his wife for something so minor as burning his dinner.

Jesus used divorce to illustrate a law that transcended the Old Testament law and his gospel of the kingdom of God. Matthew and Mark provide more of Jesus's teaching about divorce. See Matthew 5:31–32; 19:1–12; and Mark 10:11–12.

fulfilled
Matthew 5:17–18

negate
cancel, cause to be ineffective

gospel harmony

A Have and a Have-Not

LUKE 16:19–21 *"There was a certain rich man who was clothed in purple and fine linen and fared sumptuously every day. But there was a certain beggar named Lazarus, full of sores, who was laid at his gate, desiring to be fed with the crumbs which fell from the rich man's table. Moreover the dogs came and licked his sores. (NKJV)*

Jesus drew a picture of stark contrast: a rich man living at the height of luxury and a beggar existing in the depth of misery. The two were in daily eyesight of one another. The rich man's purple robes identified him as having high rank and much money. The purple dye, actually a deep crimson color with shades from red to blue, came from shellfish gathered from the floor of the eastern Mediterranean.

This parable is unique to Luke. As a physician Luke was interested in the plight of the poor and disabled. The poor were stripped of their dignity and were dependent on the compassion of others. Lazarus had to be carried to his place at the rich man's gate. There he lay, unable to help himself. People who passed by him ignored his helplessness, offering neither food nor medication for his open sores. His requests for leftovers from the rich man's table were ignored. His only companions were unclean dogs who repulsively licked his sores.

key point

The Pharisees regarded their resources as an indication that God had blessed them because of their strict adherence to the laws—many of which did not come from God but had been formulated by men. Jesus's parable proves that wealth is not necessarily proof of God's favor.

Role Reversal

LUKE 16:22–24 *So it was that the beggar died, and was carried by the angels to Abraham's bosom. The rich man also died and was buried. And being in torments in Hades, he lifted up his eyes and saw Abraham afar off, and Lazarus in his bosom. Then he cried and said, 'Father Abraham, have mercy on me, and send Lazarus that he may dip the tip of his finger in water and cool my tongue; for I am tormented in this flame.' (NKJV)*

Death changed everything. The beggar was carried by angels to lie in **paradise** at **Abraham's bosom**, whereas the rich man woke up in torment in **Hades**. The rich man looked up, recognizing Lazarus as the beggar who used to lie outside his gate. It is interesting that the two men are again within eyesight of one another—or at least the rich man could see the former beggar. The rich man called to Father Abraham to have pity on him. The rich man thought he could order people around as he had in life, so he asked to have Lazarus run an errand for him.

paradise
location of the righteous dead awaiting resurrection

Abraham's bosom
metaphor for an honored place in paradise

Hades
Greek: *Hades*, the place where the dead await final judgment

No Second Chances

LUKE 16:25–26 *But Abraham said, 'Son, remember that in your lifetime you received your good things, and likewise Lazarus evil things; but now he is comforted and you are tormented. And besides all this, between us and you there is a great gulf fixed, so that those who want to pass from here to you cannot, nor can those from there pass to us.' (NKJV)*

Abraham reminded the rich man that he had enjoyed good things in life while Lazarus had endured poverty and affliction. Now Lazarus was in comfort while the rich man was in misery. The rich man had chosen material wealth and a life of ease instead of spending time in the things of God and caring for others. But there was no way to reverse things. There are no second chances after death.

We may think we have lived a good life, believing we have not done evil deeds. But at our final judgment, we may discover that we have not done a host of good things we ought to have done. Like the rich man, we may have ignored some of the good we should have done right at our doors—our spouses, our kids, our in-laws, our neighbors.

Ghostly Request

LUKE 16:27–31 *Then he said, 'I beg you therefore, father, that you would send him to my father's house, for I have five brothers, that he may testify to them, lest they also come to this place of torment.' Abraham said to him, 'They have Moses and the prophets; let them hear them.' And he said, 'No, father Abraham; but if one goes to them from the dead, they will repent.' But he said to him, 'If they do not hear Moses and the*

go to

God's command
Leviticus 19:18

prophets, neither will they be persuaded though one rise from the dead.'" (NKJV)

The rich man accepted that Abraham could do nothing to relieve his misery in hell. Then he thought of his five brothers and asked Abraham to send Lazarus to warn them so they could avoid his plight. Notice the rich man is still thinking like a rich earthling who has errand boys!

Abraham reminded him that they already had the warnings of Moses and the prophets. The rich man thought something more spectacular would arrest their attention—a ghost or a talking dead person. But Abraham said that if they did not listen to the messengers God had already sent, they would not be persuaded even if someone spoke from the dead.

The words were sadly prophetic. Only a short while later Jesus died and rose from the dead and the Jews still rejected him. Those who reject the teachings of the Bible also reject the display of miracles done by Christ.

Both men in Jesus's parable faced eternity, but from opposite points of view.

Lazarus's name means "God, the Helper." Though this seemed a cruel mockery, Lazarus hung on in silent trust, and his faith was rewarded when he died. The rich man used his money selfishly. He focused only on his comforts, ignoring <u>God's command</u> to love his neighbor Lazarus.

The implications are clear for us today. Whether we have little or much, we are responsible to God for the money we have. How we use it has implications that will affect us after death.

Money matters—it exposes our values.

something to ponder

what others say

Lawrence O. Richards

The choices we make during this life do fix our destiny. Those who wish can scoff at Jesus' warnings of the corrupting influence of wealth. But many have pushed heaven away while grabbing greedily for this world's worthless gold.[3]

Chapter Wrap-Up

- Jesus told a parable of a dishonest manager who reduced some debts before he was fired. These people would be inclined to help him once he was out of work. The owner commended him for his shrewdness in looking out for his future. (Luke 16:1–9)

- Jesus taught that we cannot serve both God and money. Our faithfulness in using money wisely, especially with eternal rewards in view, reveals our character. (Luke 16:10–15)

- The Pharisees sneered at Jesus's teaching. They could not receive it because of their slavish love of money and their desire to impress others. (Luke 16:16–18)

- Jesus told the parable of the rich man and Lazarus to point out the importance of listening to God's Word now and acting on it, because there will be no opportunity after death to make things right. (Luke 16:19–31)

Study Questions

1. What can we learn from Jesus's parable of the dishonest manager?

2. In what way can money—whether we have little or much—be an acid test of our character?

3. Why were the Pharisees blind to Jesus's teaching about the kingdom of God?

4. What can we learn from Jesus's parable of the rich man and Lazarus?

Luke 17 Heart Attitudes

Chapter Highlights
- **Not Duty-Free**
- **Multiple Forgiveness**
- **Attitude of Gratitude**
- **Lone Thanksgiving**
- **Alert or Inert?**

Let's Get Started

We value our independence. Beginning in the <u>Garden of Eden</u> when Adam and Eve chose to <u>disobey God</u>, people have clung to the idea that they can make it on their own. We do not want to be accountable to anyone or responsible for anyone else.

Jesus says this is a false perspective. We are not islands. We are interconnected links in a chain. What we do impacts others, and we bear responsibility for that. Our standing with God has an impact on how we treat others. Jesus brings us back to where it all started in the Garden of Eden—we were created to live in a loving, dependent relationship with God that influences all our interactions with him and with others.

Garden of Eden
Genesis 2

disobey God
Genesis 3:1–13

Not Duty-Free

> LUKE 17:1–3a *Then He said to the disciples, "It is impossible that no offenses should come, but woe to him through whom they do come! It would be better for him if a millstone were hung around his neck, and he were thrown into the sea, than that he should offend one of these little ones. Take heed to yourselves.* (NKJV)

Jesus pinpointed a problem most people want to overlook. A person may act in such a way that he or she leads others into sin. Of course that person wants to avoid any blame, but Jesus says that cannot be avoided. Punishment is certain. Who wants to be weighted down in the sea with a heavy stone used for grinding grain? Jesus said that the punishment awaiting such an offender is worse than that—worse than physical death!

Jesus has special concern for "little ones." These are children and believers who are immature in their faith. Older believers, especially teachers and leaders, need to be careful that their actions and attitudes do not cause little ones to fall into sin.

go to

Lord's Prayer
Luke 11:2–4;
Matthew 6:9–15

test
Matthew 18:35

pardon
Ephesians 4:32

Multiple Forgiveness

> LUKE 17:3b–4 *If your brother sins against you, rebuke him; and if he repents, forgive him. And if he sins against you seven times in a day, and seven times in a day returns to you, saying, 'I repent,' you shall forgive him."* (NKJV)

Jesus then told his disciples how to handle people who wrong them. Confront them! Compassionately rebuke them. If they repent, then forgive them. If they repeat the wrongdoing again and again and come back to request forgiveness, forgive them again and again. In other words, forgiveness is to be done so often it becomes a habit. It is not up to the believer to decide to forgive based on the genuineness of the offender's repentance.

---

what others say

J. C. Ryle

There are few Christian duties which the New Testament dwells on so frequently as forgiving other people. It has a prominent place in the Lord's Prayer. The only thing we do in the whole prayer is to forgive those who have sinned against us. This is a test for being forgiven ourselves. The person who cannot forgive his neighbor the few trifling offenses he may have committed against him can know nothing about the free and full pardon which Christ offers us.[1]

Pumping Faith Instead of Iron

> LUKE 17:5–6 *And the apostles said to the Lord, "Increase our faith." So the Lord said, "If you have faith as a mustard seed, you can say to this mulberry tree, 'Be pulled up by the roots and be planted in the sea,' and it would obey you.* (NKJV)

Which is more difficult: to rebuke an erring person or to forgive that person who has wronged you? The standard Jesus set was so staggering that the disciples could only ask that he would increase their faith so they could fulfill his demands. They wanted a heaping bushel basket of faith, but Jesus said it need not be larger than a tiny mustard seed.

How should we deal with a standard Jesus set that is far beyond our capacity to fulfill? Some may complain while others choose to ignore that standard, explaining that Jesus probably didn't mean his words to be taken literally. The disciples did not take that route. They wisely asked Jesus to increase their faith! And that's the only way to receive the strength to obey what Jesus asks us to do. The size of our faith is not the point. Rather it is the power of the One in whom we place our faith. Faith is the key to obeying Jesus's commands.

<u>No Bragging Rights</u>

LUKE 17:7–10 *And which of you, having a servant plowing or tending sheep, will say to him when he has come in from the field, 'Come at once and sit down to eat'? But will he not rather say to him, 'Prepare something for my supper, and gird yourself and serve me till I have eaten and drunk, and afterward you will eat and drink'? Does he thank that servant because he did the things that were commanded him? I think not. So likewise you, when you have done all those things which you are commanded, say, 'We are unprofitable servants. We have done what was our duty to do.'" (NKJV)*

Jesus outlined his high standards for disciples. They were to exercise caution not to cause anyone to sin. They were to confront and rebuke those who chose to sin. They were to exercise unwavering forgiveness. They were to apply faith, not as a *cognitive* virtue but as a trust that could be employed in fulfilling Jesus's requirements.

Then, before they could feel smug or self-righteous about measuring up to Jesus's standards, he told them that even when they have fulfilled his requirements they will have done only their duty.

There are two sides to the coin of following Jesus. Here he shows one side—no matter how faithfully we serve him, we will always be unworthy disciples who at best are only doing what he asks of us.

The other side of the coin is the reward he gives—eternal blessings for all who serve him faithfully. Paul wrote of a crown <u>of righteousness</u>, which would be awarded to him. Peter wrote of a crown <u>of glory</u>. And John recorded Jesus's promise that he will bring his <u>reward</u> with him when he comes.

of righteousness
2 Timothy 4:7–8

of glory
1 Peter 5:4

reward
Revelation 22:12

go to

afar off
Leviticus 13:45–46;
Numbers 5:2

outcasts
people rejected
from living at home
or in society

what others say

Dallas Willard

An obsession merely with doing all God commands may be
the very thing that rules out being the kind of person that he
calls us to be. . . . The watchword of the worthy servant is not
mere obedience but love, from which appropriate obedience
naturally flows.[2]

Attitude of Gratitude

LUKE 17:11–13 *Now it happened as He went to Jerusalem that
He passed through the midst of Samaria and Galilee. Then as
He entered a certain village, there met Him ten men who were
lepers, who stood afar off. And they lifted up their voices and
said, "Jesus, Master, have mercy on us!"* (NKJV)

As Jesus made his way to Jesualem, he traveled along the border
between Samaria and Galilee. On the outskirts of a village ten men
tried to arrest his attention. They stood <u>afar off</u> from him, required
of **outcasts** because they had leprosy. In unison they called out,
"Jesus, Master, have mercy on us!"

what others say

William Barclay

There was no specified distance at which they should stand,
but we know that at least one authority laid it down that, when
he was to windward of a healthy person, the leper should
stand at least fifty yards away. Nothing could better show the
utter isolation in which lepers lived.[3]

Lone Thanksgiving

LUKE 17:14–19 *So when He saw them, He said to them, "Go,
show yourselves to the priests." And so it was that as they went,
they were cleansed. And one of them, when he saw that he was
healed, returned, and with a loud voice glorified God, and fell
down on his face at His feet, giving Him thanks. And he was a
Samaritan. So Jesus answered and said, "Were there not ten
cleansed? But where are the nine? Were there not any found who
returned to give glory to God except this foreigner?" And He
said to him, "Arise, go your way. Your faith has made you well."*
(NKJV)

Jesus did not respond by telling the lepers they were healed. Instead, he told them to go and show themselves to the priest as the law <u>commanded</u> those who had been healed of the disease. As the men obeyed in faith, they were healed.

Suddenly one man broke from the little procession. This man hurried back toward Jesus, calling out his thanksgiving to God.

He fell at Jesus's feet to express his thanks—and he was a Samaritan, one viewed by Jews as least deserving of Jesus's miracle. Jesus expressed amazement that since all ten men had been healed, only one returned to praise God. Jesus commended him.

While all ten men had received physical healing, only this Samaritan had faith for spiritual healing as well. We know this because Jesus used an all-encompassing word for spiritual and physical healing when he said the thankful leper was "made well." The other lepers were merely "cleansed" or healed of the filth of leprosy.

commanded
Leviticus 13:19;
14:1–11

thanks
1 Thessalonians
5:18;
Hebrews 13:15–16

glorifies
exalting God
through praise and
thanksgiving

> ## what others say
>
> ### Darryl DelHousaye
>
> Thanksgiving in everything is the key to joy. The experience of joy is all about well-being, a sense of security, a deep rest, the absence of fear. It's enjoyment! The absence of thanksgiving is what makes joy fade. It's God's design for us to give thanks lest any of our joy slip away.[4]

Luke had the practiced eye of a physician who could spot the patient most likely to regain good health. An attitude of appreciation and thankfulness goes far to ensure a full recovery. Sincere thankfulness to God banishes lethargy and depression that so frequently lingers even after a doctor has pronounced a patient well enough to resume a healthy lifestyle. Thankfulness for blessings brings additional blessings.

Is a thankful heart an endangered species? Only one man in ten expressed thanks to Jesus for healing. What would be the ratio today? Giving <u>thanks</u> to God isn't just a polite ritual—it delights God's heart and **glorifies** him.

John the Baptist
Luke 7:18–23

day of the Lord
2 Peter 3:10

If It Had Teeth, It Could Bite You!

> LUKE 17:20–21 *Now when He was asked by the Pharisees when the kingdom of God would come, He answered them and said, "The kingdom of God does not come with observation; nor will they say, 'See here!' or 'See there!' For indeed, the kingdom of God is within you." (NKJV)*

The nation of Israel had long looked for God to establish his kingdom on earth. Jesus had spoken of the kingdom, but the Pharisees were not seeing the signs they were expecting. They asked him, as John the Baptist had asked earlier, when the kingdom would come.

Jesus knew the Pharisees were looking for a political leader who would rescue them from the domination of Rome. He told them that they should not look for signs because the kingdom of God was already in their presence! The words "within you" could be better translated "among you." The unbelief that they harbored in their hearts blinded them from recognizing that their King had come.

Some of the concepts Jesus introduces in this passage are also found in Matthew 24 and Mark 13. However, the contexts in which Jesus spoke are different. In Luke he answers the question raised by the Pharisees, whereas in Matthew and Mark he is speaking only to his disciples. What Jesus had to say about his coming kingdom was so important that he no doubt taught about it on more than one occasion.

Suddenly Jesus

> LUKE 17:22–25 *Then He said to the disciples, "The days will come when you will desire to see one of the days of the Son of Man, and you will not see it. And they will say to you, 'Look here!' or 'Look there!' Do not go after them or follow them. For as the lightning that flashes out of one part under heaven shines to the other part under heaven, so also the Son of Man will be in His day. But first He must suffer many things and be rejected by this generation. (NKJV)*

Jesus then directed his teaching to the disciples. "One of the days of the Son of Man" probably refers to the day of the Lord. That event will not be secret. No one will need to peer into corners to find it. One day Jesus will come with a sudden, majestic display of lightning that will flash across the globe. But before that happens, he must suffer rejection and death on the cross at the hands of those he came to save.

go to

heavenlies
Ephesians 2:6

citizenship
Philippians 3:20

sing
Revelation 4:8

Flood
Genesis 6–8

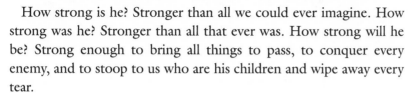

what others say

R. C. Sproul

As we look about [God's] world and see the play not yet through, we must focus on the ending. Paul tells us we are even now seated in the <u>heavenlies</u> with Christ Jesus and our <u>citizenship</u> is in heaven. We should, then, even here, <u>sing</u> with choirs of angels, "Holy, holy, holy, Lord God Almighty, who was and is and is to come!"

He is coming. And he will come in all his strength and in all his glory. Even so, come Lord Jesus.[5]

How strong is he? Stronger than all we could ever imagine. How strong was he? Stronger than all that ever was. How strong will he be? Strong enough to bring all things to pass, to conquer every enemy, and to stoop to us who are his children and wipe away every tear.

Live in a state of readiness for Jesus's return.

Alert or Inert?

> LUKE 17:26–27 *And as it was in the days of Noah, so it will be also in the days of the Son of Man: They ate, they drank, they married wives, they were given in marriage, until the day that Noah entered the ark, and the flood came and destroyed them all.* (NKJV)

Christ will come again to set up his kingdom. That is certain. When he will come has not been revealed to us. The faithful will live "on alert," ready for his arrival, but the unbelieving will be living "business as usual," assuming that life, as they know it, will go on forever.

To illustrate his point Jesus gave his hearers a history lesson. For 120 years as Noah built the ark, he warned people that God's judgment would come. But up until the <u>Flood</u> came, they refused to believe him and occupied themselves with the pleasures of life. Their actions showed their complete indifference to God, and when the Flood came suddenly, it caught them by surprise.

gospel harmony

Matthew 24:37–39 also includes Jesus's reference to the days of Noah, tying the attitudes of the unbelieving to those of people before Jesus returns. Much as the people in Noah's day were preoccupied with their daily affairs and deaf to Noah's warnings of coming judgment, so people will be so busy with the here and now that they will not heed the warning to be ready for Jesus's return.

Stop, Drop, And Run

LUKE 17:28–37 *Likewise as it was also in the days of Lot: They ate, they drank, they bought, they sold, they planted, they built; but on the day that Lot went out of Sodom it rained fire and brimstone from heaven and destroyed them all. Even so will it be in the day when the Son of Man is revealed. In that day, he who is on the housetop, and his goods are in the house, let him not come down to take them away. And likewise the one who is in the field, let him not turn back. Remember Lot's wife. Whoever seeks to save his life will lose it, and whoever loses his life will preserve it. I tell you, in that night there will be two men in one bed: the one will be taken and the other will be left. Two women will be grinding together: the one will be taken and the other left. Two men will be in the field: the one will be taken and the other left." And they answered and said to Him, "Where, Lord?" So He said to them, "Wherever the body is, there the eagles will be gathered together." (NKJV)*

Jesus pointed out that his coming will reveal what distinguishes people who seem to be very much alike. They are all occupied with everyday affairs, but those who live for the present will be preoccupied with the things of this world. Those who live for eternity will be ready to drop everything to welcome his coming.

go to

When <u>Lot's wife</u> ran away from the <u>destruction of Sodom</u>, she looked back with longing for the possessions that had made life precious to her. She became a pillar of salt. Jesus said, "Don't make the same mistake. Run toward my kingdom, not away from it."

Lot's wife
Genesis 19:26

destruction of Sodom
Genesis 19:12–26

Chapter Wrap-Up

- Jesus warned that occasions to sin would certainly come, but that we should be careful not to cause anyone—especially children or new believers—to sin. (Luke 17:1–3a)

- When someone sins against us, we should rebuke him and forgive him—even if he offends again and again and comes back in repentance again and again. (Luke 17:3b–4)

- Living the Christian life involves duties to God and others. (Luke 17:5–10)

- Faith and obedience bring spiritual as well as physical healing. (Luke 17:11–19)

- Jesus said he would return, but before he could do so, he needed to suffer rejection and death. His followers need to be always prepared for his coming. (Luke 17:20–37)

Study Questions

1. Why should we be concerned about the impact of our lives on "little ones"?

2. How should we deal with someone who sins against us?

3. Why should a faithful disciple view himself as an unworthy servant?

4. What happened to the ten lepers?

5. As we wait for Jesus's return, what do we need to be aware of?

Luke 18 People Magazine

Chapter Highlights:
- A Persistent Widow
- Let Them Come
- A Rich Ruler
- Confused Disciples
- A Blind Beggar

Let's Get Started

How do we measure people? We look at their ethnic background, physical appearance, education, economic status, accomplishments, associations—the list goes on and on. In Luke 18 we see a cross section of people—a defenseless widow; a crusty, unfair judge; a strutting Pharisee; a breast-beating tax collector; eager, accepting children; a serious-minded rich young man; disciples with questions and uncertainty; and a blind beggar determined to see.

On the surface they don't have anything in common. But take a closer look at their hearts. One essential factor that distinguishes them is their heart attitude. That's how God measures people. They are the stars in his *People Magazine*.

Luke the physician shows that he has a heart for everyone, especially those neglected by the religious hierarchy in Jerusalem—widows, publicans, little children, and beggars.

Jesus the Great Physician excludes no one who comes to him.

A Persistent Widow

LUKE 18:1–5 *Then He spoke a parable to them, that men always ought to pray and not lose heart, saying: "There was in a certain city a judge who did not fear God nor regard man. Now there was a widow in that city; and she came to him, saying, 'Get justice for me from my adversary.' And he would not for a while; but afterward he said within himself, 'Though I do not fear God nor regard man, yet because this widow troubles me I will avenge her, lest by her continual coming she weary me.'"* (NKJV)

Jesus told a parable about a widow who desperately needed justice. She had several counts against her. First, she was a woman. In her culture women did not appear in court. Second, she was a widow and had no man to appear before the judge on her behalf. Third, she was poor and had nothing to use as a bribe to gain the ear of the judge.

go to

hears
Ephesians 2:18;
3:12;
Hebrews 4:14–16

advocate
Hebrews 2:17–18;
1 John 2:1

advocate
someone who
pleads in behalf of
another

Still she persisted with her plea for justice. Finally, the judge did what he should have done in the first place—he gave her a fair decision—not because he was just but because he wanted to get rid of her.

> **what others say**
>
> **Warren W. Wiersbe**
>
> As you study this parable, try to see it in its Eastern setting. The "courtroom" was not a fine building but a tent that was moved from place to place as the judge covered his circuit. The judge, not the law, set the agenda; and he sat regally in the tent, surrounded by his assistants. Anybody would watch the proceedings from the outside, but only those who were approved and accepted could have their cases tried. This usually meant bribing one of the assistants so that he would call the judge's attention to the case.[1]

And Your Point?

LUKE **18:6–8** *Then the Lord said, "Hear what the unjust judge said. And shall God not avenge His own elect who cry out day and night to Him, though He bears long with them? I tell you that He will avenge them speedily. Nevertheless, when the Son of Man comes, will He really find faith on the earth?"* (NKJV)

Jesus's parable had a point that he did not want his disciples to miss. First, during waiting time before he would set up his kingdom, his disciples would have to endure injustice and persecution. He encouraged them to pray and not to give up. We should keep trusting and praying, even when we do not see answers immediately. If this neglected widow finally got what she deserved from an insensitive judge, how much more would Jesus's disciples receive mercy from their loving Father in heaven.

Jesus's encouragement to his disciples to pray and not give up is relevant for us today. Unlike the widow who had to plead for justice, Jesus's followers are God's children who have his ear at all times. God cares for his own as a loving Father. He <u>hears</u> their prayers. Unlike the widow who had no one to plead her cause, Jesus's followers have an **advocate** in heaven. God hears and answers prayer, not because we harass him but because he is just. He may not answer according to our timetable, but he is at work behind the scenes.

Jesus's warning is for us today. When we do not see our prayers answered we should not give up praying. Believers must persevere in faith until Jesus returns to earth.

tithed
gave one-tenth of one's goods to God

> ## what others say
>
> ### Sue and Larry Richards
>
> The parable is intended to contrast the unjust judge with the Lord, who does have compassion on people and cares deeply for the plight of widows and orphans. While God cares and will avenge his own, we need to be as persistent in prayer as the widow was in pursuing her case.[2]
>
> ### Randall D. Roth
>
> Getting to prayer is half the battle. Staying there is the other half. Either we fall asleep, or our mind wanders, or we get disenchanted. We don't see ready answers to our petitions, so we give up. But like any other wise investment, prayer requires the discipline of delayed gratification.[3]

The Purely Proud and the Humble Pure

LUKE 18:9–14 *Also He spoke this parable to some who trusted in themselves that they were righteous, and despised others: "Two men went up to the temple to pray, one a Pharisee and the other a tax collector. The Pharisee stood and prayed thus with himself, 'God, I thank You that I am not like other men—extortioners, unjust, adulterers, or even as this tax collector. I fast twice a week; I give tithes of all that I possess.' And the tax collector, standing afar off, would not so much as raise his eyes to heaven, but beat his breast, saying, 'God, be merciful to me a sinner!' I tell you, this man went down to his house justified rather than the other; for everyone who exalts himself will be humbled, and he who humbles himself will be exalted." (NKJV)*

A proud, boastful heart makes communication with God one way.

Jesus told another parable. This time he exposed the false illusions of the Pharisees who boasted of being favored by God. Two men went to the Temple to pray. The first, a Pharisee, stood up and bragged to God that he didn't do bad things. In addition, he went the second mile in earning brownie points. Though he was required to fast only one day a year, he fasted twice a week! Further, he didn't just donate a tenth of the required crops; he **tithed** his garden herbs. Surely God was pleased to hear his prayer! Standing at a distance

key point

justified
declared innocent—
"just as if" he'd
never sinned

from the Pharisee was a publican who was so aware of his short-comings that he did not dare to lift his head. He prayed, pleading with God to have mercy on him, an unworthy sinner. He knew he deserved death for his sins, but he begged for God's mercy and forgiveness.

Jesus said that the publican's prayer was answered. He went home **justified** by God, whereas the Pharisee received no word from God.

> what others say
>
> **Matthew Henry**
>
> [The publican] confesses himself a sinner by nature, by practice, guilty before God. The Pharisee denies that he is a sinner. But the tax collector gives himself no other character than that of a sinner.[4]

Let Them Come

> LUKE 18:15–17 *Then they also brought infants to Him that He might touch them; but when the disciples saw it, they rebuked them. But Jesus called them to Him and said, "Let the little children come to Me, and do not forbid them; for of such is the kingdom of God. Assuredly, I say to you, whoever does not receive the kingdom of God as a little child will by no means enter it."* (NKJV)

Jesus was so approachable that parents had no hesitation in bringing their babies to him, as they would bring them to receive a blessing from a rabbi. Jesus overrode the rebukes of the disciples and encouraged the little ones to come to him. He went on to say that the kingdom of God could be received only by people who had open, trusting hearts like little children. Unlike the boastful Pharisee, children are humble and dependent on God, as was the repentant publican in Jesus's parable.

gospel harmony

Both Matthew and Mark include this touching incident of Jesus and the little children. Matthew 19:13–15 adds that the parents wanted Jesus to pray for their children. Mark 10:13–16 says that Jesus took the little ones in his arms, placed his hands on them, and blessed them. Imagine how they snuggled close to him as he placed his hands on their heads and pronounced his Father's blessing on them.

In another context, Mark 9:36–37 tells of Jesus pulling a little child close to him and saying to his disciples that whoever welcomes a little child in Jesus's name is actually welcoming him, and in welcoming Jesus is welcoming the one who sent him—God himself!

Make room for children! Jesus says that we enter his kingdom by becoming as little children and by receiving children in his name. He wants us to cultivate traits of childlikeness and he wants us to welcome children into our lives so that we can guide them to him.

A Rich Ruler

LUKE 18:18–21 *Now a certain ruler asked Him, saying, "Good Teacher, what shall I do to inherit eternal life?" So Jesus said to him, "Why do you call Me good? No one is good but One, that is, God. You know the commandments: 'Do not commit adultery,' 'Do not murder,' 'Do not steal,' 'Do not bear false witness,' 'Honor your father and your mother.'" And he said, "All these things I have kept from my youth." (NKJV)*

One day a fine young man approached Jesus. He was wealthy, already a leader in his community, and motivated to have it all. He wanted to receive a warm welcome, so he began with some basic flattery. "Good Teacher," he said. No one addressed a rabbi this way because the greeting gave to a man qualities only God could have. (Little did he know he was being prophetic!) He continued his spiritual **faux pas** by asking what he needed to do to work his way to heaven.

Jesus's response indicates that he wanted the man to think about what he had just said. The young man had no idea the person to whom he was speaking was the true Messiah. When Jesus reminded him of the commandments given by God, the young man said, "Been there. Done that." But this guy wasn't even on first base! He did not understand that keeping the commandments was a matter of the heart, not mere outward actions. It is impossible for a human to keep all the laws perfectly.

what others say

R. C. Sproul

For a deed to be ultimately good in the biblical sense, not only must it do what the law requires, but it must be motivated by a heart that loves God completely. No human being is good in that ultimate sense, and Jesus is reminding this young man of a deeper understanding of the nature of goodness, lest his superficial understanding of goodness be the very thing that keeps him out of the kingdom of God.[5]

One Thing More

LUKE 18:22 *So when Jesus heard these things, He said to him, "You still lack one thing. Sell all that you have and distribute to the poor, and you will have treasure in heaven; and come, follow Me." (NKJV)*

Jesus looked deep into the heart of the young man. Jesus put his finger on the key issue and told the young man to sell everything and distribute his wealth among the poor. Jesus's request was designed to help the young man realize that he had not kept all the commands. He had not even kept the first commandment—"You shall have no other gods before Me" (Exodus 20:3 NKJV). His stuff had become his god. The man never considered his wealth as an opportunity to share with the needy around him and thus demonstrate that he truly loved his neighbor, as God commanded (Leviticus 19:18).

A Sad Walk into the Sunset

LUKE 18:23–25 *But when he heard this, he became very sorrowful, for he was very rich. And when Jesus saw that he became very sorrowful, He said, "How hard it is for those who have riches to enter the kingdom of God! For it is easier for a camel to go through the eye of a needle than for a rich man to enter the kingdom of God." (NKJV)*

The young man's short sprint to success skidded to a stop. He turned on his heel and left with a heavy heart. He could not part with any of the trappings of his lifestyle, let alone all of it. His very action proved that his wealth was his god.

As Jesus watched his departure he made no move to call him back. Instead, he commented sorrowfully that it is hard for the wealthy to enter the kingdom of God because they are tempted to rely on their own resources rather than God. Actually it would be easier for a camel to go through the eye of a needle than for a rich man to enter God's kingdom.

A camel and the eye of a needle? What is one to make of this **hyperbole?** Some Bible experts speak of a small gate in the wall of a city, called a needle's eye, that a camel could enter only by kneeling down and creeping through. However, other experts note that Luke used a word that referred to a surgeon's needle. Thus, he expected readers to understand the silly word picture he painted.

> ## what others say
>
> ### Lawrence O. Richards
>
> The rich ruler really did want to follow Jesus. This was not an easy choice for him. He was not like Esau, who quickly traded his birthright for a bowl of stew. Yet never mistake spiritual yearnings for true spirituality. Our spirituality is seen not in what we want to do, but in what we choose to do![6]

Both Matthew and Mark include accounts of the rich young ruler coming to Jesus. Mark 10:17–31 records that when the young man approached Jesus he ran up to him and fell on his knees before him, showing his respect. Mark also includes the insight that when Jesus challenged the young man to go sell everything he had and give to the poor, he looked at him and loved him. (See also Matthew 19:16–30.)

gospel harmony

You Can't Make It on Your Own

LUKE **18:26–27** *And those who heard it said, "Who then can be saved?" But He said, "The things which are impossible with men are possible with God."* (NKJV)

"If the rich can't make it in, how are we ever gonna get there?" the hearers asked. They thought the rich were at least five rungs above the common people on the ladder to heaven.

The young man could boast a flawless record of keeping the external demands of God's laws. He could also preen himself before others, considering his wealth an indication of God's blessing. But Jesus made it clear that the rich young ruler could not make it to heaven on his own. No person can be made ready for heaven apart from God performing in the heart what that person could not manufacture on his own. Salvation is a gift of God. Following Christ requires the choice to put him first and to give up everything else.

go to

supported
Acts 2:44–47;
4:32–37

What About Us?

> LUKE **18:28–30** *Then Peter said, "See, we have left all and followed You." So He said to them, "Assuredly, I say to you, there is no one who has left house or parents or brothers or wife or children, for the sake of the kingdom of God, who shall not receive many times more in this present time, and in the age to come eternal life." (NKJV)*

The disciples were far from rich. In fact, they had left everything, even their families and jobs, to follow Jesus. Were they wasting their time? Jesus quickly assured them that God had not overlooked them. They would be rewarded in this life and in eternity.

Jesus was grafting them into a spiritual community where they would be <u>supported</u> by fellow believers. This was fulfilled in the early church. And when they died they would receive a heavenly reward.

Confused Disciples

> LUKE **18:31–34** *Then He took the twelve aside and said to them, "Behold, we are going up to Jerusalem, and all things that are written by the prophets concerning the Son of Man will be accomplished. For He will be delivered to the Gentiles and will be mocked and insulted and spit upon. They will scourge Him and kill Him. And the third day He will rise again." But they understood none of these things; this saying was hidden from them, and they did not know the things which were spoken. (NKJV)*

Luke emphasized Jesus's determination to go to Jerusalem. He didn't want readers to misunderstand and think the events there were a terrible mistake. Jesus knew exactly what he was doing.

Jesus gave the disciples a prophecy lesson from the Old Testament. The bad news was he would be handed over to Gentiles for terrible mistreatment, which would end in his death. The good news was he would rise from the dead on the third day.

The disciples were completely mystified by his words. They had no idea what he was telling them because it was so different from their expectations. They still thought he would soon set up an earthly kingdom. In addition, Luke said, some kind of supernatural blinding kept them from understanding.

A Blind Beggar

go to

ask God
James 4:2

LUKE 18:35–43 *Then it happened, as He was coming near Jericho, that a certain blind man sat by the road begging. And hearing a multitude passing by, he asked what it meant. So they told him that Jesus of Nazareth was passing by. And he cried out, saying, "Jesus, Son of David, have mercy on me!" Then those who went before warned him that he should be quiet; but he cried out all the more, "Son of David, have mercy on me!" So Jesus stood still and commanded him to be brought to Him. And when he had come near, He asked him, saying, "What do you want Me to do for you?" He said, "Lord, that I may receive my sight." Then Jesus said to him, "Receive your sight; your faith has made you well." And immediately he received his sight, and followed Him, glorifying God. And all the people, when they saw it, gave praise to God. (NKJV)*

By this time in Jesus's life his reputation preceded him. Everywhere he went crowds followed, hanging on his words. As Jesus approached Jericho (see map in Appendix A), a blind beggar heard the commotion and discovered that Jesus of Nazareth was passing by.

The blind man called out above the noise of the crowd, "Jesus, Son of David, have mercy on me!" (Luke 18:38 NKJV).

People close to the beggar told him to shut up. But the more they rebuked him and tried to keep him quiet, the more loudly he shouted. Jesus took control of the situation. He had the man brought to him and asked, "What do you want Me to do for you?" (Luke 18:41 NKJV).

Seems like a silly question, doesn't it? What blind person wouldn't want to see? But the blind man had only asked for mercy, and in light of his view of Jesus as the Messiah a gift of mercy from Jesus could have taken many forms.

Jesus told him, "Receive your sight; your faith has made you well" (Luke 18:42 NKJV). Immediately the man could see.

Luke opened this chapter with Jesus's parable of the persistent widow and closed it with the account of a blind beggar who persisted in calling out to Jesus, even though he was told to be quiet. Both the widow and the beggar received what they needed.

something to ponder

James, usually thought of as Jesus's brother, wrote that when we struggle with selfish desires, we are never satisfied. We do not have what we need because we do not <u>ask God</u> with the right attitude.

Chapter Wrap-Up

- Jesus told a parable about an insensitive judge and a widow who persisted in her request to show how we should pray. (Luke 18:1–8)

- Jesus told another parable about a proud Pharisee and a humble tax collector to show how we should approach God. (Luke 18:9–14)

- Jesus received children with love to highlight the childlike attitudes his followers should have. (Luke 18:15–17)

- A rich young ruler sought eternal life and turned away from Jesus because the ruler loved his money more than God. (Luke 18:18–30)

- Jesus told his disciples about the Old Testament prophecies of his death and resurrection, but they didn't understand. (Luke 18:31–34)

- Jesus healed a blind beggar who called out to him for help and persisted in doing so even though he was told to be quiet. (Luke 18:35–43)

Study Questions

1. What was the point of Jesus's parable of the persistent widow?

2. Contrast the attitudes of the Pharisee and the tax collector who prayed in the Temple. Which man went home justified?

3. What attitude should we have toward children? In what way should we be childlike?

4. What did the rich young ruler want? Why did he turn away from Jesus?

5. Why did Jesus's disciples not understand what he was telling them about his approaching death and resurrection?

6. What do we learn from the blind beggar's repeated pleas for Jesus's help?

Luke 19 Loving Little People

Chapter Highlights:
• Short Climb to Success
• Give and Take
• Use It or Lose It
• Praise Parade
• Temple Business

Let's Get Started

The media place great attention on the rich and famous, the movers and shakers in business and government. But the vast majority of the world's population is made up of individuals who will never attract attention outside their little spheres of influence. The world does not notice them—but God does. In his view, there are no little people.

In this last chapter before starting his account of Jesus's final week, Luke gives us insights into Jesus's heart of love for all people, the depth of his caring, and his desire to have them enjoy the salvation he came to provide.

Short Climb to Success

LUKE 19:1–6 *Then Jesus entered and passed through Jericho. Now behold, there was a man named Zacchaeus who was a chief tax collector, and he was rich. And he sought to see who Jesus was, but could not because of the crowd, for he was of short stature. So he ran ahead and climbed up into a sycamore tree to see Him, for He was going to pass that way. And when Jesus came to the place, He looked up and saw him, and said to him, "Zacchaeus, make haste and come down, for today I must stay at your house." So he made haste and came down, and received Him joyfully. (NKJV)*

As Jesus approached Jericho, its citizens lined the roadway, eager to see him. The prominent members of the city demanded and got the spots that gave the best views. Zacchaeus was snubbed, for he was a supervisor of tax collectors who had become rich by skimming off more taxes than were required by the despised Roman Gentiles who levied the fees. People hated him.

Being creative and not afraid of ruining his dignity, Zacchaeus climbed a tree. He just planned to watch Jesus.

mercy
Matthew 5:7

plus one-fifth
Leviticus 6:5;
Numbers 5:7

Throwing etiquette to the wind, Jesus singled out Zacchaeus by inviting himself to his home. He didn't ask to visit; he said he must visit. Jesus had a divine appointment.

Zacchaeus responded by rolling out the red carpet. Jesus showed <u>mercy</u> to the least likely person in Jericho. He did this because he cared. He discerned Zacchaeus's deep hunger and desperate need, and reached out, knowing as he did so that he would receive criticism from Jericho's most respected citizens.

> **what others say**
>
> **C. Samuel Storms**
>
> No one would come right out and say it, but a lot think it: "Cursed are the merciful, for they shall be bothered!" A Roman philosopher once called mercy "the disease of the soul"; mercy, like meekness, was considered a sign of cowardice in the ancient world.
>
> Things haven't changed much. People still envy the carefree soul who is a world unto himself, far removed from the entangling complications that others' problems often bring. Many say, "Blessed is he who hasn't a care in the world." "On the contrary," says Jesus, "blessed is he who has a world of cares!" Of course he means the cares of others.[1]

Zach's Heart Transplant

LUKE 19:7–10 *But when they saw it, they all complained, saying, "He has gone to be a guest with a man who is a sinner." Then Zacchaeus stood and said to the Lord, "Look, Lord, I give half of my goods to the poor; and if I have taken anything from anyone by false accusation, I restore fourfold." And Jesus said to him, "Today salvation has come to this house, because he also is a son of Abraham; for the Son of Man has come to seek and to save that which was lost." (NKJV)*

While the citizens of Jericho criticized Jesus for choosing to dine with a "sinner," Jesus performed a heart transplant. Zacchaeus announced that he was giving back the excess tax money he had taken. The law required no more than the original amount <u>plus one-fifth</u>, but Zacchaeus was taking much more.

Jesus called Zacchaeus a son of Abraham, not only because he was biologically descended from Abraham but also because he was a true

Jew who had the same saving faith as Abraham. Jesus had come to rescue those who were lost, to <u>call sinners</u> to repentance, and Zacchaeus was certainly one of them.

Verse 10, "for the Son of Man has come to seek and to save that which was lost" (NKJV), is probably the key verse in all of Luke. The emphasis is on Jesus doing the acting. He made contact with Zacchaeus. He invited himself into Zacchaeus's home. He took out the old sinner's heart and gave him a new righteous heart.

Zacchaeus does not speak of his faith in Jesus as Savior, but he promised to give back what he had taken from taxpayers. God did not reward Zacchaeus with salvation after he did a good deed. Rather, Zacchaeus's heart was changed by the miracle of salvation and that caused him to want to do a good deed. Only by putting his trust in Jesus could Zacchaeus have had such a complete change of heart.

Does having a change of heart influence physical health? Luke the physician undoubtedly would answer yes! His opinion would be backed by personal observation as well as by statements in the book of Proverbs. A heart made <u>joyful</u> by the assurance of sins forgiven makes the face glow. Knowing one is accepted as a child of God lifts one's spirits and gives a hope that permeates every part of one's being.

go to

call sinners
Luke 5:31–32

joyful
Proverbs 15:13, 30; 17:22

restitution
Exodus 22:1, 4, 7

restitution
restoration of property previously taken away

---

what others say

Henry T. Blackaby and Claude V. King

Zacchaeus promised **restitution** to everyone he had deceived and stolen from. Zacchaeus, for the first time in his adult life, experienced love and forgiveness, grace and mercy—all in the presence of the Messiah. What society had considered to be a sinful occasion, that of Jesus staying with Zacchaeus, became an occasion of salvation. Jesus looked past the physical nature of Zacchaeus and looked into the soul of the man forsaken by society. Jesus saw someone who longed for the love of God and the chance to love other people. With Jesus, Zacchaeus stood tall.[2]

Give and Take

LUKE 19:11–15 *Now as they heard these things, He spoke another parable, because He was near Jerusalem and because they thought the kingdom of God would appear immediately.*

mina
unit of money thought to be about three months' wages

Therefore He said: "A certain nobleman went into a far country to receive for himself a kingdom and to return. So he called ten of his servants, delivered to them ten minas, and said to them, 'Do business till I come.' But his citizens hated him, and sent a delegation after him, saying, 'We will not have this man to reign over us.' And so it was that when he returned, having received the kingdom, he then commanded these servants, to whom he had given the money, to be called to him, that he might know how much every man had gained by trading. (NKJV)

Jericho was about seventeen miles from Jerusalem. The closer Jesus got the more people held their breath, hoping that at last Jesus would set himself up as king. Jesus told a parable to make clear what his followers should be doing while they waited for the kingdom of God to appear. His story had to do with a nobleman giving responsibility to his servants.

The nobleman, representing Jesus, was leaving for another country where he would be appointed king. He called in ten servants and gave them each a **mina**, which they were to invest during his extended absence and to give him a profit on his return.

Sadly, some of his subjects hated him so much they rejected him as king. These people represented the religious leaders and others of Israel who refused to recognize Jesus as the Messiah.

---

what others say

Jack Hayford

The parable is based upon a historical event. According to the historian Josephus, after the death of Herod the Great, his son Archelaus went to Rome to be confirmed as king of Judea (v. 12). The Jews, however, sent a delegation to protest the appointment.[3]

Dana Gould

God entrusts believers with the gospel, and he wants them to multiply his message so the entire world will hear it. It is the obligation of believers to be faithful stewards of the message he has entrusted us until Jesus comes.[4]

Employee Evaluations

LUKE 19:16–19 *Then came the first, saying, 'Master, your mina has earned ten minas.' And he said to him, 'Well done, good servant; because you were faithful in a very little, have authority over ten cities.' And the second came, saying, 'Master, your mina has earned five minas.' Likewise he said to him, 'You also be over five cities.' (NKJV)*

The king received reports from two of his servants who had been faithful in investing his money. The first servant had earned ten minas, a gain of one thousand percent. The king commended him and rewarded him with leadership over ten cities. The second servant reported that his mina had earned five more. The king rewarded him with leadership over five cities. God is not a taskmaster, but he does require accountability. The reward for faithful service is more responsibility.

what others say

R. Kent Hughes

The reward of Christ's faithful servants is an elevation of eternal intimacy with him. They will be his co-regents, viceroys, and confidants. What joy! Happily, the eternal reward is not rest but responsibility as we work with Christ in unimaginably vast new spiritual enterprises.[5]

Use It or Lose It

LUKE 19:20–25 *Then another came, saying, 'Master, here is your mina, which I have kept put away in a handkerchief. For I feared you, because you are an austere man. You collect what you did not deposit, and reap what you did not sow.' And he said to him, 'Out of your own mouth I will judge you, you wicked servant. You knew that I was an austere man, collecting what I did not deposit and reaping what I did not sow. Why then did you not put my money in the bank, that at my coming I might have collected it with interest?' And he said to those who stood by, 'Take the mina from him, and give it to him who has ten minas.' (But they said to him, 'Master, he has ten minas.') (NKJV)*

Another servant had done nothing, so he returned the mina to the king with bitter words about his master. The king used the hateful explanation to expose the false servant who had not expected the master ever to return. If he had, he would have put the money in a bank to earn at least a little interest. The king took the mina away from him and gave it to the servant who had earned ten minas.

Settlement

> **LUKE 19:26–27** *'For I say to you, that to everyone who has will be given; and from him who does not have, even what he has will be taken away from him. But bring here those enemies of mine, who did not want me to reign over them, and slay them before me.'" (NKJV)*

Jesus's parable has a message for everyone. We all have the same job—to live for Christ. To his followers who serve him faithfully and look for his return, Christ has amazing rewards. To those who hide his investment and do not serve him, he has shame. And to those who reject him as king, he has eternal separation from him.

gospel harmony

Matthew 25:14–30 contains a story that is similar to the one in Luke. In Matthew's account the men are given differing and larger amounts, representing people of different abilities being given serious jobs. In Luke the amounts are the same and are small, showing that each of us has the same basic job. Matthew reports that the third servant was thrown out of the kingdom. That servant represents the people in the Jewish nation who did not want the king to reign over them. He was an enemy agent on the king's staff.

Jesus's story shows that those who make good use of their opportunities will receive more opportunities. Those who do not use the opportunities that are given to them will not be given more opportunities. Jesus was primarily speaking about spiritual opportunities, not material things. In the Christian life we must use the knowledge and insight God gives us, or we will lose it.

---

what others say

William Barclay

There is no such thing as standing still in the Christian life. We either get more or lose what we have. We either advance to greater heights or slip back.[6]

Praise Parade

> **LUKE 19:28–34** *When He had said this, He went on ahead, going up to Jerusalem. And it came to pass, when He drew near to Bethphage and Bethany, at the mountain called Olivet, that He sent two of His disciples, saying, "Go into the village opposite you, where as you enter you will find a colt tied, on which no one*

has ever sat. Loose it and bring it here. And if anyone asks you, 'Why are you loosing it?' thus you shall say to him, 'Because the Lord has need of it.'" So those who were sent went their way and found it just as He had said to them. But as they were loosing the colt, the owners of it said to them, "Why are you loosing the colt?" And they said, "The Lord has need of him." (NKJV)

Jesus's triumphal entry to Jerusalem was not an event that happened spontaneously. It was carefully planned by God. Up to this point, Jesus had avoided public acclaim. Though Luke does not do so, Matthew, Mark, and John give information that leads up to Jesus presenting himself as the Messiah in the event known as the triumphal entry:

gospel harmony

- Jesus had raised Lazarus from the dead in Bethany. News of this exciting miracle had spread rapidly throughout Jerusalem. (John 11)

- Mary had anointed Jesus with costly ointment, an act considered inappropriately extravagant by some but defended by Jesus, who said plainly that she was anointing him for burial. (Matthew 26:10; Mark 14:6–9; John 12:7–8)

- Crowds gathered to see Jesus and to learn more about Lazarus, who had been miraculously raised from the dead. While many now believed in Jesus, religious leaders strategized behind the scenes how they might put Jesus—and Lazarus—to death. (Mark 14:10–11; John 12:9–11)

Amazing Preparation

Bethany was about two miles from Jerusalem. Jesus was now ready to enter the city, not as an itinerant teacher and healer from Nazareth but as the promised Messiah. On this one occasion he would arrive as their Anointed King!

He sent two disciples to borrow a donkey colt. The disciples must have been amazed that Jesus knew with absolute certainty that they would find "a colt tied, on which no one has ever sat" (Luke 19:30 NKJV), and that the owners would be prepared to make the animal available to him. Luke does not tell us how Jesus knew all this. Some Bible scholars attribute his knowledge to his divine ability to see all things. Others assume he was counting on friends who would naturally make the colt available at his request. Still others think he must have made the arrangement with the owner in advance.

Matthew, alone of the four Gospel writers, records that the disciples were instructed to bring a donkey and her colt. No one had ridden the colt before, so having its mother led along undoubtedly kept it calm (Matthew 21:1–7).

Why Not a Horse?

prophecy
Zechariah 9:9–10

praise
Psalm 118:26

messianic psalm
poem containing prophetic references to Christ the Messiah

In New Testament times a conquering king rode on a horse, a symbol of war. A donkey was a symbol of peace. Jesus deliberately fulfilled an Old Testament <u>prophecy</u> that the Messiah would ride on a donkey. He came, not as the military leader the people expected, but as the King of peace. He was their righteous, gentle King, who would some day remove war and bring peace.

A Noisy Celebration

LUKE 19:35–38 *Then they brought him to Jesus. And they threw their own clothes on the colt, and they set Jesus on him. And as He went, many spread their clothes on the road. Then, as He was now drawing near the descent of the Mount of Olives, the whole multitude of the disciples began to rejoice and praise God with a loud voice for all the mighty works they had seen, saying: "'Blessed is the King who comes in the name of the LORD!' Peace in heaven and glory in the highest!" (NKJV)*

As the crowds swelled they became caught up in the significance of Jesus's arrival on the donkey. They spontaneously threw their outer garments on the road, using a traditional way of welcoming a king. Their joyful shouts of welcome included expressions of <u>praise</u> from a **messianic psalm**.

John 12:12–13 records that crowds who had come to Jerusalem for the Passover Feast went out to meet Jesus as the parade approached the city. They carried palm branches, which represented their great longing for Jesus to deliver them from Roman rule. As they joined the parade they shouted praises to the King of Israel!

Rock Music

LUKE 19:39–40 *And some of the Pharisees called to Him from the crowd, "Teacher, rebuke Your disciples." But He answered and said to them, "I tell you that if these should keep silent, the stones would immediately cry out." (NKJV)*

The ever-present Pharisees approached Jesus and ordered him to take control of his followers and put an immediate stop to the praises. Did they feel the praise was misplaced? Probably. Or did they fear that the Romans would view the parade as a prelude to an uprising? If so, the Pharisees had a valid fear, especially since it was Passover and many visitors swelled the city.

Jesus responded that the exuberance of the crowd was so appropriate that if the people were silent, inanimate objects would take up the praise.

go to

Lazarus's grave
John 11:32–35

lamentation
vocal expression
of deep grief

> ## what others say
>
> ### Larry Sibley
>
> Whether they were critics or truth seekers, the Pharisees in the crowd were shocked by the honor the people accorded Jesus. Most likely they recognized enough scriptural allusions in the shouts of the crowd and Jesus's remarks to believe they had grounds on which to accuse him of blasphemy and heresy.[7]

The Weeping King

LUKE 19:41–44 *Now as He drew near, He saw the city and wept over it, saying, "If you had known, even you, especially in this your day, the things that make for your peace! But now they are hidden from your eyes. For days will come upon you when your enemies will build an embankment around you, surround you and close you in on every side, and level you, and your children within you, to the ground; and they will not leave in you one stone upon another, because you did not know the time of your visitation." (NKJV)*

As the parade moved toward Jerusalem, Jesus came to a ridge that gave a view of the city, which normally brought a surge of admiration and pride to a traveler. On this occasion, Jesus began to weep, not quietly as he had wept at <u>Lazarus's grave</u>, but aloud. In a heartrending <u>lamentation</u>, Jesus mourned the destruction of the city because the people within it were unrepentant and would reject him. Roman soldiers fulfilled Jesus's prophecy in AD 70 when the city was destroyed.

tax
Exodus 30:11–14

Father's house
John 2:16

tetradrachmas
shekels of Tyre;
temple money

Luke loved people, and he loved to show Jesus's love for people. All through his Gospel, Luke stressed Jesus's determined journey to Jerusalem. We would expect Jesus's parade through the city to be the climax of Luke's story, but it is not. Luke did not actually put his readers at the parade. (And all good writers know that the climax scene needs to make readers feel that they are actually seeing the events described.) Plus, Luke always said Jesus was approaching the city; he never said Jesus arrived. Instead, Luke's climax is Jesus's deep love highlighted by how he cried over Jerusalem and its people, a lament made all the more striking because of the contrasting joy in the city.

Jesus cried over Jerusalem, tears prompted by grief over the nation's coming judgment. He was ready to give his life for this people, but they did not want him as Savior-King, only as Conquering King. Judgment always follows rejection of Christ. Jesus repeated the words "you" and "your" sixteen times in four verses, showing that rejection and judgment are always personal.

Temple Business

> LUKE 19:45–48 *Then He went into the temple and began to drive out those who bought and sold in it, saying to them, "It is written, 'My house is a house of prayer,' but you have made it a 'den of thieves.'" And He was teaching daily in the temple. But the chief priests, the scribes, and the leaders of the people sought to destroy Him, and were unable to do anything; for all the people were very attentive to hear Him.* (NKJV)

Luke gives a succinct account of what must have been a dramatic event. The temple court buzzed with activity. Jews from surrounding areas made a pilgrimage to Jerusalem for the yearly Passover celebration. Booths were set up for currency exchange. To pay their temple <u>tax</u>, visiting Jews were required to change their money to **tetradrachmas**. This gave the moneychangers opportunity to make a large profit from the exchange. They had a monopoly on the market.

Adding to the confusion were the sounds of sacrificial animals and doves, which temple officials sold to the pilgrims at greatly inflated prices. It was a lucrative business, to say the least.

The crass commercialism was an insult to God in the place Jesus called his <u>Father's house</u>! Instead of worshiping God from pure hearts, the people were occupied with buying and selling, haggling energetically over their transactions, and robbing the poor who had come to worship. Enough already! Jesus took action and threw out the greedy merchants, <u>quoting</u> the Old Testament as he did so.

Does Jesus's cleansing of the Temple have anything to say to us today? We are warned to avoid anything that would detract from our focus on God and our desire to worship him. Any program or talent, any commercial venture in the name of religion, however seemingly legitimate, must not be allowed to come between us and God.

quoting
Isaiah 56:7;
Jeremiah 7:11

healing
Matthew 21:14

Poised to Pounce

The religious leaders were poised to pounce on Jesus and have him killed. But their hands were tied. Like it or not, they had to recognize that Jesus was surrounded by a growing crowd of fans who hung on his words and flocked to him for <u>healing</u>. The leaders waited for the right moment to make their move.

Chapter Wrap-Up

- Jesus sought out Zacchaeus, a Jewish tax collector. Jesus changed his heart so that he was willing to make restitution far beyond what was required in Old Testament law. (Luke 19:1–10)

- Jesus told a parable of ten servants who were entrusted with their master's resources while he was away. The servants who were faithful were given more responsibilities. The servant who was unfaithful was relieved of his responsibility. (Luke 19:11–27)

- Jesus rode on a donkey colt when he made his triumphal entry into Jerusalem, signifying his peaceful conquering as the Messiah-King. (Luke 19:28–40)

- Jesus lamented over Jerusalem because the people rejected him and the city would be judged. (Luke 19:28–44)

- Jesus became angry at the commercial enterprises he found in the temple-market and cleaned house. (Luke 19:45–48)

Study Questions

1. What made Zacchaeus an unlikely prospect for Jesus's interest and concern, and how did Zacchaeus change as a result of his encounter with Jesus?

2. What does Jesus want us to learn from his parable of the ten servants?

3. Why did Jesus ride a donkey colt on his triumphal entry into Jerusalem?

4. Why did Jesus weep as he entered Jerusalem?

5. What prompted Jesus's anger so that he cleaned out the temple-market?

Luke 20 Hostile Challenges

Let's Get Started

Jesus and the religious leaders in Jerusalem were on a collision course. While they were plotting his death, Jesus was calmly following the timetable set by his Father in heaven. They saw Jesus as guilty and were trying to hatch a plot to have him killed. Jesus, on the other hand, was preparing to <u>lay down</u> his life. He had stated that nobody would be able to take his life from him.

go to

lay down
John 10:14–18

Although the leaders were desperate to stifle Jesus, they were not dummies. They knew the crowds loved Jesus. They didn't want to cause a riot by arresting Jesus for no apparent reason. Their only solution was to throw out some bait and try to trick him into publicly saying or doing something they could use as a reason to arrest him.

Luke uses a series of dialogues to highlight these challenges and to show how Jesus handily threw the questions back into the faces of his interrogators.

Bait About Authority

> LUKE 20:1–8 *Now it happened on one of those days, as He taught the people in the temple and preached the gospel, that the chief priests and the scribes, together with the elders, confronted Him and spoke to Him, saying, "Tell us, by what authority are You doing these things? Or who is he who gave You this authority?" But He answered and said to them, "I also will ask you one thing, and answer Me: The baptism of John—was it from heaven or from men?" And they reasoned among themselves, saying, "If we say, 'From heaven,' He will say, 'Why then did you not believe him?' But if we say, 'From men,' all the people will stone us, for they are persuaded that John was a prophet." So they answered that they did not know where it was from. And Jesus said to them, "Neither will I tell you by what authority I do these things." (NKJV)*

Jesus had taken initiative that proved he had authority when he rode into Jerusalem as a king. Then he had the nerve to drive the moneychangers and merchants out of the Temple. The religious leaders were miffed. They devised what they considered a brilliant question to trap Jesus. They gathered an official posse and demanded that he give his credentials and state who gave him the authority for his recent actions.

Jesus answered their question with a question about John the Baptist. Was his baptism authorized in heaven—meaning by God—or by men? Now the religious leaders were trapped. If they answered that John's baptism was authorized in heaven, they would have to accept John's declaration that Jesus was the Messiah. If, on the other hand, they answered that John's baptism was merely from men, they would anger the multitudes who believed John's message.

The leaders could not answer Jesus, and Jesus chose not to answer them. Jesus refused to give more explanation to people who refused to accept the facts they already had. The way Jesus responded to the bait threw the religious posse for a loop. Jesus chose not to answer the question, knowing that telling the truth would lead to his death before God's time.

gospel harmony

Both Matthew and Mark include this encounter with the chief priests and teachers of the law. Mark points out that these leaders understood that the people considered John the Baptist a prophet. (Check out Matthew 21:23–27 and Mark 11:27–33.)

what others say

Warren W. Wiersbe

The chief priests claimed their authority from Moses, for the Law set the tribe of Levi apart to serve in the sanctuary. The scribes were students of the Law and claimed their authority from the rabbis whose interpretations they studied. The elders of Israel were the leaders of the families and clans, chosen usually for their experience and wisdom. All of these men were sure of their authority and were not afraid to confront Jesus.[1]

A Viny Tale

LUKE 20:9–12 Then He began to tell the people this parable: "A certain man planted a vineyard, leased it to vinedressers, and went into a far country for a long time. Now at vintage-time he sent a servant to the vinedressers, that they might give him some of the fruit of the vineyard. But the vinedressers beat him and sent him away empty-handed. Again he sent another servant; and they beat him also, treated him shamefully, and sent him away empty-handed. And again he sent a third; and they wounded him also and cast him out. (NKJV)

go to

symbol
Isaiah 5:1–7

Jesus told a parable that would clearly define his authority. The setting for the story was a vineyard, something familiar to all his listeners both as a physical feature on the landscape and as a <u>symbol</u> of their nation.

The vineyard owner followed a common practice of leasing his vineyard to vinedressers, or tenant farmers. He had every right to collect some of the harvest from his vines, but on three occasions the tenants badly mistreated the servants sent by the owner.

---

what others say

R. Kent Hughes

The vineyard/Israel connection was so much a part of their national consciousness that the very temple in which Jesus was standing sported a richly carved grapevine, seventy cubits high, sculpted around the door that led from the porch to the Holy Place. The branches, tendrils, and leaves were of finest gold. The bunches of grapes hanging upon the golden limbs were costly jewels.[2]

Making a Painful Point

LUKE 20:13–16 Then the owner of the vineyard said, 'What shall I do? I will send my beloved son. Probably they will respect him when they see him.' But when the vinedressers saw him, they reasoned among themselves, saying, 'This is the heir. Come, let us kill him, that the inheritance may be ours.' So they cast him out of the vineyard and killed him. Therefore what will the owner of the vineyard do to them? He will come and destroy those vinedressers and give the vineyard to others." And when they heard it they said, "Certainly not!" (NKJV)

beloved son
Luke 3:22

stumbled
Isaiah 8:14–15

Finally, the owner decided to send his <u>beloved son</u>, hoping the tenants would respect him. But the tenants saw this only as an opportunity to kill the heir and seize the vineyard for themselves. To be sure his listeners did not miss his important point, Jesus asked what the owner of the vineyard would do to the evil tenants. Any reasonable owner would kill them and give the vineyard to more worthy tenants.

The people got the message! The vineyard was Israel, loved and cared for by God and responsible to bear fruit for him. But Israel had mistreated God's prophets and even now its leaders were plotting to kill his Son. Jesus was saying that unbelieving Israel would not be allowed in the kingdom, but Gentiles and people considered as outcasts would become the tenants.

The listeners were horrified and said, "Certainly not!" (Luke 20:16 NKJV). They couldn't imagine that the privileges of the Jewish nation would be given to Gentiles. How dare God do such a thing!

Matthew 21:33–44 and Mark 12:1–11 include this parable with more and varied detail. Jesus tells of the great care the owner gave his vineyard to make it safe and productive. Mark gives more detail about the murder of the son.

Don't Get Stoned

LUKE 20:17–18 *Then He looked at them and said, "What then is this that is written:*
'The stone which the builders rejected
Has become the chief cornerstone'?
"Whoever falls on that stone will be broken; but on whomever it falls, it will grind him to powder." (NKJV)

Leaving the imagery of the vineyard, Jesus quoted from the Old Testament about a stone that was tossed away by stonemasons that became the cornerstone—the most significant part of a building! If they didn't believe him, how would they interpret Psalm 118:22?

Further, Jesus said the stone had destructive power. People could reject Jesus but they would suffer both in this life and eternally. They <u>stumbled</u> over Jesus by not believing on him and they would be crushed.

appointed
Ephesians 1:22–23

bow
Philippians 2:9–11

Like a builder tossing aside a stone as unusable for his building, we may ignore Jesus Christ as totally irrelevant to our lives. But God has <u>appointed</u> Jesus head over all things. He has given Jesus the most exalted place. Someday we will all <u>bow</u> before him and confess that he is Lord.

Hopping Mad

LUKE 20:19 *And the chief priests and the scribes that very hour sought to lay hands on Him, but they feared the people—for they knew He had spoken this parable against them.* (NKJV)

The religious leaders' blood pressure skyrocketed! They knew Jesus's parable had both established his authority as the Son sent from God and had pictured them as the murdering tenants rejected by God.

If only they could arrest Jesus and get rid of him—but they didn't want to start a riot and risk losing their privileges. Jesus's popularity with the crowds kept them from moving in on him.

Send in the Spies

LUKE 20:20–22 *So they watched Him, and sent spies who pretended to be righteous, that they might seize on His words, in order to deliver Him to the power and the authority of the governor. Then they asked Him, saying, "Teacher, we know that You say and teach rightly, and You do not show personal favoritism, but teach the way of God in truth: Is it lawful for us to pay taxes to Caesar or not?"* (NKJV)

Frustrated, the religious leaders sent shameful spies to get Jesus to say something against the government that would warrant his arrest.

If they couldn't catch him in religious gobbledygook, they would try to get him in trouble with the Romans. Notice the leaders weren't interested in discovering the truth. They wanted dirt. These spies used flattery to set Jesus up to give his opinion on whether it was right to pay taxes to the hated Romans.

Look at the Physical Evidence

LUKE 20:23–26 *But He perceived their craftiness, and said to them, "Why do you test Me? Show Me a denarius. Whose image and inscription does it have?" They answered and said, "Caesar's." And He said to them, "Render therefore to Caesar the things that are Caesar's, and to God the things that are God's." But they could not catch Him in His words in the presence of the people. And they marveled at His answer and kept silent. (NKJV)*

Jesus was not fooled for a minute. He asked them to show him a **denarius** and to identify the picture and the inscription on it (see Illustration #12). They had to answer honestly. Jesus then told them to give to Caesar what was his and to give to God what was his. Jesus favored neither the people who wanted to revolt against Rome nor those loyal to Rome.

The trap sprang the wrong way! The spies slunk away in silence with their tails between their legs.

Illustration #12
Denarius—A silver coin picturing on one side Tiberius Caesar, who ruled AD 14–37, and on the other side the Roman personification of peace.

The Jews bitterly resented having to pay taxes to the Roman government, which they regarded as **pagan**. Jesus did not encourage them to oppose the government or to join the **Zealots**, who wanted to fight the Romans for freedom. Instead, he taught his followers to be respectful of government and to view themselves as citizens of God's kingdom who follow his rule of righteousness and love.

Today we are called to be good citizens of our country, obeying its laws, paying the taxes, and respecting its leaders. We are also called to reach out in our country and around the world to win people to Christ and his kingdom.

unmarried brother
Deuteronomy
25:5–6

Sadducees
wealthy leaders
opposed to
Pharisees, and who
denied the afterlife,
angels, and spirits

Gilbert Bilezikian

For the people who lived in Palestine, the presence and the rule of the Romans were intolerable. But Jesus was careful not to appear anti-Roman. He acknowledged the presence of the Roman government and recognized their rights within the limits of their governmental function. But he also reminded the people that Rome could not take over that which belonged to God.[4]

How Many Angels Can Dance on a Pin?

LUKE 20:27–33 *Then some of the Sadducees, who deny that there is a resurrection, came to Him and asked Him, saying: "Teacher, Moses wrote to us that if a man's brother dies, having a wife, and he dies without children, his brother should take his wife and raise up offspring for his brother. Now there were seven brothers. And the first took a wife, and died without children. And the second took her as wife, and he died childless. Then the third took her, and in like manner the seven also; and they left no children, and died. Last of all the woman died also. Therefore, in the resurrection, whose wife does she become? For all seven had her as wife." (NKJV)*

The attempt to trap Jesus on a political issue failed. So now the **Sadducees** moved in to spar verbally with Jesus. They did not believe in any form of life after death, so they posed a ridiculous situation to entangle Jesus much the way kids love to debate how many angels can dance on the head of a pin. They didn't care about Jesus's answer. They just wanted to watch him wiggle.

First, they reminded Jesus that an <u>unmarried brother</u> was required to marry his brother's widow in order to carry on the family name and heritage. Then, they asked whose wife a woman would be if she actually married seven brothers and still had no children!

Bombing the Bluffers

LUKE 20:34–36 *Jesus answered and said to them, "The sons of this age marry and are given in marriage. But those who are counted worthy to attain that age, and the resurrection from the dead, neither marry nor are given in marriage; nor can they die anymore, for they are equal to the angels and are sons of God, being sons of the resurrection.* (NKJV)

Jesus called the Sadducees' bluff and launched a word bomb to silence them. Their clever what-if dilemma was a no-brainer. Marriage is for life on earth. After the resurrection, the relationships between husbands and wives would be on a different basis.

One of the duties of a physician is to care for the grieving spouse whose life companion has been snatched away in death. It would be a cruel blow to imply to the one in deep sorrow that there can be no reunion in heaven with the loved one. Luke was alert to note what Jesus did not say about the relationship of husbands and wives in heaven.

Chew on This

LUKE 20:37–40 *But even Moses showed in the burning bush passage that the dead are raised, when he called the Lord 'the God of Abraham, the God of Isaac, and the God of Jacob.' For*

He is not the God of the dead but of the living, for all live to Him." Then some of the scribes answered and said, "Teacher, You have spoken well." But after that they dared not question Him anymore. (NKJV)

identified
Exodus 3:15

Jesus now turned to the real issue for the Sadducees, who did not believe in life after death. He pointed out that in the Old Testament Scriptures, which they professed to accept, God had <u>identified</u> himself to Moses as "the God of Abraham, the God of Isaac, and the God of Jacob." These patriarchs had died many years before Moses, but God clearly indicates that they were alive with him.

Now there was silence in the temple court. Nobody dared to raise another question!

what others say

Personal Growth Study Bible

The Sadducees had such fun confounding the rival Pharisees with their hypothetical question ridiculing the belief in resurrection. But when they pulled out their old puzzle to trap Jesus, they were the ones left confused. What stunned the Sadducees most was the proof that Jesus drew from Moses's writings, the only part of the Old Testament the Sadducees acknowledged as God's Word. The proof rested on the tense of a single verb! God did not say to Moses, "I was the God of Abraham." He said, "I am the God of Abraham." Clearly the verb tense implies that Abraham still lived. This means that belief in resurrection is not foolish, but assured.

Think for a moment. If Jesus had such confidence in the Word of God that he rested a basic doctrine on the tense of a single verb, how much confidence should we have in God's complete Word? Jesus trusted God's Word absolutely—so can we.[7]

Dallas Willard

To one group of his day, who believed that "physical death" was the cessation of the individual's existence, Jesus said, "God is not the God of the dead but of the living" (v. 38). His meaning was that those who love and are loved by God are not allowed to cease to exist, because they are God's treasures. He delights in them and intends to hold onto them. He has even prepared for them an individualized eternal work in his vast universe.[8]

go to

David called
Psalm 110:1

hypocrisy
false impression of
desirable qualities

Jesus Makes Their Heads Spin

LUKE 20:41–44 *And He said to them, "How can they say that the Christ is the Son of David? Now David himself said in the Book of Psalms:*
'The LORD said to my Lord,
"Sit at My right hand,
Till I make Your enemies Your footstool."'
Therefore David calls Him 'Lord'; how is He then his Son?" (NKJV)

The religious leaders, their spies, and the Sadducees had raised difficult questions. Jesus had silenced them with his wisdom. Now he raised an even tougher question—one that made their heads spin.

How can the Messiah be the son of David when David called the Messiah "Lord"? In other words, how can Christ be both David's descendant and his Lord? This was outside Jewish thinking, for they held that the ancestor was always greater than any descendant. The people were silent because they could not accept the only possible answer: Christ was both God ("the Lord") and man (David's descendant).

Now a Word of Warning

LUKE 20:45–47 *Then, in the hearing of all the people, He said to His disciples, "Beware of the scribes, who desire to go around in long robes, love greetings in the marketplaces, the best seats in the synagogues, and the best places at feasts, who devour widows' houses, and for a pretense make long prayers. These will receive greater condemnation."* (NKJV)

Jesus spoke to his disciples, aware that the crowds were listening. He warned them about the **hypocrisy** of the scribes (teachers of the law), who planned their daily lives around actions that would generate approval. These leaders wore long robes that showed their place in upper-class society. Common laborers could not work in such clothing. The scribes made grand entrances at gathering places, so they could get the applause they desired. While they pretended to pray long caring prayers for defenseless widows, they actually plotted ways to make money from those defenseless women.

Again Luke includes reference to widows. The blood in his caring heart boiled as he reflected on Jesus's insight into the plight of women who had no way to defend themselves against the manipulations of greedy religious leaders. God has a tender heart for the defenseless. His heart goes out to women and children who live in fear and deprivation. He has entrusted others with the means to relieve their suffering. What are we doing about it?

Chapter Wrap-Up

- When Jesus's critics questioned where he received his authority, he asked them whether John the Baptist's authority was from heaven or from man. (Luke 20:1–8)

- Jesus told a parable about tenants of a vineyard who beat the owner's servants and murdered his son. The tale made the religious leaders furious. (Luke 20:9–19)

- When questioned about paying taxes to Caesar, Jesus gave the principle that we are to be law-abiding citizens while remembering always that we belong to his kingdom of righteousness and love. (Luke 20:20–26)

- The Sadducees wanted to make sport of the Pharisees' belief that there is life after death. Jesus's reply confounded them because he proved from Moses's writings that Abraham, Isaac, and Jacob were alive in heaven. (Luke 20:27–44)

- The teachers of the law paraded around in expensive robes and attracted attention to themselves while they plotted ways to exploit the helpless. (Luke 20:45–47)

Study Questions

1. Why did Jesus choose not to answer the religious leaders' question about his authority?

2. In what way was Israel like the tenant farmers in Jesus's parable?

3. What attitude does Jesus teach us to have toward government?

4. How did Jesus silence the Sadducees when he questioned them about the afterlife?

5. What hypocrisy did Jesus expose in the teachers of the law?

Luke 21 What Matters Most

Let's Get Started

Jesus stood in the beautiful Temple as he spoke to the crowds and the critics who gathered to hear him. After observing the people who placed their offerings in the trumpet-shaped chests provided in the Women's Court, he left with his disciples.

It is easy to get so caught up in the here and now that we ignore the reality that lies beyond the visible. This was true of the disciples. They were impressed by the grandeur of the Temple. Jesus saw beyond the showmanship of the wealthy worshipers who dropped their large offerings in the chests, making an impressive clatter. He also saw beyond the marble and gold of the Temple to the horrible destruction that would come in a few years. As he spoke about what he saw, he pointed out what matters most. He told his disciples to be alert, to persevere to the end, and to be assured that he would remain faithful to them.

evils
Luke 20:46–47

Size Doesn't Matter

> LUKE 21:1–4 *And He looked up and saw the rich putting their gifts into the treasury, and He saw also a certain poor widow putting in two mites. So He said, "Truly I say to you that this poor widow has put in more than all; for all these out of their abundance have put in offerings for God, but she out of her poverty put in all the livelihood that she had." (NKJV)*

Jesus had pointed out the <u>evils</u> of the teachers of the law who made a show of their religion and attracted attention to themselves. They offered loud and long prayers, pretending to care about the needs of widows while they were making moves to defraud them!

Now he watched the wealthy approach the thirteen trumpet-shaped chests in the Women's Court of the Temple (see a diagram of the Temple, Illustration #1). As they placed their offerings into the narrow opening at the top of the receptacle, their coins made an impressive clatter. The louder the sound, the more generous the

go to

defended
Deuteronomy 10:18

treated justly
Deuteronomy 27:19;
Isaiah 10:1–4

provided for
Deuteronomy
14:28–29; 24:19

pure and undefiled
James 1:27

distribution
Acts 6:1–7

giver! People nearby turned their heads to see what important person could afford to give such a large offering.

Then a poor widow approached. She carried two tiny coins, which barely made a clank as she placed them in the offering chest. She would have gone unnoticed by the throng, but Jesus pointed her out as having given more than the wealthy. They had given from their abundance; she had given her all. They had given to impress others; she had given to express her love to God. While we look at how much we give to God, he looks at how much of ourselves we have made available to him.

> **what others say**
>
> **Lawrence O. Richards**
>
> It's not how much we give, but our willingness to surrender all. Undoubtedly Luke purposely placed the ragged, humble widow beside the posturing, well-dressed politicians whose pretensions Jesus had just exposed. Luke wanted us to see others as God sees them. He wants us to realize that the mighty are seldom high on God's scale of values.[1]

Luke's obvious care and concern for widows shine through in his Gospel account, and give joy to God, who desires that the poor and defenseless be shown compassion.

In Bible times the plight of widows was desperate. They had no income, no way of earning a living, and had to depend on the dole of food distributed by the Temple. Even before God led the Israelites into the land of promise, he had expressed his tender concern for widows. He <u>defended</u> their cause and made it clear that widows were to be <u>treated justly</u> and <u>provided for</u>. These provisions for the fatherless and widows were reinforced by the prophets.

James describes the essence of religion that is <u>pure and undefiled</u> as watching out for the needs of orphans and widows. The early church took this responsibility so seriously that they appointed seven men known to be full of the Spirit and wisdom to serve the needs of widows who had been overlooked in the daily <u>distribution</u> of food.

Though government agencies and charities have taken over some of the services to people with needs, we each can still find ways to express God's love and care to needy individuals. We can show compassion personally to people in our communities. In addition, through donations to charities and faith-based ministries, we can reach out to widows and orphans in other places.

temple reconstruction
John 2:20

Here Today, Gone Tomorrow

LUKE 21:5–6 *Then, as some spoke of the temple, how it was adorned with beautiful stones and donations, He said, "These things which you see—the days will come in which not one stone shall be left upon another that shall not be thrown down." (NKJV)*

As Jesus left the Temple with his disciples, some of them commented on the beauty of the building and the generosity of those who had given to God for its construction. After all, the Temple had become one of the wonders of the Roman Empire!

Jesus's response must have sucked the breath out of the disciples' lungs. Workmen had labored on the <u>temple reconstruction</u> for forty-six years. Now Jesus said that not one of the huge foundation stones would be left in place. The Temple was going to be completely destroyed.

what others say

Howard Vos

The retaining walls of the Temple Mount rose 98 feet above the paved area at the foot of the mount. And in some places the lower courses of these walls, always planted on bedrock, go as far down as 65 feet below the street, making walls at such a point more than 165 feet high. Most of the stones in these walls weighed two to five tons. But in the southwest corner of the Temple Mount are stones that weigh about 50 tons apiece.[2]

What's the Timetable?

LUKE 21:7 *So they asked Him, saying, "Teacher, but when will these things be? And what sign will there be when these things are about to take place?" (NKJV)*

As Jesus led the disciples to the Mount of Olives they could hardly wait to ask him questions about the future—questions about when Jesus's prophecy would be fulfilled and what clues would come in advance. People of all generations can identify with their curiosity about what the future holds. Jesus's response is called the Olivet Discourse.

gospel harmony

Matthew 24 and Mark 13 include Jesus's prophecy about the Temple and his Second Coming. In Matthew, Mark, and Luke Jesus answered three questions raised by the disciples:

- When will the Temple be destroyed?
- What will be the sign of your coming?
- What will be the sign of the end of the age?

In answering, Jesus did not address these questions in this sequence, nor did he attach specific dates to any of them.

Be Alert

LUKE 21:8–11 *And He said: "Take heed that you not be deceived. For many will come in My name, saying, 'I am He,' and, 'The time has drawn near.' Therefore do not go after them. But when you hear of wars and commotions, do not be terrified; for these things must come to pass first, but the end will not come immediately." Then He said to them, "Nation will rise against nation, and kingdom against kingdom. And there will be great earthquakes in various places, and famines and pestilences; and there will be fearful sights and great signs from heaven. (NKJV)*

First, Jesus warned that many men would appear claiming to be Christ. They would profess to have spectacular revelations, none found in the Bible.

Then Jesus predicted international unrest—wars, revolutions, and natural disasters. Some would be alarming, but Jesus assured his disciples that none would take God by surprise. They would come, but would not necessarily indicate the end time.

day and the hour
Matthew 24:36

Some people have tried to pinpoint the date when "the end" will come, but their calculations always prove wrong. It's impossible to figure out that date. Jesus said that even he did not know nor did the angels—only the Father in heaven knows the <u>day and the hour</u>.

what others say

R. C. Sproul

Some people believe that, since we don't know when Jesus will come again, we ought not even think about the signs of the times—knowledge of such things was never intended for us. In the Olivet discourse, Jesus clearly suggests that we be vigilant and diligent and aware of what's going on around us.[3]

Philip Yancey

I confess that, despite long hours of study in the prophets, I have no clearer understanding of what will happen next year, or in 2025. But I have a much clearer idea of what God wants to accomplish in my life right now. And I am gaining, gradually, the confidence to believe in the present what will fully make sense only when seen from the future.[4]

Speechwriters Need Not Apply

LUKE 21:12–19 *But before all these things, they will lay their hands on you and persecute you, delivering you up to the synagogues and prisons. You will be brought before kings and rulers for My name's sake. But it will turn out for you as an occasion for testimony. Therefore settle it in your hearts not to meditate beforehand on what you will answer; for I will give you a mouth and wisdom which all your adversaries will not be able to contradict or resist. You will be betrayed even by parents and brothers, relatives and friends; and they will put some of you to death. And you will be hated by all for My name's sake. But not a hair of your head shall be lost. By your patience possess your souls.* (NKJV)

Jesus prepared his followers for persecution. They would face hostile questioning and physical punishment from religious and government leaders. He assured them that they were not responsible to prepare in advance to defend themselves. At the precise moment they would need that defense, Jesus would give them irrefutable words, far better than any lawyer or speechwriter could provide.

Even if his followers were betrayed by family and friends, even if they were killed because of their loyalty to him, they would be safe, for Jesus promised they would <u>never perish</u>.

Be Prepared

LUKE 21:20–24 *"But when you see Jerusalem surrounded by armies, then know that its desolation is near. Then let those who are in Judea flee to the mountains, let those who are in the midst of her depart, and let not those who are in the country enter her. For these are the days of vengeance, that all things which are written may be fulfilled. But woe to those who are pregnant and to those who are nursing babies in those days! For there will be great distress in the land and wrath upon this people. And they will fall by the edge of the sword, and be led away captive into all nations. And Jerusalem will be trampled by Gentiles until the times of the Gentiles are fulfilled. (NKJV)*

Jesus moved from long-range predictions to deal specifically with the disciples' question about when the Temple would be destroyed. He painted the picture in detail—every one fulfilled in AD 70, less than forty years later.

The Roman army moved in to surround Jerusalem. When war threatened in those days, the people who lived in the country grabbed a few belongings and headed for the protection of the closest walled city. History records that a million Jews who sought refuge inside Jerusalem died, either from starvation or from the carnage that followed when the army broke through the city walls. Jesus's followers, now called Christians, heeded Jesus's warning, escaped to the mountains before the siege, and survived.

When the Temple was destroyed, Jews fled from the surrounding areas and scattered among many nations, exactly as Jesus had predicted.

The Romans who invaded Jerusalem were followed by other occupying nations, so that for almost two thousand years the Gentiles have trampled on the land of promise. "The times of the Gentiles" (Luke 21:24 NKJV) may refer to the period when Gentiles control the land of Israel. The Jews will regain control before Christ's Second Coming.

Jesus had wept over Jerusalem, knowing that their rejection of him would bring dire consequences. Now in foretelling the scope of the destruction, his heart overflowed with compassion for the human suffering that lay ahead, especially for the women and infants who would become victims. God takes <u>no pleasure</u> in the death of the wicked. He is <u>longsuffering</u>, giving time for people to repent.

More Signs

LUKE 21:25–28 *"And there will be signs in the sun, in the moon, and in the stars; and on the earth distress of nations, with perplexity, the sea and the waves roaring; men's hearts failing them from fear and the expectation of those things which are coming on the earth, for the powers of the heavens will be shaken. Then they will see the Son of Man coming in a cloud with power and great glory. Now when these things begin to happen, look up and lift up your heads, because your redemption draws near."* (NKJV)

Jesus promised to come again and spoke with vivid language of events that would indicate his return:

- Unusual signs in the sky and on earth will indicate Jesus's imminent return. Jesus did not give specific information for this as he had given for the destruction of Jerusalem, but he left no question that the upheaval will cause great consternation among people.

- Incredible distress will come on earth. Students of Bible prophecy call this the **Tribulation**.

- Jesus will come in a cloud of glory.

Believers should welcome these signs because they announce Jesus's return and the final unfolding of believers' everlasting life with God.

go to

no pleasure
Ezekiel 33:11

longsuffering
2 Peter 3:9

Tribulation
seven years of God's judgment at history's end

---

what others say

R. Kent Hughes

The end will feature unnatural disasters. Cosmic portents—quakes in the heavens, terrestrial catastrophes, tidal disturbances, chaos—all these are part of his final appearing. This is apocalyptic language for violent change in the natural order and in human life. The result will be widespread despair and apprehension.[6]

Be Assured

Jesus returns
Titus 2:11–13;
1 John 3:2–3

LUKE 21:29–33 *Then He spoke to them a parable: "Look at the fig tree, and all the trees. When they are already budding, you see and know for yourselves that summer is now near. So you also, when you see these things happening, know that the kingdom of God is near. Assuredly, I say to you, this generation will by no means pass away till all things take place. Heaven and earth will pass away, but My words will by no means pass away.* (NKJV)

Jesus pointed to a fig tree, reminding his disciples that they could observe signs of new life in spring and know that summer was coming. The fig tree was important to the people, both for its fruit and the shade it provided, so it is understandable that people would watch for first signs of new growth. Similarly, people should be alert to signs of Jesus's kingdom.

When Jesus said, "This generation will by no means pass away" (Luke 21:32 NKJV), he may have meant a span of several lifetimes, not one thirty- or forty-year period. Jesus promised that the physical aspects of the universe would wear out and disappear, but his words would remain forever. In essence he said, "Be assured. Keep trusting in me."

Time Keeps Slipping into the Future

LUKE 21:34–36 *"But take heed to yourselves, lest your hearts be weighed down with carousing, drunkenness, and cares of this life, and that Day come on you unexpectedly. For it will come as a snare on all those who dwell on the face of the whole earth. Watch therefore, and pray always that you may be counted worthy to escape all these things that will come to pass, and to stand before the Son of Man."* (NKJV)

Jesus gave a warning that applies to all. Do not be fooled into thinking that life on planet Earth will go on forever. It won't! Be careful not to be so involved with everyday life that you are caught unprepared when the end comes and <u>Jesus returns</u>. We prepare for what Jesus predicted by being alert and prayerful.

A generation or two ago some Christians used to keep a motto on their wall that read, "Perhaps today." It was a reminder that Jesus could return any day, perhaps even today! If we took that thought seriously, what changes would we make in our lives today?

Jesus's Do-Not-Do List

We can summarize Jesus's Olivet Discourse with an eight-point do-not-do list.

- Do not be fooled by false announcements (21:8).

- Do not be alarmed by wars and natural disasters (21:9–11).

- Do not panic if you're given a hard time by authorities, friends, and family; tell them about me and count on me to give you the words to say (21:12–16).

- Do not give up even when everyone is down on you (21:17–19).

- Do not hesitate to run from Jerusalem when it is under attack. (21:20–24).

- Do not be alarmed when natural laws in the universe seem to go awry; these are signs that I am coming soon (21:25–31).

- Do not worry that my word will let you down; I guarantee it won't (21:32–33).

- Do not become preoccupied with this life. Be on alert and prayerful so you will stick by me (21:34–36).

Last Opportunity

LUKE 21:37–38 *And in the daytime He was teaching in the temple, but at night He went out and stayed on the mountain called Olivet. Then early in the morning all the people came to Him in the temple to hear Him.* (NKJV)

Only a little time was left for Jesus's teaching ministry. He wanted to spend as much time as possible with the people. Every day he went to the Temple where people gathered to hear him. Every night he camped out nearby on the **Mount of Olives** where, no doubt, he spent precious hours talking to his Father in prayer.

Mount of Olives
site of Gethsemane, Jesus's ascension, and predicted return

Chapter Wrap-Up

- At the Temple Jesus pointed out a widow who gave two tiny coins, and he said that she had given far more than others though they had poured in many large coins. (Luke 21:1–4)

- When Jesus's disciples commented on the beauty of the Temple, Jesus astonished them by saying that it would be destroyed. (Luke 21:5–7)

- In a lengthy discourse, Jesus spoke of war and natural disasters. He also warned of coming persecution. (Luke 21:8–19)

- Jesus spoke particularly of the destruction of Jerusalem and counseled believers to flee the city when armies came near. He gave additional warnings and assured followers he would remain faithful. (Luke 21:20–36)

- Jesus spent his last days teaching people in the Temple. In the evenings he went to the Mount of Olives. (Luke 21:37–38)

Study Questions

1. Why was the widow's offering so significant?

2. What three questions did Jesus answer in his Olivet Discourse?

3. What eight things does Jesus say we should avoid doing in light of his return? Which ones most apply to you?

4. How did Jesus spend his time in his last week?

Part Three
Betrayal, Death, and
Resurrection

Luke 22 The Longest Night

Chapter Highlights:
- Judas Makes a Deal
- The Lord's Supper
- An Illegal Warrant
- Peter Denies Jesus
- Mock Jewish Trial

Let's Get Started

Events moved toward the climax in which Jesus gave his life. Jesus's enemies formed plans for a coup when Judas agreed to betray Jesus in his nightly hangout. Jesus's last night as a "free man" was a long one that brought no relief when dawn came.

As we read Luke's account of Jesus's horrendous suffering, we recognize that Jesus was not a helpless victim. He knew what lay ahead for him, and he chose to give his life—for us.

Judas Makes a Deal

LUKE 22:1–6 *Now the Feast of Unleavened Bread drew near, which is called Passover. And the chief priests and the scribes sought how they might kill Him, for they feared the people. Then Satan entered Judas, surnamed Iscariot, who was numbered among the twelve. So he went his way and conferred with the chief priests and captains, how he might betray Him to them. And they were glad, and agreed to give him money. So he promised and sought opportunity to betray Him to them in the absence of the multitude.* (NKJV)

Many rival groups joined forces to nab Jesus. Prior to this point in the Gospel accounts, the Pharisees were the ones who sought ways to get rid of Jesus. In the verses above Luke says the "chief priests and the scribes" were now hot on Jesus's trail. They had the legal and political connections needed to build a case against Jesus.

Enter Satan and his new buddy Judas. Judas, one of the Twelve, took the initiative to seek out the religious leaders and arranged to betray Jesus into their hands. He knew Jesus's habits and the places he hung out when no crowds were nearby to protest the arrest. Bible experts disagree about whether Judas was possessed by Satan or just influenced by him. In either case, Judas volunteered to be the satanic pawn to place the King in check.

The religious leaders licked their evil chops in anticipation and dished out the money.

Luke states simply that Judas took action to betray Jesus after Satan entered him. Matthew 26:14–15 and John 12:4–6 fill out the picture with valuable insights into Judas's character and motivation.

price of a servant
Exodus 21:32

Judas suffered from disillusionment. Some suggest he had joined Jesus's band, thinking that he could rise to a place of prominence in a political kingdom, which he hoped Jesus would institute. He disagreed with the way Jesus ran things. This group was going nowhere fast.

Judas was dominated by love of money. As treasurer of the Twelve, he had been dipping into their limited funds. When he approached the religious leaders, proposing to hand Jesus over to them, he received thirty silver coins, the <u>price of a servant</u>.

what others say

Warren W. Wiersbe

When Judas understood that Jesus would not establish the kingdom but rather would surrender to the authorities, he turned against him in bitter retaliation.[1]

George R. Bliss

That Satan entered into Judas, means that the devil, to accomplish his malignant purposes against our Lord, took advantage of the wickedness of Judas, to direct him as a serviceable tool.[2]

Jesus Prepares His Pals

LUKE 22:7–13 *Then came the Day of Unleavened Bread, when the Passover must be killed. And He sent Peter and John, saying, "Go and prepare the Passover for us, that we may eat." So they said to Him, "Where do You want us to prepare?" And He said to them, "Behold, when you have entered the city, a man will meet you carrying a pitcher of water; follow him into the house which he enters. Then you shall say to the master of the house, 'The Teacher says to you, "Where is the guest room where I may eat the Passover with My disciples?"' Then he will show you a large, furnished upper room; there make ready." So they went and found it just as He had said to them, and they prepared the Passover. (NKJV)*

Aware that Judas had made plans to betray him to his enemies, Jesus made plans to partake of the Passover meal with his pals in private. He sent only Peter and John to a prearranged, secret location where they could prepare the meal.

The clue they would have to the location of this meal was meeting a man who would be carrying a bottle of water. They were to follow him to his house. This man would stand out in the crowded streets, because in Bible times, women carried pitchers of water while men carried water in larger, heavier water skins (see Illustration #13).

Luke refers to the Feast of Unleavened Bread as being called the

Illustration #13
Male Water Carrier—A woman carried water in a large clay jug on her head. A man carried water in a goatskin bottle on his back as shown here.

Passover. According to God's instructions for celebrations, the Passover was to be observed on a specific day in the first month of the Hebrew religious calendar followed by a week of observing the separate Feast of Unleavened Bread (Deuteronomy 16:1–8; 2 Chronicles 30:1, 21). But Luke wasn't confused. Josephus, the Jewish historian of early New Testament times, indicates that by Jesus's day the Jews had combined the two occasions into one longer celebration.

The Last Repast

marriage supper
Revelation 19:9

Passover
Exodus 11:12–14

remembering
1 Corinthians
11:23–26

LUKE 22:14–18 *When the hour had come, He sat down, and the twelve apostles with Him. Then He said to them, "With fervent desire I have desired to eat this Passover with you before I suffer; for I say to you, I will no longer eat of it until it is fulfilled in the kingdom of God." Then He took the cup, and gave thanks, and said, "Take this and divide it among yourselves; for I say to you, I will not drink of the fruit of the vine until the kingdom of God comes." (NKJV)*

Jesus had purposefully arranged to have the Passover meal in private with his disciples. He eagerly desired this because he had much to say to them and needed uninterrupted time to open his heart. He alerted them to the seriousness of the occasion by saying this was his last meal before his time of great suffering. Jesus also looked forward to the future when he would take his place beside God and would fellowship with all believers at the <u>marriage supper</u> of the Lamb.

The Lord's Supper

LUKE 22:19–20 *And He took bread, gave thanks and broke it, and gave it to them, saying, "This is My body which is given for you; do this in remembrance of Me." Likewise He also took the cup after supper, saying, "This cup is the new covenant in My blood, which is shed for you. (NKJV)*

The <u>Passover</u> meal reminded the Jews of the Exodus when the Lord literally passed over the homes of the Israelites and spared the lives of their firstborn sons and not the lives of the Egyptians' sons. Now Jesus put a new perspective on elements of the meal he ate with his disciples. They were to eat this meal to remember him.

Jesus used bread and wine that were already on the table to institute a way of <u>remembering</u> him that is still used today. He broke the unleavened bread, shared it with his disciples, and asked them to think of his body, which would soon be broken for them. He took the wine and asked his followers to think of his blood, which would soon be poured out for their salvation.

Jesus introduced a way for his followers to remember him and his sacrifice for them. He pointed forward to his death. Early Christians followed his instructions, looking back with love and gratitude to his death.

Jesus's followers continue to remember him in what is called the Lord's Supper or Holy Communion today. Jesus asked his followers to remember him in this way until his <u>return</u>. Remembering Jesus in the Lord's Supper reaffirms our relationship with him and with other believers.

apply it

what others say

Lloyd John Ogilvie

And it is here, as we break this bread and drink of this cup that we tangibly experience the central truth of life—he was broken for us that our hearts might not be splintered by the fragmentation of a multiplicity of loyalties. As we become whole through his brokenness, everything in our life begins to revolve around the central loyalty to him and his kingdom. Worry is replaced by what the poet called "the deep mysterious joy of absolute subjection"—to him rather than to the things and persons of our lives.

And the cup of the new covenant—the very word indicates that there is now a new relationship . . . When we drink of that cup, we know that we may go to him on the basis of his love and not on the basis of our adequacy.[3]

Who's the Weakest Link?

LUKE 22:21–23 But behold, the hand of My betrayer is with Me on the table. And truly the Son of Man goes as it has been determined, but woe to that man by whom He is betrayed!" Then they began to question among themselves, which of them it was who would do this thing. (NKJV)

Jesus broke into a moment of tender closeness with a stunning announcement. Within this group around the table, sharing Jesus's words about his death, was one who would be a traitor by betraying him. Jesus's use of the word *determined* shows Luke's emphasis on divine orchestration of events. Jesus would not be a victim; he would be a victor.

Judas had concealed his evil intentions, covering his tracks so well that the disciples did not know that Jesus was speaking about him. Even though God was in charge of the events, Judas was still responsible for his actions. Jesus said, "Woe to that man!" (Luke 22:22 NKJV). It was an expression of grief, like saying, "Uh-oh! Bad things are going to happen to him."

go to

return
1 Corinthians 11:26

washing
John 13:1–17

Servant Leaders

LUKE 22:24–27 *Now there was also a dispute among them, as to which of them should be considered the greatest. And He said to them, "The kings of the Gentiles exercise lordship over them, and those who exercise authority over them are called 'benefactors.' But not so among you; on the contrary, he who is greatest among you, let him be as the younger, and he who governs as he who serves. For who is greater, he who sits at the table, or he who serves? Is it not he who sits at the table? Yet I am among you as the One who serves. (NKJV)*

Instead of assuring Jesus of their loyalty and their deep caring for the suffering that lay ahead for him, the disciples began to argue. Being tops on Jesus's roster should have been the last thing on their minds, but they couldn't resist the impulse to be competitive and self-seeking. Perhaps they still thought Jesus was about to set up a kingdom on earth. Their argument broke the unity that Jesus had spoken of only minutes before when he instituted the Lord's Supper.

Jesus had made the effort to arrange this private meal so that there could be an intimate sharing of hearts. But now the interruption came from within. How disappointed Jesus must have been! Jesus patiently dealt with their argument by pointing out that humble service is the badge of leadership. He had already modeled this by <u>washing</u> their feet, a task of a lowly servant.

Self-interest and competitive scrambling for recognition and promotion lie under the surface at all times unless we consciously give Jesus first place in our lives. It's a decision we must make daily.

what others say

W. Glyn Evans

The true servant surrenders pride. Jesus described himself as "one who serves," then illustrated what he meant by washing his disciples' feet. He did not allow his equality with the Father to prevent him from doing a servant's task.[4]

Forward Thinking

LUKE 22:28–30 *But you are those who have continued with Me in My trials. And I bestow upon you a kingdom, just as My Father bestowed one upon Me, that you may eat and drink at My table in My kingdom, and sit on thrones judging the twelve tribes of Israel." (NKJV)*

With unfailing understanding of their human frailties, Jesus pointed to the future. His disciples had forgotten that God was preparing a kingdom for them. In his kingdom they would have positions of authority. The verb "<u>judging</u>" is used here in the sense of "ruling," the way "judge" is used to mean "ruler" in the book of Judges.

Jesus made a promise or a covenant with his followers. They would share a glorious future with him. There was no need to scramble for prestige and honor. There would be plenty of that for every faithful follower. But first, they must join him in humiliation and suffering.

Overconfident Simon Says

judging
Judges 2:16–18

you
here: plural, meaning all the disciples

you
here: singular, meaning Peter

LUKE 22:31–34 *And the Lord said, "Simon, Simon! Indeed, Satan has asked for **you**, that he may sift you as wheat. But I have prayed for **you**, that your faith should not fail; and when you have returned to Me, strengthen your brethren." But he said to Him, "Lord, I am ready to go with You, both to prison and to death." Then He said, "I tell you, Peter, the rooster shall not crow this day before you will deny three times that you know Me." (NKJV)*

Satan had it in for all the disciples. He was convinced they were wimps. "They will fold under pressure," he told God. "Let me test them and you'll see."

So Jesus warned Peter that he was about to be taken to the mat by Satan. This warning must have stunned the group as well as Peter, for he was their spokesman, one of the most loyal and enthusiastic of Jesus's disciples. Characteristically, he would have been the loudest in the argument they had just had. "I am the greatest!" he would have asserted.

Now Jesus was saying that he would surely fail, apart from his prayers for Peter. But when he repented, he would become an encouragement to the others.

Overconfident, Peter cried, "I'll go to the death for you, Lord!"

"No, you won't," Jesus said. Then he prophesied Peter's denial.

must ask
Job 1:6–12

no provisions
Luke 9:3; 10:4

transgressor
Isaiah 53:12

sword swipe
Matthew 26:51–52

Satan has no rights. He <u>must ask</u> God for permission to bring trials into the lives of Christians. God wields supreme control over our circumstances, our testings, and the unseen world of spirit beings. If we are willing to be humiliated for Jesus's sake, he promises we will be exalted with him.

Allies in Arms

LUKE 22:35–38 And He said to them, "When I sent you without money bag, knapsack, and sandals, did you lack anything?" So they said, "Nothing." Then He said to them, "But now, he who has a money bag, let him take it, and likewise a knapsack; and he who has no sword, let him sell his garment and buy one. For I say to you that this which is written must still be accomplished in Me: 'And He was numbered with the transgressors.' For the things concerning Me have an end." So they said, "Lord, look, here are two swords." And He said to them, "It is enough." (NKJV)

Previously, when Jesus sent his disciples out to preach, he told them to carry <u>no provisions</u>. Now, things had changed. Jesus would be arrested and executed as a <u>transgressor</u>. His followers would be suspect. He advised them to be prepared, even to the point of carrying swords.

The disciples failed to understand the implications of what he was saying, and Bible scholars have also debated the point. Was Jesus saying Christians should take up arms? That seems unlikely, especially after the way Jesus responded to one disciple's literal interpretation of the words and his <u>sword swipe</u> in the garden of Gethsemane.

Was Jesus reversing his earlier teaching when he sent out the disciples as missionaries in Luke 9:1–3 and 10:1–4? This seems unlikely as well, although Jesus is making a contrast. Before the disciples had it easy; this time things would be tough. They would face difficulties, hardships, and they would have to do without certain things. They would even face death.

what others say

R. Kent Hughes

The Last Supper closed as a vast disappointment to Jesus. The Messiah had come so eagerly to the Upper Room and had taken the Passover bread and cup and instituted the Last Supper—only to see the evening disintegrate. Judas left to betray him, the disciples fell to infighting, Jesus prophesied failure for Peter and the rest, and his final words were misunderstood due to the disciples' abysmal spiritual dullness. In dismay, Jesus despaired.[5]

go to

death
Romans 3:23

becoming sin
2 Corinthians 5:21

wrath
1 John 2:2

Agony in the Garden

LUKE 22:39–44 Coming out, He went to the Mount of Olives, as He was accustomed, and His disciples also followed Him. When He came to the place, He said to them, "Pray that you may not enter into temptation." And He was withdrawn from them about a stone's throw, and He knelt down and prayed, saying, "Father, if it is Your will, take this cup away from Me; nevertheless not My will, but Yours, be done." Then an angel appeared to Him from heaven, strengthening Him. And being in agony, He prayed more earnestly. Then His sweat became like great drops of blood falling down to the ground. (NKJV)

Jesus left the upper room and led his disciples to the Mount of Olives where they had been spending the last several nights. When Jesus entered the garden, he left his disciples, asking them to pray that they would withstand temptation. He then went to pray alone. The normal posture for prayer in that day was to stand and look toward heaven. Jesus's anguish was horrendous as he thought about what lay ahead. He knew he faced <u>death</u> as he would bear the sins of the world, actually <u>becoming sin</u> for us, and he faced his Father's <u>wrath</u> for that sin. This wrath, which was punishment for the sins he was bearing, meant that his Father would turn away from him, a separation that was far worse than physical death. He asked if it were possible to be spared this terrible pain, but affirmed that he wanted to do only his Father's will.

An angel came to him and strengthened him. Still he prayed even more earnestly so that "His sweat became like great drops of blood falling down to the ground" (Luke 22:44 NKJV). Luke is the only Gospel writer to include the description of Jesus's physical appearance as he prayed. As a physician he would be particularly sensitive to visible clues of internal distress.

what others say

Max Lucado

Never has he [Jesus] felt so alone. What must be done, only he can do. An angel can't do it. No angel has the power to

go to

temptation
1 Corinthians 10:13

break open hell's gates. A man can't do it. No man has the purity to destroy sin's claim. No force on earth can face the force of evil and win—except God.[6]

Warren W. Wiersbe

[Luke's] use of the word *like* may suggest that the sweat merely fell to the ground like clots of blood. But there is a rare physical phenomenon known as hematidrosis, in which, under great emotional stress, the tiny blood vessels rupture in the sweat glands and produce a mixture of blood and sweat.[7]

Not Standing by Their Man

> LUKE 22:45–46 *When He rose up from prayer, and had come to His disciples, He found them sleeping from sorrow. Then He said to them, "Why do you sleep? Rise and pray, lest you enter into temptation." (NKJV)*

In spite of Jesus's warning about what was ahead, in spite of his agony in prayer, the disciples did not stand by him. They fell asleep. Luke says they were depressed. Their self-centeredness added to Jesus's hardships. Jesus woke them up, urging them to pray that they would not yield to <u>temptation</u>. He knew what lay ahead for them.

gospel harmony

Matthew 26:36–46 and Mark 14:32–42 give more details to Jesus's experience in the garden. All the disciples except Judas, who had already left the group, went to the garden with Jesus. He asked Peter, James, and John to go aside with him as he prayed to his Father. He confided to them, "My soul is exceedingly sorrowful, even to death" (Matthew 26:38; Mark 14:34 NKJV). He asked them to stay by him as he prayed. However, they fell asleep. He prayed three times, and three times he found them asleep.

Kiss and Tell

> LUKE 22:47–51 *And while He was still speaking, behold, a multitude; and he who was called Judas, one of the twelve, went before them and drew near to Jesus to kiss Him. But Jesus said to him, "Judas, are you betraying the Son of Man with a kiss?" When those around Him saw what was going to happen, they said to Him, "Lord, shall we strike with the sword?" And one of them struck the servant of the high priest and cut off his right ear. But Jesus answered and said, "Permit even this." And He touched his ear and healed him. (NKJV)*

Even as Jesus was speaking with his disciples, this Judas guy—that's how Luke describes him in Greek—appeared in the garden. He was accompanied by an armed crowd sent by the religious leaders. Judas had arranged to identify Jesus by a secret signal—a kiss! He could have used any other means of identifying Jesus, but he chose to use a sign of caring and love as a signal of betrayal. It was a horrible mockery.

As the crowd grabbed Jesus and arrested him, <u>Peter</u>, true to his impulsive nature, whipped out his sword and cut off the ear of Malchus, a servant of the high priest. Peter wasn't aiming for the guy's ear! Malchus ducked to save his neck! Jesus immediately healed the man and put a stop to further violence.

Peter
John 18:10

An Illegal Warrant

> LUKE 22:52–53 *Then Jesus said to the chief priests, captains of the temple, and the elders who had come to Him, "Have you come out, as against a robber, with swords and clubs? When I was with you daily in the temple, you did not try to seize Me. But this is your hour, and the power of darkness." (NKJV)*

Jesus did not resist the arrest, but he did confront the religious leaders who arrived in the garden. Why had they come with an armed crowd to arrest him as if he were a robber? Why had they not simply taken him when he was in the temple courts? Clearly, they were doing something illegal. They were cowards who used the darkness of night to conceal their dastardly deed. But he submitted to them because of God's plan for saving sinners.

Peter Denies Jesus

> LUKE 22:54–60 *Having arrested Him, they led Him and brought Him into the high priest's house. But Peter followed at a distance. Now when they had kindled a fire in the midst of the courtyard and sat down together, Peter sat among them. And a certain servant girl, seeing him as he sat by the fire, looked intently at him and said, "This man was also with Him." But he denied Him, saying, "Woman, I do not know Him." And after a little while another saw him and said, "You also are of them." But Peter said, "Man, I am not!" Then after about an hour had passed, another confidently affirmed, saying, "Surely*

another disciple
John 18:15

home
John 18:12–23

this fellow also was with Him, for he is a Galilean." But Peter said, "Man, I do not know what you are saying!" Immediately, while he was still speaking, the rooster crowed. (NKJV)

Peter and <u>another disciple</u> followed Jesus as he was led out of the garden and into the house of Annas, the power monger behind the official high priest, Caiaphas. The other disciples fled from the scene with heart-stopping fear. Peter deserves credit for at least tagging along. But he too was scared. As he sat in the courtyard, warming himself at a fire, he was identified three times as one of Jesus's followers. Three times he vigorously denied Jesus. Then a rooster crowed.

what others say

Michael Card

Immediately after being arrested Jesus was bound and taken to the <u>home</u> of Annas, who was in all likelihood the key conspirator behind the plot to have Jesus killed. The marketplace in the temple, which Jesus had twice destroyed, was called the Bazaar of Annas. It belonged to him. Caiaphas had married Annas's daughter. Annas had been high priest some fifteen years earlier but had been removed from office by the Romans. Jesus was held here while the members of the Sanhedrin, the Jewish ruling council, could be called together.[8]

The Eyes Have It

LUKE 22:61–62 *And the Lord turned and looked at Peter. Then Peter remembered the word of the Lord, how He had said to him, "Before the rooster crows, you will deny Me three times." So Peter went out and wept bitterly. (NKJV)*

Meanwhile Jesus was probably being moved across the courtyard between the homes of Annas and Caiaphas. Just as the rooster crowed, Jesus's eyes met Peter's. Jesus looked at him with love and concern, not disgust or anger. Suddenly Peter knew that Jesus knew of his denials, and he remembered what Jesus had told him. Jesus said he would disown him three times. Regret flooded Peter's heart. He stumbled outside and bawled like a baby.

Peter failed. He failed to tell the truth. He failed to keep his promise. He failed in his loyalty to Jesus. Yet he was not destroyed. Jesus had prayed for him. Even as he wept bitterly, Jesus had not rejected him.

Jesus's prayer for Peter was not a one-time act of mercy. Today Jesus is in the presence of his Father <u>praying</u> for you and me.

Humiliation and Insults

LUKE 22:63–65 *Now the men who held Jesus mocked Him and beat Him. And having blindfolded Him, they struck Him on the face and asked Him, saying, "Prophesy! Who is the one who struck You?" And many other things they blasphemously spoke against Him. (NKJV)*

Guards let loose on Jesus. They made sport of him and beat him. So he was a prophet? Prove it! They blindfolded him and demanded that he identify the person who hit him. Then they heaped even more insults on him.

If he had chosen to, Jesus could have played their game. He could have escaped from their beatings. He could have called ten thousand angels to destroy these measly soldiers.

Mock Jewish Trial

LUKE 22:66–71 *As soon as it was day, the elders of the people, both chief priests and scribes, came together and led Him into their council, saying, "If You are the Christ, tell us." But He said to them, "If I tell you, you will by no means believe. And if I also ask you, you will by no means answer Me or let Me go. Hereafter the Son of Man will sit on the right hand of the power of God." Then they all said, "Are You then the Son of God?" So He said to them, "You rightly say that I am." And they said,*

go to

penalty
Leviticus 24:10–16

Sanhedrin
Jews' highest ruling
council

blasphemy
treating God with
contempt by reduc-
ing him to mere
human level

*"What further testimony do we need? For we have heard it our-
selves from His own mouth." (NKJV)*

Throughout the night the religious leaders held meetings and discussions, trying to figure out how to formally charge Jesus. It wasn't
legal for them to hold a trial at night. It wasn't even legal for them
to give a verdict at night on the day of a trial. But why let a little
thing like the law stop them? They were in a hurry.

As dawn broke over the city of Jerusalem, Jesus was taken before
the **Sanhedrin**. Caiaphas led the "legal" proceeding. The group
held no presumed-innocent-until-proven-guilty opinion; they had
their minds made up. All they had to do was find Jesus guilty of
some offense that would allow them to turn him over to the Romans
to be put to death. The top issue on their list was Jesus's identity.
Was he the Messiah? If they could get him to admit this, they could
accuse him of making a false claim and being guilty of **blasphemy**.
According to Jewish law, the penalty for blasphemy was death.

When they asked if he was the Messiah, he replied that they would
not believe his answer. Then he went on to say that he would soon
be seated at the right hand of the mighty God.

"Are You then the Son of God?" (Luke 22:70 NKJV) they asked in
unison. Jesus replied that they were correct in saying so.

"Enough!" They had all the testimony they needed. Now they
could turn him over to the Romans.

Chapter Wrap-Up

- Judas made a deal with the religious leaders to betray Jesus into their hands. (Luke 22:1–6)
- Jesus celebrated the Passover meal with his disciples, at which time he talked about the future and instituted the Lord's Supper. (Luke 22:7–20)
- Jesus reminded the disciples that greatness is revealed by humble service and prophesied Peter's denial. (Luke 22:21–38)
- Jesus prayed in Gethsemane, seeking strength for the suffering that lay ahead. His disciples slept. (Luke 22:39–46)
- Judas led an armed crowd into the garden and betrayed Jesus with a kiss. Jesus was arrested and led away for trial. (Luke 22:47–53)
- When Peter was questioned, he denied Jesus three times. (Luke 22:54–62)
- Jesus was mocked, beaten, and insulted. At daybreak he was led away to be questioned by the Sanhedrin. (Luke 22:63–71)

Study Questions

1. Why were the religious leaders so pleased when Judas offered to betray Jesus?

2. Why was it important for Jesus to have an uninterrupted Passover meal with his disciples?

3. What is the significance of the Lord's Supper?

4. What disturbing things did Jesus say at the Passover meal?

5. What did Jesus talk about with his Father in Gethsemane?

6. Describe Jesus's arrest, identifying the emotions of the key people involved.

7. What happened after Peter denied Jesus and the rooster crowed?

8. Where was Jesus taken through the night and how was he falsely accused and mistreated?

Luke 23 A Dark Day in History

Let's Get Started

We enter a darkened room. As we gradually become adjusted to the dim lighting, we discern some objects between the shadows. Suddenly someone opens the curtains and we are immediately horrified at the disgusting untidiness and dirt surrounding us. As we move to make a hasty exit, we begin to note some items of beauty and incredible wealth almost covered by the filth. We stop and ponder the scene.

This is the view that Luke gives us now. We have seen religious and political leaders throughout this Gospel. Now Luke pulls back the curtain and shows us what was lurking behind their shadows. He reveals the most horrendous view of men's hatred and cruelty. We can hardly bear to think of the pain Jesus endured. Yet, as we shrink from observing it, we begin to discern something more in Luke's account, something strikingly in contrast to the evil of men. We see the love of Jesus in giving his life, and we see the love of his Father in sending his Son to give his life—all for us.

Jesus endured both religious and civil trials. Although all four Gospels contain accounts of the trials, it is difficult to piece together an exact order. Each writer focuses on different things.

Matthew highlights human weakness. Mark tells about the key events. Luke emphasizes Jesus's suffering. John details Jesus's trials. Following are the most complete accounts:[1]

Jesus on Trial

Religious Trials	
Before Annas	John 18:12–23
Before Caiaphas	Matthew 26:57–68 (see also Mark 14:53–65; Luke 22:54–65; John 18:24)
Before the Sanhedrin	Matthew 27:1–2 (see also Mark 15:1; Luke 22:66–71)
Civil Trials	
Before Pilate	John 18:28–38 (see also Matthew 27:11–14; Mark 15:2–5; Luke 23:1–5)

gospel harmony

Jesus on Trial (cont'd)

Before Herod	Luke 23:6–12
Before Pilate	John 18:39–19:16 (see also Matthew 27:15–26; Mark 15:6–15; Luke 23:13–25)

Mock Roman Trial

LUKE 23:1–7 *Then the whole multitude of them arose and led Him to Pilate. And they began to accuse Him, saying, "We found this fellow perverting the nation, and forbidding to pay taxes to Caesar, saying that He Himself is Christ, a King."*

Then Pilate asked Him, saying, "Are You the King of the Jews?" He answered him and said, "It is as you say." So Pilate said to the chief priests and the crowd, "I find no fault in this Man." But they were the more fierce, saying, "He stirs up the people, teaching throughout all Judea, beginning from Galilee to this place."

When Pilate heard of Galilee, he asked if the Man were a Galilean. And as soon as he knew that He belonged to Herod's jurisdiction, he sent Him to Herod, who was also in Jerusalem at that time. (NKJV)

After a night spent dishing out interrogation, humiliation, and physical abuse, the Sanhedrin was ready to have Jesus put to death. At that time, though, Jews were not allowed to impose a death penalty. Once they had given a guilty verdict, they were required to hand the offender over to Roman authorities.

When morning came, the whole angry pack of leaders marched their prisoner to Pontius Pilate, governor of Judea. They came up with crimes, completely false accusations, which they felt would merit severe punishment from the Romans. They accused Jesus of perverting the nation, opposing paying taxes to Caesar, and claiming to be a rival king—meaning that he was a political threat to Pilate and Roman rule. None of these charges had been brought against Jesus at his trial before the Sanhedrin.

While the religious leaders wanted Pilate to view Jesus as an insurrectionist, Pilate found Jesus innocent. The Jewish leaders protested, claiming that Jesus had stirred up the people from Galilee to Jerusalem.

Pilate was no dummy. He could sense the hatred of the group toward Jesus, and he jumped at the chance to ship this hot potato off to another official. Galilee was in Herod's jurisdiction. Pilate was off the hook—or so he thought.

All four Gospel writers include accounts of the events in this chapter. John 18:28–38 gives more details of Jesus's trial before Pilate. The religious leaders would not go inside Pilate's palace because they wanted to avoid ceremonial uncleanness before eating the Passover that day. So Pilate came outside to talk with them.

Pilate questioned Jesus about the accusation that he was king of the Jews. He learned that Jesus's kingdom is not of this earth. Based on the fact that Jesus's kingship was in no way a threat to Rome, Pilate found no reason to charge Jesus with any crime.

Delighted to Meet You

LUKE 23:8–10 *Now when Herod saw Jesus, he was exceedingly glad; for he had desired for a long time to see Him, because he had heard many things about Him, and he hoped to see some miracle done by Him. Then he questioned Him with many words, but He answered him nothing. And the chief priests and scribes stood and vehemently accused Him.* (NKJV)

Sending Jesus to Herod may have been considered something of a compliment from Pilate. Pilate could have handled the case since the supposed offenses had happened in his jurisdiction, but he chose to hand the baton to his least favorite colleague.

Herod, who had imprisoned and killed John the Baptist, was delighted to have a crack at Jesus. He had heard much about the teacher and miracle worker and hoped now to see Jesus perform a miracle.

Pilate found Jesus innocent.

Any prisoner in his right mind would have milked this opportunity for all it was worth. He would have performed a few pyrotechnics on the palace plants to please Herod, with the hope of being released. Not Jesus! Jesus refused to answer Herod's many questions and he pulled no miracles out of his sleeves. Jesus had never failed to answer sincere seekers, but Herod sought only sensationalism. Although the chief priests stood close by and agitated Jesus, he remained silent.

Here He Is! Mr. King!

LUKE 23:11–12 *Then Herod, with his men of war, treated Him with contempt and mocked Him, arrayed Him in a gorgeous robe, and sent Him back to Pilate. That very day Pilate and Herod became friends with each other, for previously they had been at enmity with each other. (NKJV)*

Finally, Herod got bored. He did not take the charges against Jesus seriously. "What a jerk this guy is! Some king!" With no corner video stores, Jerusalem entertainment was often sparse, and Herod appreciated the chance for a diversion. He told the guards, "Have some fun and ship him back!" Returning the accused could have been viewed as returning Pilate's compliment. So, the former rivals became friends.

> ## what others say
>
> ### Robert L. Thomas
>
> Because much of Jesus' public ministry had been in Galilee, Pilate thought he had found a way to avoid condemning an innocent person, but Herod did not pronounce Jesus guilty or innocent. Luke had contacts within Herod's household that enabled him to describe a phase of the trial not found in the other gospels, just as John had access to information about what happened at Annas' house.[2]

Beat-and-Release Offer

LUKE 23:13–17 *Then Pilate, when he had called together the chief priests, the rulers, and the people, said to them, "You have brought this Man to me, as one who misleads the people. And indeed, having examined Him in your presence, I have found no fault in this Man concerning those things of which you accuse Him; no, neither did Herod, for I sent you back to him; and indeed nothing deserving of death has been done by Him. I will therefore chastise Him and release Him" (for it was necessary for him to release one to them at the feast. (NKJV)*

Now Pilate was in a tough spot. He tried to reason with Jesus's accusers. Since neither he nor Herod had found anything in Jesus that deserved death, he offered to beat him (to appease his accusers) and then release him.

Don't Confuse Us with the Facts!

LUKE 23:18–25 *And they all cried out at once, saying, "Away with this Man, and release to us Barabbas"—who had been thrown into prison for a certain rebellion made in the city, and for murder. Pilate, therefore, wishing to release Jesus, again called out to them. But they shouted, saying, "Crucify Him, crucify Him!" Then he said to them the third time, "Why, what evil has He done? I have found no reason for death in Him. I will therefore chastise Him and let Him go." But they were insistent, demanding with loud voices that He be crucified. And the voices of these men and of the chief priests prevailed. So Pilate gave sentence that it should be as they requested. And he released to them the one they requested, who for rebellion and murder had been thrown into prison; but he delivered Jesus to their will.* (NKJV)

Pilate's suggestion met with fury. The religious leaders demanded that Pilate release Barabbas, an insurrectionist and murderer who was currently in prison. They insisted that Jesus be crucified.

Three times Pilate attempted to have Jesus released and each time the leaders insisted that Jesus be punished with death. The crowd got louder and louder. They didn't want to listen to the facts. Pilate feared a riot. Finally, he gave in. He released Barabbas and turned Jesus over to be put to death.

Matthew is the only Gospel writer who tells us what happened to Judas (Matthew 27:3–10). When he saw that Jesus was condemned to die, Judas was overcome with horror and remorse.

gospel harmony

He met with the chief priests and elders, confessing that he had sinned in betraying Jesus, who was completely innocent. Finding the religious leaders indifferent, Judas threw the thirty silver coins down and went out to hang himself.

---

what others say

Peter Marshall

The little man did not stop running until he was outside the city gates. A picture kept flashing before his eye—he brushed his hands before his eyes but it would not leave. It was Jesus's face at that moment when he, Judas, had kissed his cheek.

"Friend," he had said gently, "wherefore art thou come? Why have you done this?"

go to

took up
Luke 14:27

Cyrene
modern Tripoli,
North Africa

> "Friend," that was what he had said. "Friend"—why have
> you done this?
> It broke Judas' heart . . . His plan had failed.
> Everything was smashed . . . his dreams . . . his hopes . . . his
> life—everything.
> There was nothing left—now. Only one way out . . .³

Even though Pilate knew Jesus was innocent and did not deserve
punishment of any kind, he allowed Jesus to be flogged and cruelly
ridiculed (John 18:39–19:16). He presented Jesus to the religious
leaders as a king—wearing a crown of thorns and covered in a purple robe.

Finally, when Pilate declared that he could find no basis for a
charge against Jesus, the religious leaders declared that he must die
because he claimed to be the Son of God.

Though this struck fear in Pilate, he still handed Jesus over to be
crucified. As Jesus was led away to die he was charged with two
"crimes": blasphemy (by the religious leaders) and claiming to be
king and thus a rival of Caesar in Rome (by Pilate).

A Forced Privilege

LUKE 23:26 *Now as they led Him away, they laid hold of a certain man, Simon a Cyrenian, who was coming from the country, and on him they laid the cross that he might bear it after
Jesus. (NKJV)*

Prisoners who were being put to death by crucifixion were publicly
humiliated by being required to carry the crossbar of their cross to the
place of death. It was a heavy piece of wood. Jesus had endured a
night of extreme emotional and physical torture, so it is not surpris-
ing that he did not have strength to carry the crossbar.

The Roman soldiers could pick any civilian to do any task. "Hey,
you, there!" they said to Simon from **Cyrene**. "Carry this cross!"
Simon was a traveler from Africa who had come to observe the
Passover in Jerusalem.

Simon could not have known the privilege the Roman soldiers had
given him. For all time he is remembered as one who literally <u>took
up</u> the cross and followed Jesus. Perhaps he was already a believer or

perhaps after this encounter he became one, because Mark 15:21 mentions Simon's sons as though readers know them.

Crucifixion Events at Calvary [4]

Following is the order of events at Calvary from the combined accounts of the Gospel writers:

- Jesus was offered drugged drink to lessen suffering (Matthew 27:34).
- Jesus was crucified (Matthew 27:35).
- Jesus cried, "Father forgive them" (Luke 23:34 NKJV).
- Soldiers gambled for Jesus's clothing (Matthew 27:35).
- Jesus was mocked by observers (Matthew 27:39–44; Mark 15:29).
- Jesus was ridiculed by two thieves (Matthew 27:44).
- One of the thieves believed (Luke 23:39–43).
- Jesus promised, "Today you will be with Me in paradise" (Luke 23:43 NKJV).
- Jesus spoke to Mary, "Woman, behold your son!" (John 19:26 NKJV).
- Darkness fell on the scene (Matthew 27:45; Mark 15:33; Luke 23:44).
- Jesus cried, "My God, My God . . ." (Matthew 27:46; Mark 15:34 NKJV).
- Jesus cried, "I thirst!" (John 19:28 NKJV).
- Jesus cried, "It is finished!" (John 19:30 NKJV).
- Jesus cried, "Father, into Your hands . . ." (Luke 23:46 NKJV).
- Jesus released his spirit (Matthew 27:50; Mark 15:37).

gospel harmony

Don't Cry for Me, Jerusalem

LUKE 23:27–31 *And a great multitude of the people followed Him, and women who also mourned and lamented Him. But Jesus, turning to them, said, "Daughters of Jerusalem, do not weep for Me, but weep for yourselves and for your children. For indeed the days are coming in which they will say, 'Blessed are the barren, wombs that never bore, and breasts which never nursed!' Then they will begin 'to say to the mountains, "Fall on us!" and to the hills, "Cover us!"' For if they do these things in the green wood, what will be done in the dry?"* (NKJV)

Executions were public events, and the one this sad day probably drew an even larger number of spectators. The city was packed because of Passover, and Jesus had been a popular teacher. Reports of his miracles had circulated for three years. Pilate had feared a riot. What he got was a bunch of crying women. They mourned and wailed as if Jesus were already dead.

Characteristic of his selflessness, Jesus expressed his concern for them, not himself. "Don't worry about me, ladies," he said. "You're the ones who will have to deal with the consequences."

Luke is the only Gospel writer to include the account of the women who followed Jesus weeping and wailing in their distress for him. These were kindhearted women from Jerusalem who, historians suggest, may have been professional mourners and were prepared to provide medications to ease the pain of the men being executed. Luke reports Jesus's counsel to them. Incredible suffering was ahead for them when God would fulfill prophecy by destroying Jerusalem in AD 70.

what others say

Robert C. Girard

He [Jesus] said, "For if men do these things when the tree is green, what will happen when it is dry?" (Luke 23:31). This was a Jewish proverb meaning "If today God pours his wrath on his Son—an innocent 'green tree'—what will conditions be when he pours his wrath on the world that spurned his love and rejected his Son?"[5]

Crime and Punishment

LUKE 23:32–34 *There were also two others, criminals, led with Him to be put to death. And when they had come to the place called Calvary, there they crucified Him, and the criminals, one on the right hand and the other on the left. Then Jesus said, "Father, forgive them, for they do not know what they do." And they divided His garments and cast lots.* (NKJV)

Crucifixion was an incredibly painful and humiliating form of execution. Two criminals were crucified with Jesus that day, one on either side of him. Unlike anyone who had ever been executed, Jesus prayed aloud, asking his Father to forgive his Roman executioners who had no idea of the enormity of the wrongs that were being done to the sinless Son of God that day. What love and grace!

Unaware of the significance of what was occurring, the soldiers followed their custom of dividing the clothes of the men being executed. Rather than cutting the one garment that remained, they gambled over it.

Cruel Mockery

> LUKE 23:35–38 *And the people stood looking on. But even the rulers with them sneered, saying, "He saved others; let Him save Himself if He is the Christ, the chosen of God." The soldiers also mocked Him, coming and offering Him sour wine, and saying, "If You are the King of the Jews, save Yourself." And an inscription also was written over Him in letters of Greek, Latin, and Hebrew:*
>   **THIS IS THE KING OF THE JEWS.** (NKJV)

Onlookers began to mock Jesus. They reminded him that through his miracles he had helped others, now he could prove who he really was by saving himself from death.

Roman soldiers joined in the mockery. Even the notice that was nailed to the cross above his head was a mockery, for it identified Jesus, in Aramaic, Latin, and Greek, as king of the Jews.

Cross Conversation

> LUKE 23:39–43 *Then one of the criminals who were hanged blasphemed Him, saying, "If You are the Christ, save Yourself and us." But the other, answering, rebuked him, saying, "Do you not even fear God, seeing you are under the same condemnation? And we indeed justly, for we receive the due reward of our deeds; but this Man has done nothing wrong." Then he said to Jesus, "Lord, remember me when You come into Your kingdom." And Jesus said to him, "Assuredly, I say to you, today you will be with Me in Paradise." (NKJV)*

Paradise
Revelation 2:7

enter
Hebrews 9:7

direct contact
Hebrews 10:19–22

One of the criminals joined the mockery, gasping out insults at Jesus and challenging him to save the three of them—if he was the Christ.

The second criminal rebuked him, pointing out that both of them had done deeds deserving punishment, but Jesus had done nothing wrong. Then with amazing insight he asked Jesus to remember him when he established his kingdom. Jesus promised far more. He said on that very day he would be with Jesus in <u>Paradise</u>.

Unexplained Events

> LUKE 23:44–45 *Now it was about the sixth hour, and there was darkness over all the earth until the ninth hour. Then the sun was darkened, and the veil of the temple was torn in two.* (NKJV)

Unexpectedly at the sixth hour, noon, an eerie darkness came over the scene and remained for three hours. There is no record of an eclipse, but certainly the darkness was most unusual.

In Jerusalem the beautiful curtain that hung in the Temple was torn from top to bottom. The curtain separated the most holy place in the Temple, called the Holy of Holies, from the rest of the building (see Illustration #1). No one could explain how or why this occurred. Only an act of God could take a heavy woven drape and rip it apart from top to bottom.

The curtain kept people from the holy place where God had promised to reside. Once a year the high priest was permitted to <u>enter</u> that Holy of Holies and offer blood for his sins and for the sins of his people. When that curtain was torn, it signified that Jesus's death provided the way that all people could actually enter God's presence.

Today we have the privilege of <u>direct contact</u> with God. Because Jesus has opened the way for us, we can come near to God, having our hearts cleansed by Jesus's sacrifice of his life for us.

Volunteer Victory

> LUKE 23:46 *And when Jesus had cried out with a loud voice, He said, "Father, 'into Your hands I commit My spirit.'" Having said this, He breathed His last.* (NKJV)

Ordinarily, someone close to dying from crucifixion would not be able to speak anything more than a low groan. But Jesus spoke loudly, calling to his Father in prayer and committing his spirit into God's loving hands. His words mirror Psalm 31:5. Then he died, not in defeat as a victim, but in victory. He had accomplished what he had been <u>born to do</u>—and actually what he had planned to do from the <u>foundation</u> of the world! He voluntarily gave up his life.

go to

born to do
Mark 10:45

foundation
1 Peter 1:18–20

Our eyes brim as we read of Jesus's suffering—it was horrendous. We are aghast at the cruel and unjust way he was tried and killed. But never forget his words: "I lay down My life that I may take it again. No one takes it from Me, but I lay it down of Myself" (John 10:17–18 NKJV).

Awe-Filled Onlookers

> LUKE 23:47–49 *So when the centurion saw what had happened, he glorified God, saying, "Certainly this was a righteous Man!" And the whole crowd who came together to that sight, seeing what had been done, beat their breasts and returned. But all His acquaintances, and the women who followed Him from Galilee, stood at a distance, watching these things. (NKJV)*

A Roman centurion who had observed the whole execution was so filled with awe that he confessed audibly that without doubt Jesus was a righteous man. This caused him to praise God. Other onlookers were deeply impressed and left expressing their grief and consternation at what had happened.

Luke makes special note of the role of women at the cross. He points out that those who knew and loved Jesus separated themselves from those who mocked him, and stood at a distance. In this group were women who had followed him from Galilee, including Mary, Jesus's mother, his mother's sister, the wife of Clopas, and Mary Magdalene.

Borrowed Tomb for a King

Luke 23:50–54 *Now behold, there was a man named Joseph, a council member, a good and just man. He had not consented to their decision and deed. He was from Arimathea, a city of the Jews, who himself was also waiting for the kingdom of God. This man went to Pilate and asked for the body of Jesus. Then he took it down, wrapped it in linen, and laid it in a tomb that was hewn out of the rock, where no one had ever lain before. That day was the **Preparation**, and the Sabbath drew near. (NKJV)*

Where were Jesus's disciples? We do not know. But one man, Joseph, approached Pilate and obtained permission to bury Jesus. Joseph was a wealthy member of the Sanhedrin, but Luke notes that Joseph had not voted to condemn Jesus. Perhaps Joseph's views were known and his fellow Sanhedrin members conveniently "forgot" to wake him up for the mock trial. Joseph took Jesus's body down from the cross, wrapped it in many yards of linen cloth, and placed it in a cave-like tomb, which was for a private family burial.

Rushed Burial

Luke 23:55–56 *And the women who had come with Him from Galilee followed after, and they observed the tomb and how His body was laid. Then they returned and prepared spices and fragrant oils. And they rested on the Sabbath according to the commandment. (NKJV)*

The women who had stood at the scene of Jesus's crucifixion followed Joseph to the tomb where he laid Jesus's body to rest. There was no time to follow the proper burial customs, for it was time to observe the Sabbath laws of rest.

Again Luke highlights the role of women. When Joseph, a secret believer in Jesus, received permission to bury Jesus's body,

<u>Nicodemus</u>, another secret believer, supplied myrrh and aloes to be bound in the lengths of linen wound around his body. This was not enough for the women. Their deep grief had to find some expression, so they planned to prepare more spices and perfumes to bring to the grave after the Sabbath.

All four Gospel writers recorded details about Jesus's burial. They made it clear that Jesus had indeed died since the glorious truth of Jesus's resurrection required acceptance of his death (Matthew 27:57–61; Mark 15:42–47; and John 19:38–42).

Why did Jesus die? He could have avoided it, but he did not. Why? "God demonstrates His own love toward us, in that while we were still sinners, Christ died for us" (Romans 5:8 NKJV). "In this the love of God was manifested toward us, that God has sent His only begotten Son into the world, that we might live through Him. In this is love, not that we loved God, but that He loved us and sent His Son to be the propitiation for our sins" (1 John 4:9–10 NKJV).

Nicodemus
John 19:39–40

gospel harmony

something to ponder

Chapter Wrap-Up

- The Jews took Jesus to Pilate for sentencing. They charged Jesus with undermining the nation, opposing payment of taxes to Rome, and claiming to be Christ, a king (Luke 23:1–7).

- Pilate found Jesus innocent. Since Jesus was a Galilean, Pilate sent him to Herod, who ruled that province. When Jesus did not satisfy his curiosity, Herod sent him back to Pilate after allowing Jesus to be ridiculed and mocked (Luke 23:8–12).

- Pilate gave in to the demands of the religious leaders and sentenced Jesus to death (Luke 23:13–25).

- Jesus was crucified between two criminals. Groups of people gathered around the cross to watch the agonizing death process (Luke 23:26–49).

- After Jesus died, Joseph, a secret follower of Jesus, went to Pilate and asked for Jesus's body. He laid it in his own tomb (Luke 23:50–56).

Study Questions

1. Why did the religious leaders take Jesus to Pilate?

2. Why was Herod happy when Pilate sent Jesus to him?

3. Why did Pilate turn Jesus over for execution even though he was convinced that Jesus was innocent?

4. What crime was Jesus charged with by (a) the religious leaders, and (b) Pilate?

5. While groups of people watched the agonizing death process, what was happening unseen and spiritually as Jesus voluntarily gave his life on the cross? What does this mean to you?

6. What happened to Jesus's body after he died?

Luke 24 A Bright Day Dawns

Chapter Highlights:
- Rising Up
- Three Is Not a Crowd
- Amazing Appearances
- rising to the Occasion

Let's Get Started

We look forward to a happy event with almost impatient expectancy, whether it's a graduation, a promotion, a wedding, or the birth of a longed-for child. The happiest event of all history was about to occur. It had been promised, even to the timing, but nobody really expected it to happen!

rise
Luke 18:31–34

Jesus had told his disciples that he would die and that in three days he would <u>rise</u> from the dead. But after his death and burial, who stood outside the tomb in a countdown to be an eyewitness to his coming alive again? Nobody! All his followers were so confused and depressed, so crushed by grief, that they could not imagine how soon their mourning could be turned to joy.

Luke, in the closing chapter of his Gospel, gives a factual account of individuals who had firsthand experiences of meeting the risen Christ.

Rising Up

> **LUKE 24:1–3** *Now on the first day of the week, very early in the morning, they, and certain other women with them, came to the tomb bringing the spices which they had prepared. But they found the stone rolled away from the tomb. Then they went in and did not find the body of the Lord Jesus.* (NKJV)

Observing the Sabbath law of rest must have been an ordeal for the women who were determined to express their love for Jesus by placing fragrant spices around his body. They couldn't wait for the Sabbath to be over. They may have rushed around Friday gathering ingredients or mixing potions. It was the least they could do! Finally, Sunday came. They got up while it was still dark. As dawn broke they were making their way to the tomb, worrying about how they would move the stone that covered the entrance to the tomb (see Illustration #14).

executed
Acts 12:19

Imagine their amazement as they approached the tomb and found the stone rolled away. Imagine their shock and consternation at finding no body inside!

Soldiers who were guarding the tomb's sealed entrance reported that while they were sleeping, Jesus's disciples came and stole his body. But the soldiers weren't telling the truth. Any soldier who fell asleep while on guard duty was <u>executed</u>. So why would these soldiers openly confess that they had fallen asleep? Further, if they were asleep, how could they report convincingly that they knew Jesus's disciples had broken the seal, rolled back the stone, and removed the body? If they knew this to be a fact, how could they explain that they did not do their duty in preventing the theft? The only reasonable answer is that the soldiers' report was pure fiction, a tale they were bribed to tell (Matthew 27:62–66; 28:11–15).

Illustration #14
Tomb—Jesus's body was laid in a cave-like tomb such as this one. A large stone was rolled to cover the entrance.

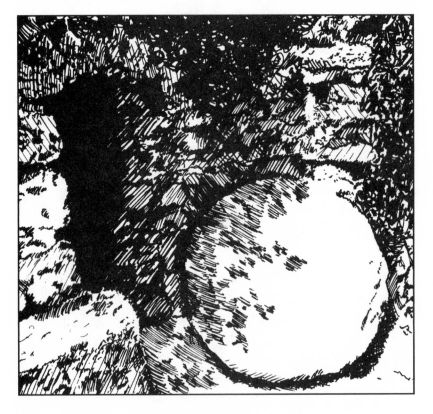

Matthew 28:2–4 gives the true account of how the tomb was opened. The ground was shaken and an angel rolled back the heavy stone that covered the entrance so that Jesus's followers could see for themselves that Jesus body was not there. The guards who were charged with keeping the tomb sealed saw the angel and were terrified.

Astonished by Two Angels

> LUKE 24:4–8 *And it happened, as they were greatly perplexed about this, that behold, two men stood by them in shining garments. Then, as they were afraid and bowed their faces to the earth, they said to them, "Why do you seek the living among the dead? He is not here, but is risen! Remember how He spoke to you when He was still in Galilee, saying, 'The Son of Man must be delivered into the hands of sinful men, and be crucified, and the third day rise again.'" And they remembered His words.* (NKJV)

promise
Matthew 16:21

Holy Spirit
John 14:15–26

Suddenly two angels appeared, filling the astonished women with fear. The heavenly messengers reminded them of what Jesus had clearly told them. Their understanding had been clouded then, so that they had not really understood his <u>promise</u> that he would be raised from the dead on the third day.

The angels made an excellent point. To understand what God is doing and to have our questions answered, we need to remember what Jesus has said. There may be much we do not understand in the Bible, but Jesus promised to send the <u>Holy Spirit</u> to teach us the truth and to clarify what Jesus has said. Understanding grows through careful study of the Bible and obedience to what is shown to us.

Serious Sorrow and Supposed Scuttlebutt

> LUKE 24:9–11 *Then they returned from the tomb and told all these things to the eleven and to all the rest. It was Mary Magdalene, Joanna, Mary the mother of James, and the other women with them, who told these things to the apostles. And their words seemed to them like idle tales, and they did not believe them.* (NKJV)

go to

resurrection
John 11:25–26

The women hurried back to Jerusalem where the disciples and other followers of Jesus were grieving their loss. These women, who had been sharing their loss, were now bubbling with excitement as the good news tumbled out of their mouths. So full of sorrow were Jesus's disciples that they could not even take in the news. In fact, the women's announcement seemed to them like hysterical nonsense. Sorrow and doubt prevented the disciples from hearing the women's announcement.

> **what others say**
>
> **Darryl DelHousaye**
>
> The church of Jesus Christ, in honor of his rising from the dead on the first Easter, gathers every Sunday to celebrate the victory of her Lord over death, and the hope we therefore have. For He promises, "I am the <u>resurrection</u> and the life; he who believes in me shall live, even if he dies."[1]

Peter's Checkup

LUKE 24:12 *But Peter arose and ran to the tomb; and stooping down, he saw the linen cloths lying by themselves; and he departed, marveling to himself at what had happened. (NKJV)*

Peter heard the women—at least enough that he ran to the tomb to check out what they had reported. He looked in the opening and saw an amazing sight. There was no question where Jesus's body had been laid to rest. The strips of linen were there, the head covering was in its place, and the separate body covering was in its place. But the body was missing! He walked away scratching his head.

> **what others say**
>
> **William MacDonald**
>
> We are not told whether [the cloths] were unwound, or still in the shape of the body, but we are safe in presuming the latter. It appears that the Lord may have left the grave-clothes as if they had been a cocoon.[2]

Three Is Not a Crowd

LUKE 24:13–18 *Now behold, two of them were traveling that same day to a village called Emmaus, which was seven miles from Jerusalem. And they talked together of all these things which had happened. So it was, while they conversed and reasoned, that Jesus Himself drew near and went with them. But their eyes were restrained, so that they did not know Him. And He said to them, "What kind of conversation is this that you have with one another as you walk and are sad?" Then the one whose name was Cleopas answered and said to Him, "Are You the only stranger in Jerusalem, and have You not known the things which happened there in these days?" (NKJV)*

The day of the Resurrection two of Jesus's followers were walking from Jerusalem to Emmaus. As they went they rehearsed all that had happened while they were in Jerusalem. The painful sights and sounds were seared in their hearts. The events gripped them and their grief required an outlet.

Suddenly, they were joined by Jesus, who appeared to them as just another traveler. They were stunned when he asked them what they were talking about. How could he not have heard about the tragic events of the past few days?

Spilling Their Guts

LUKE 24:19–24 *And He said to them, "What things?" So they said to Him, "The things concerning Jesus of Nazareth, who was a Prophet mighty in deed and word before God and all the people, and how the chief priests and our rulers delivered Him to be condemned to death, and crucified Him. But we were hoping that it was He who was going to redeem Israel. Indeed, besides all this, today is the third day since these things happened. Yes, and certain women of our company, who arrived at the tomb early, astonished us. When they did not find His body, they came saying that they had also seen a vision of angels who said He was*

unmitigated
not lessened or
relieved

alive. And certain of those who were with us went to the tomb and found it just as the women had said; but Him they did not see." (NKJV)

When Jesus asked what had happened, the two unburdened their hearts. They recounted their love for Jesus of Nazareth, the incredible injustice and cruelty of his trial and crucifixion, their shattered hopes that he would be the Messiah to rescue Israel, their amazement at the women's news—and their **unmitigated** sorrow because they had not seen Jesus.

apply it

Why did Jesus draw close to two obscure disciples? He read their hearts and knew their needs. He joined them and gave them opportunity to pour out their confusion and disappointment. He has not changed. He will draw close to us and listen as we tell him what troubles us.

Clues for the Clueless

LUKE 24:25–27 *Then He said to them, "O foolish ones, and slow of heart to believe in all that the prophets have spoken! Ought not the Christ to have suffered these things and to enter into His glory?" And beginning at Moses and all the Prophets, He expounded to them in all the Scriptures the things concerning Himself. (NKJV)*

Jesus must have shaken his head and said, "Guys, get a clue!" Then patiently he reminded them of the Old Testament Scriptures that foretold how the Messiah would come and suffer before he would arrive to establish his kingdom. The phrase "all the Scriptures" may mean that these two had focused only on the prophecies about the Messiah's glory and not his prior suffering. Jesus set them straight. Jesus opened the Scriptures to the two. He will do the same for us today.

> **what others say**
>
> **G. Campbell Morgan**
>
> Then he opened to them all the Scriptures as they applied to himself. From their standpoint we see these two, then, listening to a stranger interpreting to them the Scriptures which they thought they knew, but the deep meaning of which they had never apprehended. Moreover, they were listening to this

stranger interpreting to them the events through which they had recently passed in the light of Messianic foretelling.[4]

Tantalizing Tip-Off

LUKE 24:28–32 *Then they drew near to the village where they were going, and He indicated that He would have gone farther. But they constrained Him, saying, "Abide with us, for it is toward evening, and the day is far spent." And He went in to stay with them. Now it came to pass, as He sat at the table with them, that He took bread, blessed and broke it, and gave it to them. Then their eyes were opened and they knew Him; and He vanished from their sight. And they said to one another, "Did not our heart burn within us while He talked with us on the road, and while He opened the Scriptures to us?" (NKJV)*

As the two travelers approached the end of their journey, the stranger appeared to be going on. Traveling in the dark was too difficult and dangerous. "Have dinner and spend the night with us," they said. As they began to share the evening meal, they suddenly recognized who Jesus was. At that moment he disappeared.

What tipped off the men to Jesus's identity? Did they see his nail-scarred hands as he broke the bread? Did they recognize something in his voice and phrasing as he prayed? Did God simply choose that moment to allow them to see Jesus?

what others say

Elisabeth Elliot

The two who sat with [Jesus] had not been pessimists. They had indeed had hopes. But what puny hopes theirs had been. In their wildest optimism they could not have dreamed of the glory they now saw. A resurrection, the ultimate contradiction to all of the world's woes, had taken place. They saw Jesus with their own eyes. What must their own words have seemed to them if they thought about what they had said: "We were hoping . . ."? They could not deny that those hopes had died, but what insane dreamer could have imagined the possibility that had become a reality here at their own supper table? Their savior had come back. He had walked with them. He was in their house. He was eating the very bread they had provided.[5]

Not Running on Empty

LUKE 24:33–35 *So they rose up that very hour and returned to Jerusalem, and found the eleven and those who were with them gathered together, saying, "The Lord is risen indeed, and has appeared to Simon!" And they told about the things that had happened on the road, and how He was known to them in the breaking of bread.* (NKJV)

There was not a moment to lose. The two hurried back to Jerusalem to share with Jesus's friends their most amazing discovery. They didn't finish their meal and they didn't care that it was getting dark. Their news couldn't wait. Jesus was indeed alive again!

When they arrived, they discovered their encounter with Christ was not unique. Peter had also seen the Lord. The disciples had not believed the women who went to the tomb, but now the truth sank in.

Amazing Appearances

LUKE 24:36–43 *Now as they said these things, Jesus Himself stood in the midst of them, and said to them, "Peace to you." But they were terrified and frightened, and supposed they had seen a spirit. And He said to them, "Why are you troubled? And why do doubts arise in your hearts? Behold My hands and My feet, that it is I Myself. Handle Me and see, for a spirit does not have flesh and bones as you see I have." When He had said this, He showed them His hands and His feet. But while they still did not believe for joy, and marveled, He said to them, "Have you any food here?" So they gave Him a piece of a broiled fish and some honeycomb. And He took it and ate in their presence.* (NKJV)

Suddenly Jesus appeared with them and greeted them. The group was taken aback, thinking they had seen a ghost. Assuring them of his identity, Jesus invited them to touch his hands and feet. Still they did not believe their eyes, so Jesus asked them for some food. He ate a piece of fish and some honeycomb to prove that he was not a ghost.

what others say

Max Lucado

It was a moment the apostles would never forget, a story they would never cease to tell. The stone of the tomb was not enough to keep him in. The walls of the room were not enough to keep him out.[6]

We may wish Luke included more information about Jesus's resurrected body. We would like to know how Jesus could enter a <u>locked</u> room and how he could suddenly appear and disappear. His body was solid flesh and bones. He invited his disciples to touch his body and to look closely at the prints of the nails, which were evident on his hands and feet. He even ate.

Luke does not satisfy our curiosity. Instead, he leaves it up to us to focus on the fact that Jesus is alive today and we are to be witnesses to this truth.

go to

locked
John 20:19

transmutation
change from one
state to another

> ### what others say
>
> ### Larry Richards
>
> The Gospels report several incidents where Jesus brought the dead back to life. This was not resurrection, but resuscitation. In resuscitation biological life is restored. But the individual remains mortal, and must experience biological death again. On the other hand resurrection is not a restoration of biological life. It is a transformation of the individual; a **transmutation** from mortality to immortality. The resurrected never again die, but live forever with the Lord. The resurrected are not subject to suffering or pain, or to the limitations that restrict mere men.
>
> Christ entered into the glory of the resurrected life when he burst triumphant from his tomb.[7]

Clue Review

LUKE **24:44–49** *Then He said to them, "These are the words which I spoke to you while I was still with you, that all things must be fulfilled which were written in the Law of Moses and the Prophets and the Psalms concerning Me." And He opened their understanding, that they might comprehend the Scriptures. Then He said to them, "Thus it is written, and thus it was necessary for the Christ to suffer and to rise from the dead the third day, and that repentance and remission of sins should be preached in His name to all nations, beginning at Jerusalem. And you are witnesses of these things. Behold, I send the Promise of My Father upon you; but tarry in the city of Jerusalem until you are endued with power from on high." (NKJV)*

Jesus then reviewed what he had told them. He opened their minds as he went over the Old Testament Scriptures that had foretold his death and resurrection. If Jesus had not died and been raised to life again, there would be no message to take to all nations.

Holy Spirit
Acts 1:8

Pentecost
Acts 2:1–13

Pentecost
Feast of Weeks held
fifty days after
Passover

Then He gave them their assignment. They were to stay in Jerusalem until they received spiritual power to bear witness for him to all nations. The needed power would come in the person of the Holy Spirit at **Pentecost**.

Events on Resurrection Day

- Before sunrise, an angel rolls away the stone covering Jesus's tomb (see Matthew 28:2–4).
- Women discover the tomb is empty (see Matthew 28:1; Mark 16:1–4; Luke 24:1–3; John 20:1).
- Mary Magdalene leaves to give the news to Peter and John (John 20:1–2).
- Other women who stay at the tomb see two angels who tell them Jesus has risen from the dead (see Matthew 28:5–7; Mark 16:5–7; Luke 24:4–8).
- Peter and John visit Jesus's tomb (see Luke 24:12; John 20:3–10).
- Mary Magdalene returns to the tomb; Jesus appears to her (Mark 16:9–11; John 20:11–18).
- Jesus appears to Mary, mother of James, Salome, and Joanna (see Matthew 28:8–10).
- Guards are bribed into giving a false report instead of saying the angel rolled away the stone at the tomb (Matthew 28:11–15).
- Jesus appears to Peter (1 Corinthians 15:5).
- Jesus appears to two disciples on the road to Emmaus (Mark 16:12–13; Luke 24:13–32).
- Two disciples tell the others that they have seen Jesus (Luke 24:33–35).
- Jesus appears to disciples in a locked room (Luke 24:36–43; John 20:19–25).

Rising to the Occasion

LUKE **24:50–53** *And He led them out as far as Bethany, and He lifted up His hands and blessed them. Now it came to pass, while He blessed them, that He was parted from them and car-*

ried up into heaven. And they worshiped Him, and returned to Jerusalem with great joy, and were continually in the temple praising and blessing God. Amen. (NKJV)

Holy Spirit
Acts 1:8

every nation
Revelation 14:6

Jesus led his followers out of the city where he blessed them. His actions remind us of a priest who blessed the people when he came out of the Temple and give Christians an image of Jesus as high priest today, interceding with God on their behalf (Luke 1:22; Hebrews 1:3; 4:14).

Then Jesus left the disciples. He returned to the One who sent him, his Father, and to his home in heaven. This time the disciples were not thrust into mourning. They worshiped him and returned to Jerusalem with joy. They stayed there to wait for the coming of the <u>Holy Spirit,</u> who would empower them to be Jesus's witnesses.

Luke's concise conclusion to his book emphasizes Jesus as the Son of God and shows what should be our logical response. For the continuation of Luke's story we need to read the book of Acts, which he also wrote for Theophilus. The disciples were eyewitnesses to Jesus's resurrection. Their fears turned to joy, and after Jesus ascended to his Father, they became enthusiastic witnesses for him. Empowered by the Holy Spirit, they led many in Jerusalem to believe on Jesus, and thus the church was born.

Today Jesus has witnesses scattered around the world preaching the Gospel, teaching, ministering in acts of Christlike compassion to physical needs, preparing people from <u>every nation</u> to stand before Christ and sing his praises.

Chapter Wrap-Up

- On the first day of the week women approached the tomb, bringing spices to lay on Jesus's body. They found the tomb empty. Angels announced that Jesus had risen from the dead. (Luke 24:1–8)

- The women reported the astounding news to the disciples, but they did not believe. Peter ran to the tomb, saw that it was empty, and left wondering. (Luke 24:9–12)

- Jesus appeared to two disciples as they walked from Jerusalem. (Luke 24:13–35)

- Jesus appeared to more disciples and opened their minds and hearts to the Scriptures. He commissioned them to be witnesses for him around the world. (Luke 24:36–49)

- When Jesus ascended to his Father in heaven, the disciples returned to Jerusalem with great joy and praises to God. (Luke 24:50–53)

Study Questions

1. Who first learned that Jesus had risen from the dead?

2. What amazing discovery did two obscure disciples have as they left Jerusalem in confusion and disappointment?

3. How did Jesus convince his disciples that he was alive again and had a mission for them?

4. How did the disciples respond when Jesus left them to return to his Father?

Appendix A – Map of Israel in Jesus's Day

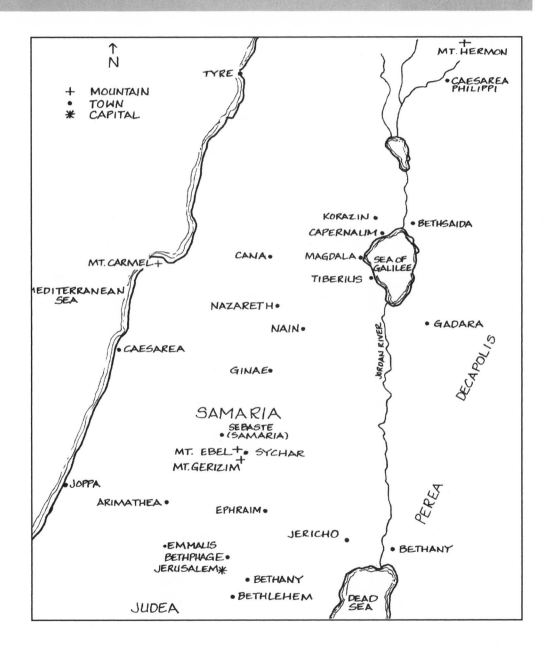

Appendix B – Map of Jesus's Trial and Crucifixion

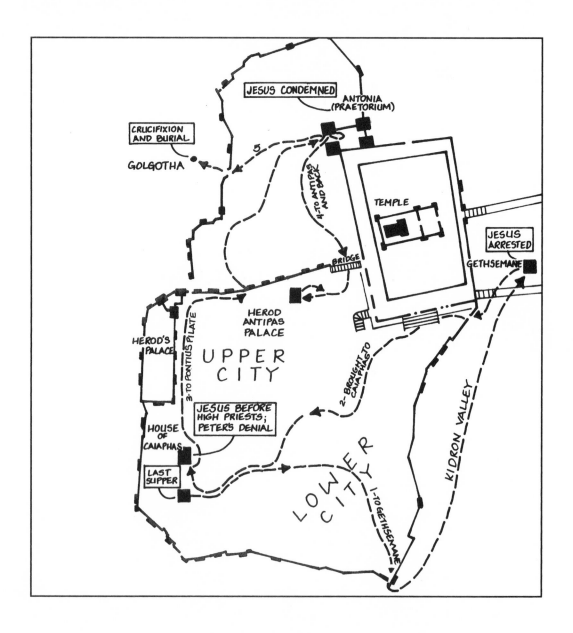

Appendix C - The Answers

Chapter 1: Luke 1—Visitors from Heaven

1. God sent the angel Gabriel on two separate occasions. First, to speak to Zacharias, as the priest offered incense in the Holy Place. Gabriel announced that Zacharias and Elizabeth would have a child. This child would be called John and would have the mission of preparing people to receive the long-awaited Messiah. Then Gabriel announced to Mary, a young virgin, that by the overshadowing of the Holy Spirit she would be the mother of the Messiah.
(Luke 1:5–20; 26–38)

2. When Gabriel made his announcements to Zacharias and Mary, they both responded with fear. Zacharias raised a question, reflecting doubt that God could keep his promise to give him a son. Mary, on the other hand, raised a question for clarification but immediately submitted herself to whatever God willed for her.
(Luke 1:11–19; 29–38)

3. John's unique mission would be to bring people back to the Lord and to prepare them to receive the coming Messiah. (Luke 1:14–17)

4. While Zacharias was unable to speak, he could not express further doubts about God's ability to keep his promise to send a son to him and Elizabeth in their old age. (Luke 1:18–20)

5. If we cannot accept and believe in the virgin birth of Jesus, we cannot accept and believe anything else that is recorded in the New Testament about who Jesus is and how he can be our Savior from sin.

6. Events connected with the birth of John led people to watch him for further evidences that the Lord's hand was on him: his birth to Zacharias and Elizabeth, who were past child-bearing years, and the astounding way in which both Elizabeth and Zacharias confirmed that the baby's name would be John, though custom dictated that he should have been called Zacharias.
(Luke 1:57–66)

Chapter 2: Luke 2—Birth and Boyhood

1. God caused Caesar Augustus to decree a census. This required all Jewish males to return to their ancestral towns to be registered, which forced Joseph to go to Bethlehem, where Jesus was born. This fulfilled the prophecy of Micah. (Micah 5:2; Luke 2:1–7)

2. Jesus was born in a stable, which could have been a cave or an open courtyard in which animals were kept. He was born there because Mary and Joseph could not find space to stay in the inn. (Luke 2:7)

3. God chose to send his angel messenger to announce to humble shepherds that Jesus had been born. This was significant because many Bible students believe they were tending temple sheep which would be offered as sacrifices. Jesus had come to give his life as the Lamb of God. Thus, temple offerings would no longer be needed. (Luke 2:8–14)

4. Both Simeon and Anna recognized that the baby Mary and Joseph presented at the Temple was the promised Messiah. Simeon took the baby in his arms and praised God for allowing him the privilege of seeing the Savior who would bring salvation to the Gentiles as well as the Jews. Anna also recognized who Jesus was, gave thanks to God, and shared this good news with others in the Temple who were also looking for the Messiah. (Luke 2:25–38)

5. Jesus visited Jerusalem for the Feast of Passover when he was twelve years old. While there, he visited the Temple and entered a discussion with the religious leaders. They were amazed at his insights and the wisdom reflected in the questions he raised. When Mary asked why he had stayed at the Temple when they were anxiously searching for him, Jesus asked in return why they were searching for him. They should have known that he "must be about My Father's business." This indicated his awareness that God in heaven was his real Father. Still, he returned to Nazareth with Mary and Joseph and submitted himself to live in obedience to them. (Luke 2:41–52)

Chapter 3: Luke 3—A Desert Call

1. John's God-given mission was to prepare the hearts of people to receive the coming Messiah.

He preached repentance and turning to God, baptized the people in the Jordan River, and called for them to prove their change of heart by their everyday actions and attitudes. (Luke 3:1–14)

2. Personal answers will vary. What might John say to those who carelessly waste earth's resources, businesses that overcharge the poor so they can live in luxury, individuals who exploit the poor and the elderly with false offers and outright lies? (Luke 3:7–9)

3. Personal answers will vary. Everyone who professes to have turned to God is called to stand for justice for others and to share what they have in time, influence, and material resources with people who have needs. (Luke 3:10–14)

4. John's baptism signified repentance and turning to God, whereas Jesus would baptize with the Holy Spirit, creating inner cleansing and transformation. John considered himself so inferior to the Messiah that he was not worthy to assume the humble role of a slave by untying the thongs of Messiah's sandals. (Luke 3:15–18)

5. After John baptized Jesus, the Holy Spirit came on Jesus in the form of a dove, and a voice spoke from heaven confirming that Jesus was God's dearly loved Son, and was fully approved by God. (Luke 3:21–22)

6. Matthew traces Jesus's ancestry back through Abraham and King David, showing that as the legal son of Joseph, Jesus had the right to the throne of David. Luke, on the other hand, traces Jesus's ancestry through Mary back to Adam, the Son of God. In doing so, Luke confirms that Jesus was truly human, bearing our weaknesses. (Matthew 1:1–17; Luke 3:21–37)

Chapter 4: Luke 4—Temptation and Triumph

1. The Holy Spirit led Jesus into the desert to be tempted because by this means Jesus proved his humanness and his complete commitment to God. The temptations prepared him for ministry. (Luke 4:1)

2. Jesus's forty days in the desert run parallel to the Israelites' forty years of wandering in the desert after the Exodus.

3. Jesus was tempted in the general areas of (1) not relying on God's promised provision and care, (2) seeking success apart from God's plan, and (3) testing God.

4. The people of Nazareth rejected Jesus because they refused to believe he was who he claimed to be unless he would perform miracles for them. Also, they became angry when he told them that God's grace extended to Gentiles as well as to Jews. (Luke 4:14–30)

5. Jesus proved his authority over evil spirits by commanding them to keep silent and by ordering them to leave their victims. (Luke 4:31–37)

6. Jesus showed compassion to people with physical needs by touching and healing them. (Luke 4:38–44)

Chapter 5: Luke 5—Breaking the Rules

1. Experienced fishermen knew better than to attempt to catch fish in deep water during the day. But when Simon obeyed, Jesus performed a miracle by providing a huge catch of fish. This led Simon to recognize Jesus's power and his own sinfulness. More than anything Jesus taught that day, the nets overflowing with fish convinced Simon and his three companions to leave all and follow Jesus. (Luke 5:1–11)

2. In healing the man with leprosy, Jesus showed compassion and divine power. In reaching out to touch the man, Jesus showed his disregard for Old Testament laws. In commanding the man not to tell others of his healing, Jesus wanted him to go directly to the priest to be pronounced clean. Possibly Jesus also wanted to delay the surge of crowds coming for healing once the news was out. (Luke 5:12–16)

3. Jesus raised questions by claiming to be able to forgive sins—an act that was not visually verifiable to his critics. He healed the paralyzed man, thus proving he had power both to heal and to forgive sins. (Luke 5:17–26)

4. The Jews in Jesus's day were prejudiced against their fellow Jews who represented the hated Roman government as tax collectors. Not only did Jesus refuse to condemn Levi, but he also called him to be a disciple. Jesus also accepted Levi's invitation to honor him at a banquet in Levi's spacious home where he socialized with Levi's friends and fellow tax collectors—all who were considered outcasts by the religious leaders. (Luke 5:27–32)

5. Jesus's critics observed that while their disciples and those of John the Baptist fasted and prayed regularly, Jesus's followers joined him in enjoying an active social life. Jesus replied that he had come to replace the old legalistic system with something much better. (Luke 5:33–39)

Chapter 6: Luke 6—Jesus, Ph.D.

1. Jesus spoke out against man-made laws that turned observing the Sabbath into a burden. As Lord of the Sabbath, he showed that it should be a day of rest, delighting in God, and doing good to others. (Luke 6:1–11)

2. Jesus chose twelve men to be his disciples. A disciple is a learner who becomes like his master. An

apostle is sent out to represent his master. (Luke 6:12–16)

3. Jesus pronounced his followers to be blessed when because of their loyalty to him they experienced poverty, hunger, pain, and persecution. In contrast, people would be under judgment who enjoyed prosperity and popularity with no regard for heavenly values. (Luke 6:20–26)

4. Disciples who demonstrated God's love and generosity to the undeserving would be rewarded by becoming more like their Father in heaven. (Luke 6:27–36)

5. We will stand firm in times of temptation if our lives are built on the foundation of putting Jesus's words into practice. (Luke 6:46–49)

Chapter 7: Luke 7—Jesus, M.D.

1. The centurion was a Gentile who had learned to love the Jews so much that he had built a synagogue for them. Though he felt unworthy to approach Jesus directly, he sent Jewish elders to request that Jesus come to heal his dying slave. Then he sent friends to ask Jesus just to "say the word" of healing. He understood that Jesus's word would be effective because Jesus was under God's authority. Even Jews had not shown such understanding and faith. (Luke 7:1–10)

2. Jesus has great compassion for the poor, for all who suffer and grieve. He still has compassion for all who are in need of his touch. We convey his compassion when we reach out to people who hurt. (Luke 7:11–17)

3. John wrestled with doubt that Jesus was the Messiah whose coming he had announced. Jesus's reply was proof that he was fulfilling the prophecy of the Messiah. He had a blessing for John if he kept trusting, in spite of the disappointment that Jesus had not yet fully established his kingdom. (Luke 7:18–23)

4. John was great because he had the privilege of preparing people to receive Jesus. The "least" in his kingdom would have blessings that John only announced would be coming. (Luke 7:24–28)

5. Jesus's religious critics complained about the messengers: John was too severe and Jesus was too relaxed. Actually, they refused both messengers because they didn't want to hear the truth from anyone. (Luke 7:29–35)

Chapter 8: Luke 8—The Way of Jesus

1. Women who had received Jesus's healing touch were especially devoted to him. They traveled with him and his band of twelve disciples, sharing their personal finances to provide practical assistance to them. (Luke 8:1–3)

2. The seed is the "word of God." The packed-down path represents people with hard hearts who are not open to the truth. The rocky soil represents people who accept the Word but reject it when they are tested. The thorny soil represents people who give more attention to this life than to eternal values. The good soil represents people who receive and obey God's message. (Luke 8:4–15)

3. Jesus is the light of the world. We who believe in him are like lamps shining in a dark world. Jesus's light also shines within us, exposing our secrets. If we conceal them instead of confessing and forsaking them, he will expose them. (Luke 8:16–18)

4. We become members of Jesus's spiritual family by hearing and obeying God's Word. (Luke 8:19–21)

5. Jesus wanted his disciples to trust him even when everything seemed hopeless and death was certain. He proved his authority to calm the tempest, thus proving to them that he was the Lord over creation. (Luke 8:22–25)

6. The woman was desperate for help. After twelve years of physical misery, being declared ceremonially unclean and spending money on doctors who could not help her, she took a daring step of faith—she touched the tassels of Jesus's cloak and was healed immediately. (Luke 8:43–48)

7. Though Jesus was delayed in arriving at Jairus's home, he encouraged Jairus to have faith and believe that his daughter would be restored to him. On arriving at Jairus's home, he found the mourning in progress. He was not deterred by the mockery of the group in the home, but took the parents and three of his disciples into the room and raised the girl from the dead. (Luke 8:40–56)

Chapter 9: Luke 9—Who Jesus Is

1. The disciples realized they had been given power and authority by Jesus. Their preaching was effective and they were able to perform miracles of healing. They also experienced God's provision for their needs. (Luke 9:1–6)

2. Peter identified Jesus as the Christ of God, an insight he had received from God. Jesus cautioned the disciples not to talk about this truth. He had yet to suffer rejection, death, and resurrection. (Luke 9:18–22)

3. Having identified Jesus as the Christ of God, the disciples expected to share in his glory in some way. But the time was not yet. In the meantime, they needed to follow his standards of discipleship. They needed to deny themselves, take up

their cross, and follow him. They should be willing to lose their lives in his service—and save their lives. And they were not to be ashamed of Jesus and his words. (Luke 9:23–27)

4. Jesus took Peter, James, and John with him up a mountain. As he prayed, he was changed so that his true glory shone brightly. Moses and Elijah appeared and talked with Jesus about his approaching suffering and death. God spoke from a cloud, confirming that Jesus was his Son and the disciples should listen to him. (Luke 9:28–36)

5. Jesus knew the disciples were arguing about who was the greatest. So he brought a child to stand next to him. He pointed out that true greatness was reflected in their attitude toward a child—or anyone needing their care and protection. If they cared for a child they would be welcoming Jesus himself. Among the disciples, the one who was least, as a child, would be the greatest. (Luke 9:46–50)

Chapter 10: Luke 10—Significant Decisions

1. Jesus sent out seventy-two to precede him to Judea. On their return they reported great joy that even demons submitted to them. Jesus said that they should find even greater joy in the fact that their names were written in heaven. (Luke 10:1–20)

2. God chooses to reveal the truths of Scripture to only those who come with childlike hearts—humble and dependent on him. He hides the truths from the wise who rely on themselves without any sense of need to depend on him. (Luke 10:21–24)

3. The expert in the law hoped to trick Jesus into giving an answer that would be a basis for accusing him. Jesus responded with a question and a story. The expert learned that there was nothing he was capable of doing that would earn him eternal life. He simply could not truly love a neighbor because he did not totally love God. (Luke 10:25–37)

4. To fulfill the law, the expert in the law should express his love for God by being a neighbor to anyone who has need. (Luke 10:25–37)

5. Both Martha and Mary loved Jesus and welcomed him. Martha expressed her love by preparing an elaborate meal for Jesus, wearing herself out to the point that she was frustrated and angry with Mary and Jesus. On the other hand, Mary left the kitchen to sit at Jesus's feet and listen to him. Jesus said Mary had chosen what was better because listening to him was more important than serving him without first hearing him. (Luke 10:38–42)

Chapter 11: Luke 11—Candid Conversations

1. Jesus's pattern for prayer included approaching God as Father, desiring that his name be honored, asking help to do his will and extend his kingdom throughout the earth, depending on him for everyday needs, trusting him to forgive our sins, as we are willing to forgive others, and asking him to keep us from yielding to temptation. (Luke 11:1–4)

2. Jesus pointed out that Satan would never weaken his kingdom by casting out his demons. (Luke 11:17–26)

3. While Jesus did not detract from Mary, he pointed out that when we hear God's Word and act on it, we are even more blessed. (Luke 11:27–28)

4. Jesus condemned those who insisted on a sign from heaven, saying that the Queen of Sheba and the wicked citizens of Nineveh had more faith than they did. He said they would get a sign: as Jonah was in the deep for three days, he would be buried for three days and would come alive again. (Luke 11:29–32)

5. Jesus condemned the Pharisees (1) for not showing justice and mercy to the poor, (2) for parading their self-righteousness and seeking praise from people, and (3) for spreading unbelief and false teaching. (Luke 11:42–44)

6. Jesus condemned the experts in the law (1) for burdening people with rules and not helping them, (2) for honoring the memory of God's prophets while harboring in their hearts the evil attitudes of their murderers, and (3) for not wanting the truth of Scripture and for keeping others from receiving it. (Luke 11:45–52)

Chapter 12: Luke 12—Wise Words

1. The yeast of the Pharisees is hypocrisy, pretending to be something that does not reflect the real person inside. Jesus warned his disciples that hypocrisy was a danger if they faked their relationship with him. (Luke 12:1–3)

2. Greed blinds us to our duty to share our prosperity with others who have needs. Greed also keeps us from building treasure in heaven. (Luke 12:13–21)

3. Jesus's followers should seek his kingdom first, which includes taking care of the needs of others. As they do this, God will take care of their needs of food and clothing. (Luke 12:22–34)

4. Jesus gives his followers assignments to do while he is away. They need to be faithful in their duties, always on alert for his return. We need to do the same. (Luke 12:35–48)

5. Allegiance to Jesus must have first place in the

hearts of his followers. Sometimes this causes divisions in family relationships when some members follow Jesus and some reject him. (Luke 12:49–53)

Chapter 13: Luke 13—Going Against the Grain

1. People assumed that the victims of a massacre and the victims of an accident had been punished by God. Jesus pointed out that they were no more guilty than his listeners. Each person needed to repent and avoid eternal judgment. (Luke 13:1–5)

2. When Jesus healed a woman on the Sabbath, the synagogue ruler became furious and told people not to seek healing on the Sabbath. Jesus pointed out his hypocrisy. Sabbath laws allowed compassion for the needs of an animal. Was it not lawful to show compassion on a human? (Luke 13:10–17)

3. God's kingdom is like a tiny mustard seed and a small amount of yeast. Though both seem to be insignificant, in time both would grow and have wide influence. (Luke 13:18–21)

4. Jesus spoke of the narrow door as the only way to enter God's kingdom. Many in Jesus's day assumed that they would enter simply because they were descendants of Abraham, Isaac, and Jacob. Jesus pointed out that unless they accepted him and his teaching, they could not be part of the kingdom. The same applies to us today. (Luke 13:22–30)

5. Jesus thought about his goal of dying on the cross and of Israel's rejection of him. He knew the Jews faced terrible eternal consequences and that made him sad because he loved them. (Luke 13:31–35)

Chapter 14: Luke 14—Relating to People

1. When Jesus healed the man with dropsy on the Sabbath, he silenced the Pharisees by saying they had more concern for an ox falling into a well on the Sabbath than they had for a man who was suffering from a disease. (Luke 14:1–6)

2. The guests at the Pharisee's dinner who pushed their way to the seats of honor showed that they were proud. The Pharisee who invited only those guests who could repay him showed that he did not care about social outcasts. God rewards those at the resurrection who show kindness and generosity to others. (Luke 14:7–14)

3. The Pharisees understood Jesus's parable about the banquet to picture God's kingdom. The law-abiding Jews thought they had a secure place there. But Jesus pointed out that when he came to invite them to commit themselves to the kingdom, they made flimsy excuses. The host sent his servant out to bring in the social outcasts and to go further and bring in even more guests. Jesus was saying that God would welcome those Jews whom the Pharisees considered unworthy and would expand his kingdom to include Gentiles. (Luke 14:15–24)

4. Jesus said that anyone who wanted to be his disciple must count the cost of total commitment to him. Jesus must come before every human relationship and the disciple must be willing to suffer and even give his life for his uncompromising loyalty to Jesus. (Luke 14:25–35)

Chapter 15: Luke 15—Lost and Found

1. The Pharisees were critical of Jesus for welcoming sinners, whom they despised. Jesus told the parables to show that God loves and welcomes each sinner who comes to him. (Luke 15:1–2)

2. The shepherd tirelessly searching for the lost sheep pictures God's love for each lost person. He seeks us and rejoices when we come to him. (Luke 15:3–7)

3. The woman's search for the lost coin pictures God's search for people because they are precious to him. (Luke 15:8–10)

4. We are loved by God the Father but have chosen to go our own way and are indifferent to the pain we cause the Father. When we turn to God in repentance, we are welcomed with love. (Luke 15:11–24)

5. We may pride ourselves in living according to God's rules but miss enjoying his perfect love and demonstrating it to others. (Luke 15:25–30)

6. The father loved both sons and longed to have a close relationship with them. He was quick to forgive the sinning son and longed for the older son to repent of his bitterness and self-righteousness and come home to his father's love. (Luke 15:31–32)

Chapter 16: Luke 16—Money Matters

1. When the dishonest manager was advised that he was facing an audit and certain termination, he called in the rich man's debtors and significantly reduced the amounts owed. In so doing, he bought the friendship of the debtors and guaranteed for himself their favor after he was without employment. Jesus taught that we can learn from his shrewdness by using our money to build his kingdom on earth. After death we will be welcomed in heaven by people who are there because we have invested in the spread of the Gospel. (Luke 16:1–9)

2. How we view and use what money we have reveals our character—whether we use it on our-

selves for comfort in this life or faithfully invest it in Christ's kingdom. (Luke 16:10–15)

3. The Pharisees were blind to Jesus's teaching about the kingdom because they were preoccupied with money and their obsession to be highly regarded by others. (Luke 16:16–18)

4. In Jesus's parable of the rich man and Lazarus, we learn that we need to take God's Word seriously and act on it, because there are no second chances after death. We are responsible to use our resources for the relief of others' needs. (Luke 16:19–31)

Chapter 17: Luke 17—Heart Attitudes

1. Jesus has special love for children and new believers. Because he knows the influence we have on them, he warns that punishment awaits us if we cause "little ones" to sin. (Luke 17:1–3a)

2. When someone sins against us, we need to take the initiative to confront him. If he repents, we are to forgive him—even if he repeats the sin and the repentance again and again. (Luke 17:3b–4)

3. A disciple is called to do whatever the Lord asks of him. When he has done that, he is an "unprofitable servant" because he has done only what was expected. (Luke 17:5–10)

4. Jesus healed ten lepers. One returned to thank him—a Samaritan and a "foreigner" to the Jews' concept of God. Jesus said his faith had healed him. (Luke 17:11–19)

5. While we wait we need to beware of false predictions of when and where he will return. We also need to beware lest we give priority to everyday concerns and not be prepared in our hearts for his appearance. (Luke 17:20–37)

Chapter 18: Luke 18—People Magazine

1. God loves us and listens to our prayers. Unlike the insensitive judge, he works for our good. Like the widow, we need to be persistent in our prayers and not give up. (Luke 18:1–8)

2. The Pharisee was proud of his outward religious acts. He felt superior to the tax collector. The tax collector came humbly with sincere repentance. He went home justified. (Luke 18:9–14)

3. We should welcome children and seek to lead them to Jesus, who loves them and can bring blessing into their lives. We need to be like children, who have open, trusting hearts that are willing to depend on God's love and care. (Luke 18:15–17)

4. The rich young ruler wanted eternal life but was not willing to give up his wealth and follow Jesus with an undivided heart. (Luke 18:18–30)

5. The disciples thought Jesus was going to set up Messiah's kingdom. Luke says, "Its meaning was hidden from them." (Luke 18:31–34)

6. Jesus does not discourage us from being bold in seeking him, though those around us may want to discourage us. (Luke 18:35–43)

Chapter 19: Luke 19—Loving Little People

1. Zacchaeus was despised because he, a Jew, was a tax collector for the Roman government. After his encounter with Jesus, he volunteered to make restitution—going far beyond what was required in the Old Testament law. (Luke 19:1–10)

2. Jesus told a parable about ten servants who were entrusted to care for their master's resources while he was away. When he returned, he asked them to give account. Jesus has entrusted us to serve him loyally while he is away. Someday he will return and will ask us to give an account of our service. (Luke 19:11–27)

3. Jesus chose to ride into Jerusalem on a donkey colt. He fulfilled Zechariah's prophecy that he would ride on a donkey, thus signifying that he was coming as the righteous, gentle Messiah-King who would bring peace, in contrast to the conquering kings who rode on horses to signify their power and authority. (Luke 19:28–40)

4. Jesus wept as he lamented over Jerusalem because the people rejected him and were heading toward the unavoidable consequences of their sins. Within forty years the Roman army would level the city and destroy its people. (Luke 19:41–44)

5. When Jesus came to the Temple he found a market set up to make high profit from the out-of-town people who came to worship. The temple entrepreneurs cheated the visitors when they forced them to exchange their currency for the required Galilean shekels. They also forced the worshipers to buy sacrificial animals and doves at steep prices. (Luke 19:45–48)

Chapter 20: Luke 20—Hostile Challenges

1. Jesus knew the evil motivation behind the question of his authority. He raised the question about John the Baptist, knowing that his critics could not answer it without falling into a trap. (Luke 20:1–8)

2. Like the tenant farmers who rejected the owner's servants, Israel rejected the prophets God had sent. Like the farmers, Israel was preparing to kill God's Son. (Luke 20:9–19)

3. Jesus's followers should be good citizens by respecting positions of authority and paying taxes while at the same time living as citizens of

Christ's kingdom of righteousness and love. (Luke 20:20–26)

4. The Sadducees did not believe in life after death, so Jesus confounded them by proving from Moses's writings that God referred to Abraham, Isaac, and Jacob as alive in heaven. (Luke 20:27–44)

5. Jesus exposed the hypocrisy of the teachers of the law who wore expensive robes and made a show of greeting people. They prayed for widows while plotting to exploit them. (Luke 20:45–47)

Chapter 21: Luke 21—What Matters Most

1. In giving her two tiny coins, the widow gave her all. Others gave much more money, but kept plenty for themselves. The widow kept nothing for herself. (Luke 21:1–4)

2. Jesus answered three questions raised by the disciples: (1) When will the Temple be destroyed? (2) What will be the signs of your coming? (3) What will be the sign of the end of the age? (Luke 21:5–7)

3. Don' be fooled by imposters, don't be alarmed about wars, don't worry about what to say, don't give up, don't hesitate to run from Jerusalem, don't be alarmed when natural laws fail, don't worry that I will fail, and don't be preoccupied with this life. (Luke 21:8–36)

4. Jesus spent his time teaching in the Temple. In the evening he went to the Mount of Olives to pray and spend the night. (Luke 21:37–38)

Chapter 22: Luke 22—The Longest Night

1. The religious leaders couldn't arrest Jesus during the day because they feared a riot from the crowds that followed Jesus, and they did not know how to find him when he was alone with his disciples. Judas would lead them to Jesus. (Luke 22:1–6)

2. Jesus wanted to prepare them for what was soon to happen and to institute the Lord's Supper. (Luke 22:7–18)

3. The Lord's Supper is Jesus's way of helping us remember him, his death for us, and his promised return. We celebrate it today because Jesus asked us to do this until he comes back. (Luke 22:19–20)

4. At the Passover meal (1) Jesus announced that he would be betrayed by one of the Twelve. (2) The disciples argued about which of them was the greatest. (3) Jesus told Simon Peter that he would deny him. (4) Jesus warned his disciples that they would need to be resourceful after he was arrested. (Luke 22:21–38)

5. In Gethsemane Jesus went to pray alone. He was in anguish as he asked if it were possible to be spared the terrible suffering that lay ahead, but he would do his Father's will. (Luke 22:39–46)

6. Judas led an armed crowd into the garden of Gethsemane to arrest Jesus. Judas betrayed Jesus with a kiss, a cruel mockery. The disciples were terrified, but drew their swords to protect him. One disciple cut off the ear of a servant of the high priest. Jesus calmly healed him and put an end to any attempted violence. Throughout the arrest, Jesus remained calm and "in charge." (Luke 22:47–53)

7. Jesus's eyes met Peter's, and Peter was overwhelmed with regret and sorrow for his failure. He went out and wept bitterly. (Luke 22:54–62)

8. Jesus was taken to the high priest's house at night. No one read a charge against him. Later, soldiers mocked and beat him. At daybreak Jesus was led before the Sanhedrin for questioning. (Luke 22:63–71)

Chapter 23: Luke 23—A Dark Day in History

1. Under Roman law Jews were not permitted to execute criminals. The religious leaders sent Jesus to Pilate for sentencing on false charges. (Luke 23:1–7)

2. Herod had long wanted to meet Jesus. He welcomed the opportunity to see him, hoping to see Jesus perform a miracle. (Luke 23:8–12)

3. Pilate sentenced Jesus to death, knowing that Jesus was innocent, because he feared a riot if he didn't. He gave in to the demands of the religious leaders. (Luke 23:13–25)

4. Jesus was charged with two crimes. The Jews charged him with blasphemy because he claimed to be the Son of God and Pilate charged him with claiming to be king and thus a rival of Caesar in Rome. (Luke 23:1–25)

5. What observers could not see was the transaction that was taking place as Jesus took our sins on himself and thus made the way for us to be welcomed in God's presence. (Luke 23:26–49)

6. Joseph, a secret believer, obtained permission to take Jesus's body and lay it in a tomb, wrapped in linen cloth. Women went home to prepare spices and perfumes to place around the body after the Sabbath. (Luke 23:50–54)

Chapter 24: Luke 24—A Bright Day Dawns

1. Women came early in the morning to place spices on Jesus's body. They worried how they could roll back the heavy stone that closed the entrance to the tomb, but found the stone rolled away and

the tomb empty. Angels told them that Jesus was alive again and sent them to share the good news with Jesus's disciples. (Luke 24:1–12)

2. As two disciples went away from Jerusalem they were overtaken by Jesus, whom they did not recognize. As they poured out their confusion and disappointment to him, he opened their hearts as he explained the Old Testament Scriptures that showed that Jesus would die and come back to life again. Only as he shared a meal with them did he reveal his identity to them. (Luke 24:13–35)

3. Jesus appeared to the frightened disciples and convinced them that he was indeed alive again as he ate with them and showed them the nail prints on his hands and feet. He reminded them of what he had taught them and commissioned them to take the good news of the Gospel to all nations of the world. (Luke 24:36–49)

4. When Jesus ascended to his Father the disciples did not grieve. Instead, they returned to Jerusalem with great joy and praises to God. (Luke 24:50–53)

Endnotes

Introduction
1. Larry Sibley, *Luke: Gospel for the City* (Colorado Springs, CO: David C. Cook, 1988), 10.
2. Ken Gire, *The Reflective Life* (Colorado Springs, CO: Chariot Victor, 1998), 12.

Chapter 1: Luke 1—Visitors from Heaven
1. Paul N. Benware, *Luke: Everyman's Bible Commentary* (Chicago: Moody Press, 1985), 9.
2. John F. Walvoord and Roy B. Zuck, eds., *The Bible Knowledge Commentary* (Colorado Springs, CO: Chariot Victor, 1985), 202.
3. J. C. Ryle, *Luke: The Crossway Classic Commentaries* (Wheaton: Crossway Books, 1997), 22.
4. R. C. Sproul, *A Walk with Jesus* (Fearn, Rossshire GB: Geanies House, 1999), 15.
5. Gilbert Bilezikian, *Christianity 101* (Grand Rapids, MI: Zondervan, 1993), 63.
6. Charles C. Ryrie, *Basic Theology* (Colorado Springs, CO: Chariot Victor, 1987), 242.
7. Benware, *Luke: Everyman's Bible Commentary*, 31.
8. Sibley, *Luke*, 18.
9. Walvoord and Zuck, *The Bible Knowledge Commentary*, 206.
10. Stephen Fortosis, *Great Men and Women of the Bible* (New York: Paulist Press, 1996), 106.

Chapter 2: Luke 2—Birth and Boyhood
1. R. Kent Hughes, *Luke*, vol. 1 (Wheaton, IL: Crossway Books, 1998), 83.
2. William Barclay, *The Gospel of Luke*, Revised Edition, The Daily Study Bible Series (Louisville, KY: Westminster John Knox Press, 1975), 17.
3. Ryle, *Luke*, 39–40.
4. Frederick Buechner, *Peculiar Treasures* (San Francisco: Harper & Row, 1979), 157.
5. John Piper, *A Hunger for God* (Wheaton, IL: Crossway Books, 1997), 88.
6. Sproul, *A Walk with Jesus*, 41.

7. Leon Morris, *Luke: Tyndale New Testament Commentaries* (Grand Rapids, MI: Eerdmans, 1988), 102.
8. Oswald Chambers, *Still Higher for His Highest* (Grand Rapids, MI: Zondervan, 1970), 77.

Chapter 3: Luke 3—A Desert Call
1. Hughes, *Luke*, vol. 1, 111.
2. Bilezikian, *Christianity 101*, 159.
3. Benware, *Luke: Everyman's Bible Commentary*, 40.
4. Robert C. Girard, *The Life of Christ—The Smart Guide to the Bible™* (Nashville, TN: Thomas Nelson, 2007).
5. Ibid., 62.
6. Lawrence O. Richards, *Illustrated Bible Handbook* (Nashville, TN: Thomas Nelson, 1997), 516.
7. Girard, *The Life of Christ*.
8. *The Zondervan NIV Matthew Henry Commentary* (Grand Rapids, MI: Zondervan, 1992), 226.

Chapter 4: Luke 4—Temptation and Triumph
1. William MacDonald, *Believer's Bible Commentary* (Nashville, TN: Thomas Nelson, 1995), 30.
2. Sproul, *A Walk with Jesus*, 59.
3. Piper, *A Hunger for God*, 58.
4. Raymond B. Dillard and Tremper Longman, *An Introduction to the Old Testament* (Grand Rapids, MI: Zondervan, 1994), 66.
5. Derek Prime, *Jesus—His Life and Ministry* (Nashville, TN: Thomas Nelson, 1995), 44–45.
6. Warren W. Wiersbe, *Be Compassionate* (Colorado Springs, CO: Chariot Victor, 1988), 46.
7. Ibid.
8. John Piper, *A Godward Life* (Sisters, OR: Multnomah, 1997), 86–87.

Chapter 5: Luke 5—Breaking the Rules
1. Hughes, *Luke*, vol. 1, 161.
2. Larry Richards, *Bible Difficulties Solved* (Grand Rapids, MI: Fleming H. Revell, 1993), 235.

3. Philip Yancey, *The Jesus I Never Knew* (Grand Rapids, MI: Zondervan, 1995), 173.

4. Michael Card, *Immanuel: Reflections on the Life of Christ* (Nashville, TN: Thomas Nelson, 1990), 116.

5. Barclay, *The Gospel of Luke*, 62.

6. Yancey, *The Jesus I Never Knew*, 174–75.

7. Max Anders, *Jesus—Knowing Our Savior* (Nashville, TN: Thomas Nelson, 1995), 63.

8. Larry Richards, ed., *The Personal Growth Study Bible* (Nashville, TN: Thomas Nelson, 1996), 1247.

9. Wiersbe, *Be Compassionate*, 56.

Chapter 6: Luke 6—Jesus, Ph.D.

1. Joy Davidman, quoted in Kathy Collard Miller, *Since Life Is a Game, These Are God's Rules* (Lancaster, PA: Starburst Publishers, 1999), 8; Joy Davidman, *Smoke on the Mountain* (Philadelphia, PA: Westminster Press, 1953), 16.

2. Richard J. Foster, *Seeking the Kingdom* (San Francisco: HarperSanFrancisco, 1995), 66.

3. Hughes, *Luke* vol. 1, 208.

4. Peter Kreeft, *Making Sense Out of Suffering* (Ann Arbor, MI: Servant Books, 1986), 142.

5. John Piper, *Desiring God* (Sisters, OR: Multnomah, 1996), 234.

6. Marcus Borg, beliefnet, "What Would Jesus Think of King's Protests? New scholarship about 'turning the other cheek,'"<http://www.belief.net/story/6/story_689_1.html> (22 August 2001).

7. Bock, *Luke: The NIV Application Commentary*, 191.

8. Benware, *Luke: Everyman's Bible Commentary*, 60–61.

9. John Piper, *Future Grace* (Sisters, OR: Multnomah, 1995), 164.

10. Oswald Chambers, *Studies in the Sermon on the Mount* (London: Simpkin Marshall, Ltd., n.d.), 97.

11. Dallas Willard, *The Divine Conspiracy* (San Francisco: HarperSanFrancisco, 1998), 276.

Chapter 7: Luke 7—Jesus, M.D.

1. G. Campbell Morgan, *The Great Physician* (London: Marshall, Morgan and Scott, 1937), 138.

2. Wiersbe, *Be Compassionate*, 73.

3. Bock, *Luke: The NIV Application Commentary*, 215.

4. Charles R. Swindoll, *Hope Again* (Dallas: Word Publishing, 1996), 17.

5. Morris, *Luke: Tyndale New Testament Commentaries*, 158.

6. Sue and Larry Richards, *Every Woman in the Bible* (Nashville, TN: Thomas Nelson, 1999), 164.

Chapter 8: Luke 8—The Way of Jesus

1. Richards and Richards, *Every Woman in the Bible*, 188.

2. Helmut Thielicke, *The Waiting Father* (New York: Harper and Row, 1959), 60.

3. Max Lucado, *Just Like Jesus* (Nashville, TN: Word Publishing, 1998), 42.

4. Barclay, *The Gospel of Luke*, 105.

5. Wiersbe, *Be Compassionate*, 90–91.

6. Sproul, *A Walk with Jesus*, 161.

7. Lawrence O. Richards, *The Bible Reader's Companion* (Colorado Springs, CO: Chariot Victor, 1991), 659.

8. Barclay, *The Gospel of Luke*, 114.

9. Lawrence O. (Larry) Richards, *The 365 Day Devotional Commentary* (Colorado Springs, CO: Chariot Victor, 1990), 725.

Chapter 9: Luke 9—Who Jesus Is

1. *Zondervan NIV Matthew Henry Commentary*, 243.

2. Hughes, *Luke*, vol. 1, 324.

3. Jack Hayford, ed., *Spirit-Filled Life Bible*, New King James Version (Nashville, TN: Thomas Nelson, 1991), 1437.

4. Walter L. Liefeld, quoted in Kenneth L. Barker and John R. Kohlenberger III, eds., *Zondervan NIV Bible Commentary*, vol. 2: New Testament (Grand Rapids, MI: Zondervan, 1994), 244.

5. Wiersbe, *Be Compassionate*, 107.

6. Liefeld, *Zondervan NIV Bible Commentary*, 247.

7. Bock, *Luke: The NIV Application Commentary*, 283.

8. Jerry White, quoted in Robert Crosby, *More Than a Savior* (Sisters, OR: Multnomah, 1999), 55.

Chapter 10: Luke 10—Significant Decisions

1. Morris, *Luke: Tyndale New Testament Commentaries*, 199.

2. Walvoord and Zuck, *The Bible Knowledge Commentary*, 233.

3. John Piper, *The Pleasures of God* (Sisters, OR: Multnomah, 2000), 271.

4. Piper, *Desiring God*, 279.

5. Willard, *The Divine Conspiracy*, 110.

6. Gary A. Haugen, *Good News About Injustice* (Downers Grove, IL: InterVarsity, 1999), 143.

7. Richards, *The Bible Reader's Companion*, 661.

Chapter 11: Luke 11—Candid Conversations

1. Richard J. Foster, *Prayer: Finding the Heart's True Home* (San Francisco: HarperSanFrancisco, 1992), 135.

2. Willard, *The Divine Conspiracy*, 243.

3. Darryl DelHousaye, *Today for Eternity: 365*

Powerful Daily Readings (Sisters, OR: Questar, 1991), September 27.

4. Jack Hayford, ed., *Spirit-Filled Life Bible*, New King James Version, 1536.

5. Anders, *Jesus: Knowing Our Savior*, 30–31.

6. Ibid., 31.

Chapter 12: Luke 12—Wise Words

1. R. Kent Hughes, *Luke*, vol. 2 (Wheaton, IL: Crossway Books, 1998), 38.

2. Sproul, *A Walk with Jesus*, 228–29.

3. Wiersbe, *Be Compassionate*, 139.

4. Leon Morris, *The Gospel According to St. Luke: Tyndale New Testament Commentaries* (Grand Rapids, MI: Eerdmans, 1974), 213.

5. Bob Benson, *See You at the House* (Nashville, TN: Generoux, 1986), 95.

Chapter 13: Luke 13—Going Against the Grain

1. Charles C. Ryrie, *So Great Salvation* (Colorado Springs, CO: Chariot Victor, 1989), 45.

2. MacDonald, *Believer's Bible Commentary*, 1423.

3. Lawrence O. Richards, *The Revell Bible Dictionary* (New York: Wynwood Press, 1990), 718–19.

4. Tom Sine, *The Mustard Seed Conspiracy* (Waco, TX: Word Books, 1981), 12.

5. Yancey, *The Jesus I Never Knew*, 160.

Chapter 14: Luke 14—Relating to People

1. Richards, *The 365 Day Devotional Commentary*, 738.

2. Willard, *The Divine Conspiracy*, 109.

3. Thielicke, *The Waiting Father*, 185–86.

4. Hughes, *Luke*, vol. 2, 125.

5. Oswald Chambers, *My Utmost for His Highest* (New York: Dodd, Mead, and Company, 1935), 184.

6. Benware, *Luke: Everyman's Bible Commentary*, 104.

Chapter 15: Luke 15—Lost and Found

1. Bilezikian, *Christianity 101*, 149.

2. Phyllis Kilbourn, *Children in Crisis: A New Commitment* (Monrovia, CA: MARC Publications, div. of World Vision, 1996), 14.

3. Lawrence O. Richards, *The Teacher's Commentary* (Colorado Springs, CO: Chariot Victor, 1987), 685.

4. Walvoord and Zuck, *The Bible Knowledge Commentary*, 245.

5. Henri J. M. Nouwen, *The Return of the Prodigal Son* (New York: Image Books, Doubleday, 1995), 52.

6. Piper, *The Pleasures of God*, 189.

7. Max Lucado, *In the Grip of Grace* (Dallas: Word Publishing, 1996), 71.

8. Nouwen, *The Return of the Prodigal Son*, 71.

Chapter 16: Luke 16—Money Matters

1. Barclay, *The Gospel of Luke*, 208.

2. Charles R. Swindoll, *The Quest for Character* (Portland, OR: Multnomah, n.d.), 117.

3. Richards, *The 365 Day Devotional Commentary*, 744.

Chapter 17: Luke 17—Heart Attitudes

1. Ryle, *Luke: The Crossway Classic Commentaries*, 219.

2. Dallas Willard, *Hearing God* (Downers Grove, IL: InterVarsity, 1999), 11–12.

3. Barclay, *The Gospel of Luke*, 218.

4. DelHousaye, *Today for Eternity*, reading for November 26.

5. R. C. Sproul, *Almighty Over All* (Grand Rapids, MI: Baker Books, 1999), 184.

Chapter 18: Luke 18—People Magazine

1. Warren W. Wiersbe, *Be Courageous* (Colorado Springs, CO: Chariot Victor, 1989), 62.

2. Richards and Richards, *Every Woman in the Bible*, 262.

3. Randall D. Roth, *Prayer Powerpoints* (Colorado Springs, CO: Chariot Victor, 1995), 12.

4. *Zondervan NIV Matthew Henry Commentary*, 285.

5. Sproul, *A Walk with Jesus*, 294–95.

6. Lawrence O. Richards, *The Bible Reader's Companion* (Colorado Springs, CO: Chariot Victor, 1991), 669.

Chapter 19: Luke 19—Loving Little People

1. Storms, *To Love Mercy*, 178.

2. Henry T. Blackaby and Claude V. King, ed., *The Experiencing God Study Bible—New King James Version* (Nashville, TN: Broadman and Holman, 1994), 1541.

3. Hayford, *Spirit-Filled Life Bible*, 1554.

4. Dana Gould, ed., *Shepherd's Notes: Luke* (Nashville, TN: Broadman and Holman, 1998), 70.

5. Hughes, *Luke*, vol. 2, 234.

6. Barclay, *The Gospel of Luke*, 238.

7. Sibley, *Luke*, 66.

Chapter 20: Luke 20—Hostile Challenges

1. Wiersbe, *Be Courageous*, 84.

2. Hughes, *Luke*, vol. 2, 255.

3. MacDonald, *Believer's Bible Commentary*, 1444.

4. Bilezikian, *Christianity 101*, 70.

5. Morris, *Luke*, 316.

6. Richards, *The Bible Reader's Companion*, 671.

7. Larry Richards, ed., *The Personal Growth Study Bible* (Nashville, TN: Thomas Nelson, 1996), 1351.

8. Willard, *The Divine Conspiracy*, 84.

Chapter 21: Luke 21—What Matters Most

1. Richards, *The 365 Day Devotional Commentary*, 751.

2. Howard Vos, *Nelson's New Illustrated Bible Manners and Customs* (Nashville, TN: Thomas Nelson, 1999), 406.

3. R. C. Sproul, *Now That's a Good Question!* (Wheaton, IL: Tyndale, 1996), 490.

4. Philip Yancey, *The Bible Jesus Read* (Grand Rapids, MI: Zondervan, 1999), 195.

5. Piper, *Desiring God*, 226.

6. Hughes, *Luke*, vol. 2, 302.

Chapter 22: Luke 22—The Longest Night

1. Wiersbe, *Be Courageous*, 107.

2. George R. Bliss, quoted in *Gould, Shepherd's Notes*, 80.

3. Lloyd John Ogilvie, *The Cup of Wonder* (Wheaton, IL: Tyndale, 1976), 87.

4. W. Glyn Evans, *Don't Quit Until You Taste the Honey* (Nashville, TN: Broadman Press, 1993), 50.

5. Hughes, *Luke*, vol. 2, 331.

6. Max Lucado, *The Final Week of Jesus* (highlights from *And the Angels Were Silent*) (Sisters, OR: Multnomah, 1994), 93.

7. Wiersbe, *Be Courageous*, 119.

8. Michael Card, *The Parable of Joy* (Nashville, TN: Thomas Nelson, 1995), 213.

9. Lucado, *In the Grip of Grace*, 125.

Chapter 23: Luke 23—A Dark Day in History

1. Richards, *Illustrated Bible Handbook*, 537.

2. Robert L. Thomas, ed., *The NIV Harmony of the Gospels* (San Francisco: HarperSanFrancisco, 1988), 222.

3. Peter Marshall, *The First Easter* (Lincoln, NE: Chosen Books, 1959), 66, 69.

4. Richards, *Illustrated Bible Handbook*, 537.

5. Robert C. Girard, *The Life of Christ*.

6. Chambers, *My Utmost for His Highest*, 325.

7. Larry Richards, *The Bible—The Smart Guide to the Bible™* (Nashville, TN: Thomas Nelson, 2007).

Chapter 24: Luke 24—A Bright Day Dawns

1. DelHousaye, *Today for Eternity*, reading for April 12.

2. MacDonald, *Believer's Bible Commentary*, 1457.

3. Morris, *Luke*, 367.

4. G. Campbell Morgan, *The Great Physician*, 318.

5. Elisabeth Elliot, *Keep a Quiet Heart* (Ann Arbor, MI: Servant Publications, 1995), 76.

6. Max Lucado, *Six Hours One Friday* (Sisters, OR: Multnomah, 1989), 72.

7. Richards, *The 365 Day Devotional Commentary*, 755.

Index

A

Aaron
 sons of, 6
Abba
 definition, 151
able to help, 48
Abraham
 definition, 44
 descendants of, 180
 Father, 213
 Jesus as descendant of,
  45
 Jesus's family tree, 44
 parable of Lazarus and
  rich man, 213, 214
 same faith as, 239
Abraham's bosom
 definition, 212, 213
abyss
 definition, 111
 Jesus cast demons into
  the, 111
Adam and Eve, 196, 217
 chose to disobey God,
  217
adultery, 211, 231
advocate
 definition, 228
altar
 definition, 6
altar of incense
 illustration #2, 8
analogy, 93, 196
ancient world
 false missionaries in, 122
 sign of cowardice, 238
Anders, Max
 on Jesus's moral
  authority, 159
 on the Pharisees vs.
  Jesus, 72
 on the stubbornly
  unbelieving, 158

angels
 announced the birth of
  Christ, 35, 172
 choir of, 26
 Gabriel, 11, 12, 13, 17,
  27
 God appeared as an, 7
 visit the temple, 5
animals
 sacrificial, 246
Anna
 daughter of Phanuel,
  30, 31
announce, 38, 97, 132
anoint, 19, 100
Anointed King, 243
Anointed One
 of God, 26
 Messiah, 3, 23
another disciple, 284
anti-Roman, 255
apocalyptic language, 267
apostle
 definition, 4
 Jesus selected twelve, 80
 Paul was one, 4
 Peter was one, 285
appointed, 253
Aramaic, 151, 297
Ark
 Noah built, 223
ashamed, 126, 165, 203
Asher tribe, 30
ashes (and sackcloth), 139
ask God, 11, 117, 156,
  235
austere
 definition, 98
 John's lifestyle, 98
authority
 allegiance with Satan, 50
 ancient teachers, 70
 definition, 121
 from Moses, 250

 of Gabriel, 9
 healing the man with, 71
 Jesus proved his, 112
 Jesus spoke with, 111
 Jesus taught with, 58
 positions of, 39, 279
 power and, 121, 129,
  140

B

Babylon, 33
Balaam
 definition, 19
 prophesied, 19
baptism
 administered by temple
  priests, 42
 definition, 38
 Jesus's, 43
 public statement of
  repentance, 38
bar mitzvah, 33
Barclay, William
 on the birth of
  children, 28
 on Christian life, 242
 on falsifying finances,
  208
 on Jesus and the sea,
  110
 on a leper's isolation,
  220
 on sin and suffering, 71
 on someone in need, 115
battle of prayer, 229
Beelzebub
 another word for Satan,
  48
 definition, 109, 153
 Jesus empowered by,
  109, 154
 Jesus was in league
  with, 153

believers
 don't speak against the
  Holy Spirit, 166
 expect God to care for
  them, 169
 immature in their faith,
  217
 must persevere in faith,
  229
 perspective on death, 30
Benson, Bob, 169
Benware, Paul N.
 on Mary and Elizabeth,
  15
 on removal of sins, 41
 on response to evil, 85
 on salt and the believer,
  192
 on why Peter wrote, 4
Bethlehem, 23, 24, 25,
  26, 27, 28, 32, 35, 36
Bethsaida, 123, 124, 139
Bible Knowledge
 Commentary
 on barren women who
  have children, 7
 on the birth of John
  the Baptist, 18
 on Jesus and sinners,
  200
 on three persons of the
  Godhead, 141
Bilezikian, Gilbert
 on Jesus and Rome, 255
 on Love, 196
 on the significance of
  the virgin birth, 14
 on sin and repentance, 39
birth
 announcements, 13, 35
 to a "holy" child, 13
 of Jesus Christ, 4, 22,
  23, 25, 27, 35
 virgin, 14

servants, 241
on the disciples, 81, 122
on the end, 267
on Jesus's word, 68
on John's language, 39
on Judgment Day, 164
on the Last Supper, 280
on the manger, 24
on our first loyalty, 190
on the vineyard/Israel
parable, 251
husband, 211, 256
hyperbole
definition, 233
hypocrisy
definition, 163, 258
hypocrites, exposed, 158,
173, 177

I

Immanuel
definition, 12
Incarnation
definition, 14
incense
definition, 6
indignation, 177, 178
ineluctable
definition, 59
Isaac, 7, 10, 44, 180,
256, 257, 260
Israelites, 49, 50, 51, 52,
56, 144, 199

J

Jacob
God of, 256, 257
house of, 11, 12
Isaac and, 180, 260
Jairus, 95, 103, 114, 116,
119, 120
daughter, 95, 116, 120
Jehovah
equal with, 11
view of, 199
Jesus
perfectly balanced, 35
returns, 52, 224, 229,
268
special concern for
"little ones," 217
on trial, 289, 290
Joanna

sons of, 44
wife of Chuza, 103
Job, 177
John
"whom Jesus loved," 5
Jordan River, 38, 40, 46
Joseph (father of Jesus),
24, 28, 31
Judah (person), 44
Judah (place), 14
Judea, 5, 11, 17, 23, 82, 94
and Jerusalem, 53, 70,
82
"judging," 279
judgment, 39, 138, 155,
164
judgment day, 164
justice, 3, 40, 144, 158,
160, 227, 228
justified, 98, 229, 230
definition, 230

K

Kilbourn, Phyllis, 197
kindred hearts, 14
King, Claude V., 239
KING OF THE JEWS,
THIS IS THE, 32,
297
Kingdom of God, 61, 82,
103, 133, 138, 178,
211
definition, 138
King
God, 61, 103, 126,
133, 138, 178, 211,
291, 297
of the Jews, 32, 290
of Judea, 5, 240
Kreeft, Peter, 83

L

lackeys
definition, 143
Lake of Fire, 112
Lake of Gennesaret
definition, 65
Lamb of God, 26, 317
Lamb's Book of Life, 140
Lamech, 44
lamentation
definition, 245
last

days, 270
promise, 90
law
God's, 5, 17, 21, 47,
159, 178, 233
of Moses, 28, 72, 74
Sabbath, 78, 186, 300,
303, 321
Lazarus, 117, 145, 212,
213, 214, 215, 243
leaven
definition, 163
legion, 111, 112
definition, 111
Levi, 71, 72, 75, 76, 81
Levite, 142, 146
definition, 142
liberty, 53, 57
lilies
definition, 168
Longmann, Tremper, 52
longsuffering, 267
Lord's
Prayer, 151, 218
Supper, 273, 276, 277
lost, the, 196, 197, 204,
205
lots
definition, 6
"lover of God," 4
lovingkindness, 10, 16, 21
Lucado, Max
on agony in the garden,
281
on grace, 202
on missing the
message, 107
on Peter, 285
on the resurrection, 310

M

MacDonald, William
on the result of satanic
activity, 177
on the resurrection, 306
on the sinless redeemer,
48
on the stone, 253
Magnificat, the
definition, 16
"make every effort," 180
Malchus, 283
male water carrier
illustration #13, 275

manger, 24, 25, 26, 27, 32
definition, 24
marriage, 11, 17, 223, 255
supper, 277
Marshall, Peter, 293
Martha's hospitality, 144
Mary Magdalene, 300,
312
Mary, mother of James,
305, 312
Master
definition, 66
Mediterranean Sea, 212
Menan, 44
mercy, 15, 17, 18, 19,
138, 143, 220, 235
Messiah
definition, 3
Promised, 12, 22, 26,
35, 41, 55, 173
messianic, 141, 244, 309
messianic psalm
definition, 244
metaphor, 213
Micah, 23, 36, 317
millstone, 217
mina, 240, 241
definition, 240
miracle
definition, 10
Jesus's, 67, 68, 221
misfortune, 96, 176
missionary (missionaries),
4, 5, 65, 121
journey, 5
moon, 267
Morgan, G. Campbell
on the centurion, 93
on Jesus and the
Scripture, 308
morning, 61, 80, 269, 290
Morris, Leon
on God's servants, 138
on Jesus's coming, 97
on Jesus's messiahship,
34
on resurrection, 307
on Sadducees, 256
on sins and greed, 168
Moses, 10, 28, 49, 51,
127, 128
Law of, 28, 33, 72, 74
Mother Teresa, 69
Mount Hermon, 127
Mount Meron, 127

illustration #1, 6
temple money, 246
Temple Mount, 263
temple reconstruction, 263
temple tax, 132, 246
temptation, 47, 48, 52, 282
tempted, 47, 52, 62, 164
definition, 47
terror, 7, 30, 39
test
our character, 215
of faith, 110
God's, 51
tetradrachmas
definition, 246
tetrarch, 37, 42, 122, 124
thanksgiving, 221
theft, 304
Thielicke, Helmut
on the invitation, 189
on spiritual growth, 107
Thomas, Robert L., 292
threshing floor, 40
throne, 11, 12, 15, 45, 60, 279
times of the Gentiles, 266
tithed
definition, 229
tithes
definition, 158
title, 4, 23, 86, 121
tomb, 110, 111, 159, 300, 303, 304, 305
illustration #14, 304
transfiguration, 121, 126, 128, 129, 135
definition, 126
transfigured, 116
definition, 116
transform our hearts, 161
transforming a person's life, 41, 157
translation, 16
transmutation
definition, 311
transparency, 163, 164
definition, 163
treasure in heaven, 169, 174, 232
tribulation
definition, 267
twelve, the, 4, 5, 81, 121,

124, 137, 273
twelve world changers, 77, 80
Tyre, 82, 139, 246

U

unbelief, 10, 13, 56, 94, 154, 222
unbelieving, 30, 98, 101, 135, 175, 223
undefiled, 262
unleavened bread, 273, 274, 275, 276
unmarried brother, 255
unmitigated
definition, 308
unprepared, the, 172, 268

V

valid, 98, 132, 245
Valley, Kedron, 51
vineyard, 176, 251, 252
virgin, 11, 12, 13, 14, 21, 22, 31, 37
virgin birth, 12, 13, 14, 22
vision, 10, 307
voice from the cloud, a, 128
Vos, Howard, 263

W

wail, 94, 95, 296
wall, 233, 263, 266, 270
war, 191, 244, 266, 270
against another king, 191
bring peace, 244
and natural disasters, 270
wealth, 40, 208, 212, 232, 255
wealthy, 75, 83, 232, 255, 261

weeds, 105
weep, 82, 248, 295
weeping and gnashing of teeth, 180
weeping king, 245
White, Jerry, 134
wickedness, 157, 274
Wiersbe, Warren W.
on the disciples and faith, 110
on grace, 56
on Jesus, 94
on Jesus's death, 282
on Judas, 274
on the parable of the unjust judge, 228
on students of the law, 250
on temple tax, 132
on truth-haters, 57
on wealth, 167
on the wedding feast, 74
Willard, Dallas
on good Samaritans, 144
on obedience and love, 220
on physical death, 257
on prayer, 150
on the "Rock," 89
on showing kindness and generosity, 188
wineskin
illustration #6, 75
new wine would burst, 74
wrath,
God's, 39, 281, 296
wringing their hands, 92, 129

Y

"Yahweh is gracious," 18
"Yahweh remembers," 18
Yancey, Philip
on being unwanted, 69
on emotional pain, 182
on forgiveness of sin, 71
on the future, 265

Z

Zacharias and Elizabeth, 7, 17, 21, 37
a child in their old age, 17
their barrenness, 7
Zealots, 80, 81, 254
definition, 254
Zebedee's sons, mother of, 66, 80
Zechariah, 8, 9, 20, 22, 60, 159, 244
Zerubbabel, 44